A FAMOUS ANTIENT
SEED-PLOT OF LEARNING

GATEWAY TO WOLSEY'S COLLEGE, IPSWICH.

Published by F. Jawsey, Ipswich.

Fred. Russel.   Ant. Hafreen.

A FAMOUS ANTIENT
SEED-PLOT OF LEARNING

A History of Ipswich School

JOHN BLATCHLY

PUBLISHED BY IPSWICH SCHOOL

2003

*This book is dedicated to the School's earlier historians upon whose
shoulders the author stands*

W. H. Richardson FSA
C. S. Partridge FSA OI
V. B. Redstone FSA
Miss Nina Layard FSA
I. E. Gray FSA OI
W. E. Potter OI
and particularly
W. M. Morfey OI

*The book's title is taken from the printed appeal to Parliament, c. 1620,
of one of the school's most faithful pupils and masters, James Leman,
originally a poor scholar from Whitton.*

Frontispiece: Wolsey's Gate etched by Wat Hagreen after F. B. Russel.

set in 10/15.5pt Parable

Published by Ipswich School,
25 Henley Road, Ipswich, Suffolk IP1 3SG
Printed in Ipswich by The Five Castles Press
Designed and typeset by S. J. M. Watson OI

Contents

Preface

Gray and Potter's *Ipswich School 1400-1950* was a model for its time, more generously and imaginatively illustrated than many contemporary school histories. It will long remain an excellent work of reference. The two Old Ipswichian authors missed very little evidence, despite living and working away from Suffolk; Irvine Gray was at first in the Essex Record Office but then became the first County Archivist for Gloucestershire. Teddie Potter taught physics and was a housemaster at Bryanston. Both gave their free time over five years to the research and the writing, claiming a modest fifteen pounds each for their expenses. When the book appeared and the authors received no word whatever from the then headmaster, they felt responsible for the publisher's loss when only half the 1250 copies sold in three years. When the governors paid sixty pounds for one hundred copies at one-fifth discount (to give as school prizes), Gray nobly took out a seven-year five-pound covenant which, with interest, would offset the governors' outlay. This only shows how perilous the school's finances were in those austere post-war days. The authors' deep-seated love of their school and the many skills they brought to their joint work enabled them to demonstrate with ease that the school had a long and interesting history, thoughtfully leaving clues to other aspects of the story.

Before Gray and Potter, there existed only Nina Frances Layard's *Brief Sketch of the History of Ipswich School 1477–1851* of 1901. Miss Layard was a cousin of Layard of Nineveh and in 1921 became one of the first women Fellows of the Society of Antiquaries of London. Her *Sketch*, though brief, preserves some valuable reminiscences, and helped A.F. Leach with his account of the school in the Victoria History of the county in

1907. In 1950, the school had been independent for only five years and a new and energetic spirit was abroad with the arrival from Radley of Patrick Mermagen as headmaster. Here was a man capable of transforming the school, despite the problems of the times, and of establishing it firmly over his twenty-two years on a completely new footing. Meanwhile, Wallace Morfey was working on aspects of the history of his old school, compiling a list of all its members traceable up to 1857. Since that date the records are complete. Morfey founded the *Old Ipswichian Magazine*, edited it for fourteen years and enlivened it with entertaining historical articles. The reader will be referred to most of these at appropriate points. In 1982, the ancient town library of Ipswich came back to the school to be cared for, as it had been from 1612 until 1802, by successive headmasters. Its detailed examination revealed rich details about the school, particularly during the seventeenth century, and other discoveries are continually being made in other fields. The Morfey Museum and archive rooms house materials, which, added to the events of over half a century since the Gray and Potter history, more than justify the writing of another. To have known Gray, Potter and Morfey well, as I did, gave me the stimulus to attempt this task. Indeed, in 1987 Gray wrote 'You – if ever you can find the time, with all your interests – or someone else, will have to produce a second edition of the history'.

More than most school histories, ours has its wistful aspects; too often it is a case of 'if only...' or 'what if...'. The mists which surround the earliest days of the school have yet to be totally dispersed; perhaps they never will be. We now know more about Richard Felaw, whose bequest of house and lands in 1483 was the first of many, but can only lament the demolition of his house in Foundation Street. This occurred in 1963, after which the site remained waste ground for thirty years, well into the era when conservation would have been automatic. What a tourist attraction a fifteenth-century schoolhouse would be today!

It is also regrettable that, in about 1850, the claustral buildings of the Blackfriars, opposite Felaw's house, were pulled down. They had provided the schoolroom from 1612 to 1842, first in the refectory and then the dormitory. In Norwich, St Andrew's Hall is an almost complete Blackfriars church. The Ipswich church came down at the Dissolution, but all the domestic buildings of the Dominican friary could have been preserved.

Who, interested in Ipswich and in her most spectacularly ambitious son, has not felt '*If only* Wolsey had continued to please King Henry VIII and lived until his Ipswich college was well enough established to make its future secure'? His intention was that it should always rival the colleges, also dedicated to the Blessed Virgin Mary, at Eton and Winchester.

Winchester College
§ founded by William of Wykeham in 1387
§ Warden, 10 fellows, 3 chaplains, 16 choristers, 70 scholars.
§ Linked with New College, Oxford

Eton College
§ founded in 1441 by Henry VI from revenues of suppressed alien priories
§ Provost, 10 priests, 4 clerks, 6 choristers, schoolmaster, 25 poor scholars, 25 bedesmen. Linked with King's College, Cambridge

Ipswich College
§ founded by Thomas Wolsey in 1528
§ Dean, 12 priest fellows, 8 lay clerks, 8 children (choristers), grammar-schoolmaster, usher, 50 scholars, 12 poor bedesmen.
§ Linked with what is now Christ Church, Oxford

If, on his way from the station to lay the foundation stone of the new buildings in Henley Road, Prince Albert had not been jeered at by an unusually outspoken Suffolker, there would have been no royal interdict on Ipswich for the next seventy-five years and Albert's memorial in Suffolk would surely have been an enlarged Ipswich School. At least the 1851 buildings and later additions are the finest the school has ever inhabited. It is reassuring that, in his *Buildings of England: Suffolk,* Nikolaus Pevsner quoted, and thus endorsed, the 1864 *Handbook* of Ipswich: 'There is probably no such fine line of modern Elizabethan buildings elsewhere in the Eastern counties'.

There is in the school museum a panel which divides the history between the seven great schoolrooms in which pupils have gathered at different times:

1. 1483–1528 and 1531–1614	Felaw's House
2. 1528–30	The Cardinal's College
3. 1614–1767	The former Blackfriars' refectory
4. 1767–1842	The former Blackfriars' dormitory
5. 1842–1852	The Lower Brook St Great School
6. 1852–1957	The Henley Road Great School
7. 1957 to date	The Ivry Street Great School
	and since 1989 the Little School adjoining

Just as the School has had several locations, so it has been variously named but its history is nevertheless continuous. Here are most of them, with the periods or dates when they are known to have been used. During some headships more than one name was in use.

The Guild Merchant School	*Possibly from 1200 or earlier*
The Corpus Christi Guild School	*Probably from c.1327*
or The Grammar School of Ipswich	*1412 or earlier*
The Free School of Ipswich	*1483–1528*
The Cardinal's College of St Mary in Ipswich	*1528–30*

The King's Majesty's School	*1531*
Ipswich School (on a printed title-page)	*1697*
King Henry VIII School, Ipswich (*ditto*)	*1722*
Queen Elizabeth's Grammar School, Ipswich	*1851*
Queen Elizabeth's School, Ipswich }	{ *Both names used by*
Ipswich Grammar School }	{ *Rigaud and Holden*
Ipswich School	*since 1883*

The 1950 history contains useful full transcripts of certain important documents, which I have only summarised. In the spirit of their times, Gray and Potter imposed long embargoes on some facts which can now be faced. Just as the *Dictionary of National Biography* of 1900 varnished over a great deal which its successor in 2004 will not hesitate to state plainly, so this history will attempt to present the full facts fairly. The main chapters will follow in chronological order but certain topics, sport, performance and art and artists will be treated across the whole of the school's long history. It will soon become clear that the earliest explicit evidence comes from a dispute between the first two named masters, a reminder that history becomes most interesting when things are going wrong. Fortunately, therefore, much went awry in every period until the most recent, to the advantage of the narrative. If there seems to be too much about masters and ushers, the smaller the school and its staff, the greater their influence, and the experiences of boys were only by chance recorded before *The Elizabethan* appeared, a pioneer school magazine, in 1852. Headmasters are often asked whether they disproportionately influence their schools. During long periods of poor governance in the nineteenth and early twentieth centuries, it can only have been the vision and drive of great heads that saved the school.

The title of the book comes from a headmaster's printed petition to Parliament in about 1620. Its author, James Leman, boy, usher and master, was of humble origins, supported through school and at Cambridge by benefactions. After an ignominious dismissal, he fought tirelessly to defend the school and Felaw's endowments against those who would divert them to other purposes, saving both but sacrificing his own career. He has emphatically earned this prominent latter-day remembrance. The corporation's treatment of Leman nearly four hundred years ago sprang from a realisation, even then, that one small school for boys only could never educate the youth of the town. Nowadays, the school is fully co-educational and, with about fifty other schools within the borough boundaries, shares the task of preparing all the girls and boys of Ipswich for the next stages of their education and careers which take them all over the globe. We are bold enough to claim as a pupil Thomas Eldred, who accompanied Thomas Cavendish of Grimston Hall near Felixstowe, a year his senior, on a circumnavigation in 1586-87. They, and generations of young men of this town on the Orwell, will have been drawn to the bustle on the quays and in the shipyards only a few hundred yards from the school. There is little to attract today's pupils in that direction, but young men and women leave well-equipped to further their studies and succeed in an ever-widening range of professions. They should know that learning is lifelong and of the need to be flexible in the light of change. The modern school – since Rigaud, but particularly in the last fifty years – will also have taught them how to use their leisure fully and constructively.

ADVERTISEMENT.

Acknowledgements

First of all, I am most grateful to Ian Galbraith, the headmaster, and the governing body for inviting me to write a new history, and to Peter Boughton, the bursar, for ready help in practical ways. Several people read the later chapters: David Coe, Ian Galbraith, Andrew Gregory, Ian Prior and David Warnes, and were encouraging. Andrew Gregory undertook the compilation of Chapter 22, bringing it up to date, and Alex Burnett gave guidance on Chapter 23. Graham Peck and Alan Gibson gave me the freedom of the archives during the work, and Sally Dawson recovered information from her records. Norman Scarfe made valuable improvements to early drafts as far as 1800, and Rodney Garratt gave the whole text a check for errors and conventions. My wife Pam has nobly read most of the text more than once and spotted several errors and infelicities; for those which remain the blame is entirely mine.

John Ridgard, Colin Richmond, Peter Northeast, Keith Wade, Tom Loader, David Jones, Derek Culley and Derek Williams have all given me the benefit of their specialist knowledge and assistance. Inge Mermagen generously allowed her watercolour of the school in 1853 to be photographed for the jacket. The late Birkin Haward reconstructed the elevation of the Blackfriars facing Felaw's House across Foundation Street (then Edmund Pountney Lane), and Philip Aitkens produced a revealing reconstruction of Felaw's House by collating the available evidence. Michael Broadbent generously had the drawings in Charles Keene's Homer's *Iliad* photographed for reproduction. David Allen kindly transcribed the earliest documentary references to the school, and Marion Allen was largely frustrated in her search for more early material. Joan Corder and Tony Copsey have for nearly thirty years opened their libraries to my searches, and members of staff of the Suffolk Record Office have been unfailingly helpful. Finally, I believe that readers will share my gratitude to Stephen Watson OI, who chose the type and designed the layout in preparation for the book's printing by Mike Castle at his Five Castles Press in Ipswich.

John Blatchly

The Headmaster and the author wish to thank the following for their kind permission to reproduce illustrations: the Bibliothèque nationale de France, 10; the British Library, 42, 109; Michael Broadbent, xii, xiii, 151, 360; A.T. Copsey, 45; Victor Gollancz, 237, 362; the Houghton Library, Harvard University, 55; Ipswich and Norwich Co-operative Society Limited, 14; Ipswich Borough Council Museums and Galleries, 50, 51, 57, 66, 105, 123, 127, 140, 153; National Portrait Gallery, 270; Norfolk Record Office, 12; Master and Fellows of Pembroke College, Cambridge, 74; Public Record Office, 26, 30, 36; Society of Antiquaries of London, 73; Suffolk Record Office, 40, 84, 112, 158, 181 and 182; F.H. Browne Papers, Van Volkenburg-Browne Collection, Special Collections Library, University of Michigan., 206, 208, 323.

CATECHESIS

Ecclesiæ Anglicanæ

UNA

Cum precibus aliquot Selectis in
Usum Scholæ,

REGIS *HENRICI*

Ejus Nominis OCTAVI,

IN

Burgo *Gippovicensi.*

*Instrue puerum pro ratione viæ ipsius, etiam cum
senuerit non recedet ab câ.* Prov. 22. 6.

GIPPOVICI:
Typis *Joannis Bagnall.* 1722.

See page 117

Epigrammatum

ET

POEMATUM

Sacrorum et

PSALMORUM.

Delectus.

EX

AUDOENO,
BARLÆO,
BUCHANANO
Decerptus.

In Usum Scholarum.

Lectorem delectando, pariterq; monendo.

GIPPOVICI:
Typis *Joannis Bagnall.* 1722.

See page 117

I

The School before 1480

While it is possible to argue for such dates as 1200, 1325 and the 1390s for the beginnings of the school, the first two grammar schoolmasters, whose names we know, fell out while changing over in 1412 and the school itself is mentioned four years later. The earliest recorded collations of masters by the bishop of Norwich but chosen by the corporation were: a song school master in 1445 and a grammar school master in 1477. That was the year when fees were fixed for boys at the three main stages of the curriculum but no precise location for the school can be stated. Only the corporation itself and some of the medieval churches can claim longer continuous histories than the school.

THE TRUE BEGINNINGS of our most ancient schools are hard to pin down and the older they are the more their origins are obscured. Ipswich School has certainly been in existence for more than six, probably seven, and possibly eight hundred years. The school at Dunwich in 631 has been claimed as the earliest recorded in England but nothing is known of it after about 1100, a reminder that it is one thing for a school to be ancient, but far more important that it should continue to flourish as does Ipswich School today. A.F. Leach, the first serious student of medieval education, believed that there were schools at Thetford by 1075 and Bury St Edmunds in 1081 and, for him, Ipswich comes next.

'Ipswich,' Leach wrote, 'which had a Guild merchant in the days of King John, probably had a grammar school in days

1

equally early'[1] but proof is needed, though reference to a town school at Colchester in a deed of 1206 supports the possibility. Nicholas Orme, almost a century later, suggests that, staffed from the great abbey at Bury, schools sprang up at Beccles and Mildenhall in about 1235 and at Botesdale in 1389. Hadleigh owed its grammar school foundation in 1382 to the deanery there being a Canterbury peculiar and there was a reading and song school for the choristers of the collegiate church at Stoke-by-Clare from 1422.[2]

The Suffolk medieval historian John Ridgard has found a grammar school at Framlingham by 1387, run by a married schoolmaster whose wife brewed and sold ale.[3] The 'keeper of the lodgings of the school of Clare' is listed with those who took part in the Peasants' Revolt of 1381 at Cavendish Green.[4] Geoffrey Martin found 'Thomas scholemayster' at Colchester paying the poll tax which led to those riots but, unfortunately, the corresponding lists for Ipswich went astray in the nineteenth-century. In 1206, the Colchester school came under the bishop of London, not because the town was in his diocese but because the school was in his *soke*.[5] In the early fifteenth-century, Dame Alice de Bryene of Acton was sending her clerks to Lavenham to learn Latin grammar.[6] With so many schools with

---

1   A.F. Leach wrote the article on the grammar schools in the county in *Victoria History of the Counties of England, Suffolk*, vol.ii, (1907) 325–36.

2   Nicholas Ormes' *English Schools in the Middle Ages*, 1973 is now the standard work, and the dates cited are his.

3   Bodley Suffolk Charter 1303.

4   PRO KB9/166/1.

5   Geoffrey Martin wrote *The History of Colchester Royal Grammar School* for *The Colcestrian* of March 1947, just as he was leaving the school for Merton College, Oxford. The introductory essay 'The Governance of Ipswich from its origins to c.1550' which he contributed to David Allen's *Ipswich Borough Archives 1255-1835* SRS, 43, 2000, has greatly helped the author with this chapter.

6   Private communication from Dr John Ridgard.

ancient origins nearby, it is surely only mischance that no mention of Ipswich School has so far been found earlier than 1412.

King John's Charter to Ipswich and the Guild Merchant
In 1200, the burgesses of Ipswich met in the churchyard of St
Mary le Tower on 29 June to receive their first Charter, which
had been sealed by King John near Rouen on May 25 and
brought to Ipswich with all haste. What makes the occasion of
its arrival unusually interesting is, that the town's Great
Domesday Book contains a full account of the proceedings
then and at several subsequent gatherings that summer and
autumn, when the newly autonomous corporate borough
chose its first officers under the new constitution. Most signif-
icant for the beginnings of education in Ipswich was the
licensing of the guild merchant (with the implication that it
already existed) and the election of an alderman and three
associates to run it. It was about a century later that the guild
became the Guild of Corpus Christi, in association with the
two Augustinian houses and the three friaries.

We learn from later records that the principal burgesses,
who made up the craft and trade companies under the guild,
appointed chaplains to celebrate mass for them, probably in St
Mary le Tower. Chaplains were given the task of organising
Corpus Christi festival pageants each June on three days in the
week after Trinity Sunday, collecting members' dues for the
expenses of the feasts and maintaining the costumes and properties used in three days of processions. There was, right into
Stuart times, a role for the master of the school in arranging for
his pupils to entertain the corporation and visitors of importance and the early guild chaplains were, perhaps, the best people to undertake the education of the leading townsmen's sons.
Unfortunately, none of the guild records survived the Dissolu-

tion, certainly depriving us of primary sources of information about the early school.

The roll of benefactors, read by the headmaster at the school's annual service of Commemoration of Benefactors in the town's civic church of St Mary le Tower (a comparatively recently established tradition), begins with the words: 'The brothers and sisters of the Guild of Corpus Christi, who cared for the school in its earliest days'. It is reassuring to know that the guild rules specified that wives of burgesses should also enjoy guild feasts; only for other guests was an extra payment required. The order of procession gives a complete list of the leading crafts and trades, with the pageant they presented. The parents of the school's early pupils presumably plied colourfully diverse occupations:

> *How every occupation or craftsman should order themselves in their going with their pageants in the procession of Corpus Christi.*[7]
> Gentlemen, pewterers, plumbers, sadlers, masons, tilers and armourers *with the pageant of St George.*
> Tailors *with the pageant of St John.*
> Goldsmiths, blacksmiths, locksmiths and bladesmiths *with the pageant of St Eligius.*
> Barbers and waxchandlers *with the pageant of St Thomas à Becket.*
> Glaziers, painters, carpenters, carvers, bowyers, fletchers, wheelwrights, coopers, patternmakers, turners and scriveners *with the pageant of St Luke the Evangelist.*
> Weavers, fullers, cappers and hatmakers.
> Shoemakers and tanners.
> Fishmongers *with a model dolphin.*
> Butchers and tallowchandlers *with a bull.*
> Skinners, glovers, pursers and cardmakers.

7 This transcript from *Liber Quartus* of Richard Percyvale's Great Domesday of 1521 (SROI C/4/1/4), is collated with the list in English added in a sixteenth-century hand to the fourteenth-century White Domesday (SROI C/4/1/2).

Clothmakers, drapers, dyers and shearmen *with the pageant of the Assumption of Our Lady.*
Mercers, poynters [collar makers] and haberdashers.
Merchants, mariners and brewers *with a ship.*
Bakers and waferers.
Then the religious orders: Whitefriars, Greyfriars, Blackfriars; Priests;
THE TABERNACLE CONTAINING THE HOST
Secular priests; Canons of Holy Trinity Priory; Canons of St Peter and Paul Priory; Brethren of the Guild of Corpus Christi; Four Aldermen of the Guild; The Borough Corporation: Twenty-four Common Councilmen, twelve Portmen, including two Bailiffs, the joint chief justices.

Early references to education locally

When chance references are found to schooling in or around Ipswich, particularly once the guild merchant became the guild of Corpus Christi and employed a chaplain, we can reasonably assume that it took place at a school in Ipswich. The south aisle of St Mary le Tower church had secular uses for many centuries and may have been used for teaching; the claims of other places must also be considered.

Several early mentions of schooling in the Ipswich area have been found, the first in a will made and proved in 1312. The family called Reymes originated at the Norman village of Rames near the forest of Lillebonne. Roger de Rames was established as a baron by William I in 1086, with lands in several eastern counties, particularly in Suffolk.[8] There were knightly de Reymes in Wherstead, Wenham and Higham in the 13th and 14th centuries and, when Robert of Little Wenham, younger son of William de Reymes of Higham, made his

---

8   A.L. Raimes, 'The Family of Reymes of Wherstead in Suffolk' in *PSIA*, xxiii, (1938) 89–115 gives a full English translation of the whole Latin will, as well as a illustrated account of the wealth and distinction of the family who presumably sent a youngster to the school in 1312.

long will[9] in 1312 he had no wife or children, so that many relatives benefited, including his elder brother John and his sons. To one of these nephews, Robert, he left '52 shillings for his maintenance at school for one year to come'. His non-family bequests were concentrated on churches and monastic establishments in and close to Ipswich. Nowhere further afield is mentioned. It seems very probable that the boy was sent from Higham to Ipswich, boarding there with his schoolmaster. As early as this, by a peculiar Ipswich custom, a child over fourteen wishing to buy or sell property was tested by 'numbering and measuring'. In 1315, Mabel Toke and John, her son, were able to grant a house in the Quay parish to Thomas le Rente when John satisfactorily passed this test. In a specific case in the Petty Pleas Court in 1344, a boy of nineteen counted out twenty shillings and measured 12 ells of cloth 'well and sufficiently' and the transfer was legal. Education was already important.

Another reference to schooling, in and before 1399, is found in Petty Court actions between John Blast and Alice Gamen.[10] Alice had supplied John with board, shoes and bed clothes for his schooling and maintenance during his youth but, still in 1407, the account was unsettled. She claimed £6 but he, now a merchant, disclaimed any debt. The dispute was eventually brought to arbitration but the result went unrecorded. In 1389 Thomas and Alice Gamen lived in St Nicholas parish in a house fronting St Nicholas Street and Thomas died in 1410. The question remains, whether the Gamens were running the school John Blast attended; why else should Alice be claiming money for these purposes?

9   SROI HD 210/3/1.
10   SROI C/2/3/1/40, membrane 8r.

The first schoolmasters named in the records

The first firm evidence for the existence of a grammar school in Ipswich comes from Court records, when successive masters had business there. The first two masters, whose names we know for certain, have left nothing but particulars of debts and disagreements and nothing at all about their qualifications or fitness for the post. On 8 October 1412, RICHARD PENYNGTON, the outgoing Master, paid fourpence for leave to sue NICHOLAS SCHOLEMAYSTER for trespass in the Court of Petty Pleas.[11] To him, Scholemayster was presumably an unwelcome intruder on the benefits he had been enjoying. Penyngton owed a master butcher, Geoffrey Balley, the not inconsiderable sum of five shillings and the following month the same Petty Court, as Penyngton persistently failed to attend, gave leave for his goods to be distrained, i.e. taken in lieu of the debt. The affair dragged on to the next February, when Balley (in Penyngton's absence again) gave the court an account of their violent argument (they may have come to blows). Penyngton's goods to the value of ten pounds were seized, and they included grammar books. As this was forty years before printing began in England, the grammar books must have been handwritten copies. Amongst Penyngton's other property, 'togas' were mentioned, perhaps academic gowns. The records for March 1414 show that four townsmen owed money and chattels to Scholemayster, who, that September, paid fourpence for leave to sue a priest called William Gryslee; at least he never appears as debtor himself.

11   SROI C/2/3/1/45, 46, 47.

The grammar school first mentioned

Scholemayster did not last long in the post but we know that his successor was one WILLIAM BURY, clerk, though not in full priestly orders as he was a married man. The costs of one very interesting pupil lodging with the Burys for the year from Michaelmas 1416 were found in his family's accounts in the British Library and they make the first mention of the grammar school itself.[12] On their arrival in Ipswich in June 1414, Bury and his wife Margery formally engaged one Stacia Stroop as maid [*ancilla*] for one year, running from the following Christmas. She only stayed a week, denying any contract with the Burys, who tried to claim five pounds in damages but the justices thought fourpence sufficient, despite the fact that she had done the same thing before. The dates and sums involved in this action seem peculiar but that is what the vellum Petty Court rolls show.[13]

The school bill for 1416–17 is for Alexander de la Pole, from Wingfield Castle, who would certainly have been able to entertain his fellows with stirring stories. His grandfather Michael, earl of Suffolk, died, exiled for treason, in Paris in 1389, to be succeeded by his son and Alexander's father Michael II, who had the earldom restored to him in 1399. Michael II died of dysentery at Harfleur in 1415, just five weeks before Agincourt. There the next earl, Michael III, Alexander's eldest brother but only 23, 'distinguished above all the courtiers', wielded his axe at Agincourt but was killed. A second brother, William, was now the earl and head of the family but the boy's grandmother was his guardian at Wingfield. The details from the accounts

---

12 Norman Scarfe found the school bill in British Library Egerton MS 8776, membranes 3-6, and wrote 'Ipswich School in the time of Henry V' for the *Ipswichian* in 1977.

13 SROI C/2/3/1/48.

are in Latin and the translation is given in full, except that dates are modernised:

> And in expenses of the same Alexander, the lord's son, in riding to Ipswich to study there in the month of September 1416, paid in good faith by the hand of John Hedon,   4s 6d
> And paid to master William Bury, master of the School there, for the sojourn of the said Alexander with him, staying there from Sunday 27 Sept. until 18 July 1417, that is to say for 42 weeks, taking per week 20d.,   70s
> And for four pairs of shoes bought for the said Alexander during the said time, costing 4d. per pair,   16d
> And in [church] offerings of the said Alexander on various occasions within the same time,   9d
> And in candles bought in the school for the same time in the winter,   6d
> And delivered to the same Alexander by the hand of Thomas Lathome, for his sport and small expenses etc.,   20d
> And paid to a barber of Ipswich, both for medicines applied by him to the said Alexander and for shaving his head,   2s
> And given to Master William Bury, for teaching the said Alexander for 3 terms of the year,   5s
> And given to the wife of the said Master William, for her good work done concerning the said Alexander,   6s 8d

At the end of the year it was time for Alexander to proceed to Cambridge:

> And in expenses of the said Alexander on the 20 September, and of Robert Bolton, Esquire and others riding with the said Alexander to Cambridge to study there, with the expenses of the said Robert and the others returning thence to Wingfield,   14s 8d

Alexander was, as his name perhaps suggests, intended for a soldier but he did not have a long career. In 1429 he and his brothers, William and John, were laying siege to Orléans. William was one of the most experienced commanders in France but he was outmanoeuvred by the young, almost legendary,

Joan of Arc, who pursued the English up the Loire and trapped them in Jargeau.

Joan of Arc at the Siege of Orléans (Bibliothèque Nationale de France, MS Français 2679, fol. 66)

There, on 12 June, Earl William and John were taken prisoner and poor Alexander was killed. The earl's ransom was £20,000, the equivalent of millions today. He was eventually exchanged for his brother Thomas, a priest, who died in captivity four years later. William became a leading advocate of peace with France at Court, and erected a magnificent tomb to his parents and their children in Wingfield church. Had not the small named statues of the children been taken off the tomb, we would have at least a stylised image of the first of the school's pupils known for certain.

In September 1417, the Burys were selling a tenement with garden and curtilage in St Nicholas parish, the bounds of which are defined in the Ipswich recognizance roll[14] but with reference to Couloteslane to the west, not a street name otherwise encountered. 'East head on highway' probably indicates that the house had its frontage on the modern St Nicholas Street.

N		lately John Hoxne	
W —+— E	Couloteslane	THE BURYS' HOUSE	The Highway (St Nicholas St)
S		Margaret Starlyng	

14 SROI C/2/4/1/62.

This is likely to have been the schoolhouse and the place where Alexander de la Pole boarded. William Bury may not long have been content to be the master, for he was one of the two borough coroners (who acted with the bailiffs as the town's justices) for five years from 1421. To hold this office, Bury must have been a free burgess, and therefore probably son of another freeman, with the right to educate William in the town's school.

Regulations and the bishop of Norwich involved

There follows a fifty-year gap before the next master can be named but then at last the school's affairs were put on a regular footing. The bishop of the diocese, at that time Norwich, was to set the fees and approve and license the masters, who would be nominated by the corporation. The bishops' involvement continued, at least in theory, until 1881 but the registers running from 1290 to 1700 contain only two relevant entries. The first master, collated by the surrogate acting for Bishop James Goldwell of Norwich, was JOHN BESETT, MA, who was also a graduate in Canon Law at Cambridge but without a college specified. Besett's *Collacio scholarum grammaticalium in villa Gippewici* took place on 22 June 1477.[15] He was to have custody and direction of the grammar school in the town, on condition that he provide his scholars with sound teaching, always employing the utmost diligence.[16] There was at the time no endowment and Besett would live on the fees paid by the parents of the pupils. The reason for this formal appoint-

---

15   Oddly, the translation is strictly collation of the grammar school, rather than of the master. The plural 'scole grammaticales' means 'grammar school', singular. NRO DN/Reg 7 Registers of the Bishops of Norwich, Book 12, p.55. The register entry is reproduced overleaf by kind permission of the Norfolk County Archivist.

16   The term *diligence* was only replaced by *effort* in the school in the early 1970s.

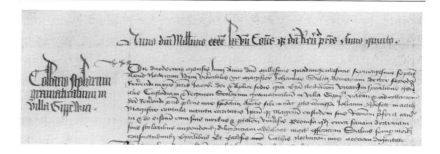

ment appears from a resolution made at the Great Court meeting three months earlier on 23 March 1477:[17]

> Ordinacio: Et quod magister scole gramaticalis de cetero habebit jurisdiccionem et gubernacionem omnium scolarium infra libertatem et procinctum istius ville, exceptis petytis vocatis Apeseyes et Songe, tantum capiendo pro suo salario de quodlibet gramatico saltario et primario secundum taxacionem Domini Episcopi Norwicensis, videlicet pro gramatico xd quarteragii, saltario viijd et primario vjd.

> *It is ordered that the master of the grammar school shall henceforth have jurisdiction and governance of all scholars within the liberty and precinct of this town except only petties called Apesyes & Songe, taking for his salary from each grammarian, psalterian, and primerian, according to the rate fixed by the Lord Bishop of Norwich, viz. for a grammarian 10d a quarter, for a psalterian 8d and for a primerian 6d.*

A junior master, therefore, was responsible for the youngest boys while they learnt their alphabet and singing and the other entry in the bishop's register shows that the implied arrangement of senior and junior schools had existed as early as 1445.[18] This much earlier collation made no mention of the grammar school or its master, but gave WILLIAM GODYNG, clerk (not *dominus*

17   British Library Add. MS 30158 *s.v.* the Monday before Lady Day.
18   NRO DN/Reg 7 Registers of the Bishops of Norwich, Book 10, p. 62. The entry headed 'Scole can' Gippe" is dated 9 October 1445.

or *magister*, so probably a non-graduate) custody and direction of the song school of Ipswich. Apeseyes must be a corruption of ABCs; in other places they were called Abecedarians. Primerians studied the standard late medieval Latin primer of Aelius Donatus. It was not until 1487 that Caxton printed an edition of *Donatus melior*, and so the books used ten years earlier must still have been in manuscript. The learning of the psalter as an intermediate stage between the primer and the grammar scholars is unique to Ipswich, a musical school from the first.

Besett's tenure did not last long and he may have died in 1479, because his successor took office then, and the next year the widow of a recent schoolmaster suffered at the hands of a local parson. The Sessions Roll[19] for 14 July 1480 records that on 1 May and on many other days, Edward Valentyn, rector of Freston, clerk, with force and arms, *viz.* a stick and a knife, attacked Joan, the widow of 'le olde Scolemayster', and had carnal knowledge of her 'against the King's peace'. Another woman suffered the same fate a month later. Valentyn was fined a shilling on each count. Perhaps the unfortunate Joan was the widow of Besett.

19 SROI C/2/9/1/1/1/12.

Bonmachers   Parminters   Cox Lane

This Victorian photograph will help to dispel the Donachers myth, which was begun by Vincent Redstone and taken up by Gray and Morfey. A Tudor deed refers to the house next to Parminters in Carr Street, on the corner of Cox lane, as Donachers. They hoped that the name might be a corruption of Donatus, author of the standard Latin grammar text, and the house the place where boys studied. Unfortunately for this thesis, earlier deeds call the same house Bonmachers, obviously belonging to the Bonmarche family prominent in fifteenth-century Ipswich. As Cox Lane was often referred to in early deeds as the lane leading from Carr Street to the Grammar school house these buildings would have been a familiar sight to boys making their way to school from the north of the town.

The steep-gabled house built for the Preparatory School near the Ivry Street entrance to the Lime avenue in 1908 was from about 1950 called Donachers to keep the old name alive, for which reason it was enclosed in the 1970 building there, like an insect in amber.

II

John Squyer, Richard Felaw and John Howard
The Clerk, the Merchant Benefactor
and the Duke of Norfolk

The School, in 1480, still lacked a designated schoolhouse. Thanks to a partnership between a versatile priest schoolmaster, his wealthy and nationally influential patron and the most powerful noblemen in eastern England, a suitable house facing the convent of the Blackfriars was given to the school in 1483. Felaw's house housed the school of over one hundred boys for all but three years of the next century and a half.

FOR A SCHOOL TO PROSPER it needs permanent premises and the means to attract good masters. Even when, in 1477, the corporation had fixed the fees to be charged and the bishop of Norwich had approved them and their choice of John Besett as master, the school did not immediately flourish, perhaps because the latter was ailing and the school was not yet adequately housed.

The first we hear of JOHN SQUYER, clerk, in whose time all this would change, is a legacy in the 1472 will of a rich widow of the Quay parish.[1] In July 1475, he was presented to the living of

---

[1] SROI IC/AA2/2/235: Will of Dame Alice, late wife and executrix of Thomas Andrew, who was giving Richard Felaw the first option to purchase her houses in Harwich. A John Squyer clerk was found in Bodleian Library MS Top. Suff. b.2 at the final proof stage. Peter Le Neve notes him Receiver General of the lands of William (De la Pole), duke of Suffolk in a deed of exchange of lands in Saxmundham in April 1450. If this is our Squyer he can hardly have taken the school into the 16th century as tentatively suggested below.

Akenham, only two miles north of Ipswich, by Gilbert Deben-ham Esq. of Little Wenham. Unfortunately, Squyer has not been found in the lists of Oxford or Cambridge graduates, though his title 'dominus' in the bishop's register and 'Sir' in wills implies that he held a bachelor's degree. In May 1479, he freely resigned his Akenham benefice, probably to succeed Besett; the following September, the corporation great court ruled that he should have a life interest in the profits of all millstones, quernstones 'also all stones known as Doggestonys[2] and grinstonys' coming to the 'town or port of Orwell'. From this income, he was to find a 'suitable and honest chaplain' to celebrate mass for the Guild of Corpus Christi, who would be paid an annual stipend of nine marks, that is £6. The profits of the trade in imported stone had, since 1200, been the means of rewarding the aldermen of the Guild for their work on its behalf. It appears that Squyer wanted to succeed Besett as master of the grammar school but did not wish to be Guild chaplain as well. If so, we shall eventually con-clude that he may have been the longest serving headmaster in the school's history and the one whose influence with the first founder and benefactor made him a benefactor also.

Five years after the school fees had first been set, in October 1482, the corporation ordered them to be reduced, to bring Ips-wich fees in line with those of schools elsewhere. 'Every bur-gess shall pay to the master of the grammar school, for a boy, 8 pence a quarter and no more, and [perhaps to make up the loss to him] that the said grammar school master shall celebrate mass, for the whole term of his life, for the Guild of Corpus Christi.' The school educated the sons of the ruling burgesses of the town at these modest fees. Presumably the master could charge more to those who were not so entitled; we have seen

---

2 dog-stone, 'a stone used for a millstone', *OED*.

that, in the case of Alexander de la Pole and perhaps Robert Reymes, far higher charges, including board, were paid for the sons of the east Suffolk nobility and gentry.

Squyer's close association with the school's earliest known benefactor, Richard Felaw, culminated in his being appointed one of his executors; the other, James Hobart, was later knighted as attorney-general. Felaw gave the school its first proper home and lands at Whitton (next to Akenham, which may explain how he and Squyer first met) to produce income. In his will, he left his house in St Edmund Pountney Lane, now Foundation Street, as a place where the master could live and keep the school. Here, in the parish of St Mary Quay, the school prospered from sometime after Felaw's death in January 1483 until 1612,[3] when it moved across the road to the refectory of the former Blackfriars and the house was put to other uses.

Richard Felaw was born about 1420, son of John and Agnes Felaw of Ipswich. His crucial interest in the school is likely to have arisen from its having given him sufficient education in the 1430s to rise to the highest positions in Ipswich and to become highly influential nationally. John Felaw was bailiff in 1439 but Richard served in that office eight times, returning himself as one of the two burgesses to Parliament in 1449 and again in 1460–62. He purchased Crewches Hall, in Harwich, and became bailiff there towards the end of his life. He married Agnes, daughter of Thomas Denys, another Ipswich bailiff; their only child Agnes married John Fastolf of Pond Hall, opposite King John's Ness on the Orwell, at the seaward extent of the borough bounds.[4] Felaw's merchant ships brought salt and

3 Not counting the brief excursion in the 1520s to Wolsey's college in St Peter's parish.
4 J. C. Wedgewood, *History of Parliament* 1439–1509 (2 vols. London, 1936), vol. 1, *s.v.* Fellowes, Richard, 315.

fish from Scandinavia, wine from Gascony and iron from Spain. As collector of customs and subsidy from 1458, he was the senior officer of the crown in Ipswich. His chief strength, however, lay in his close association with Sir John Howard of Tendring Hall, Stoke-by-Nayland, later of Framlingham Castle, who as a loyal Yorkist, was made the first Howard duke of Norfolk in 1483 but killed at Bosworth two years later. Howard was Lord High Admiral in 1461, when he engaged Felaw and others to provision the king's ships; this led to Felaw serving (with the archbishop of Canterbury and others) as commissioner to raise a fleet of six ships against the king's enemies – France and Scotland. Felaw shared Howard's Yorkist loyalty and was his trusted business agent in Ipswich, provisioning ships and supplying materials for his building projects, and Howard was no stranger to Felaw's house, where he is known to have come on business. Despite the Felaws giving generous gifts to the Blackfriars, for which their names were to be placed in the martyrology of the convent and commended among the foremost benefactors every week, they were buried in their parish church of St Mary Quay.

Since Felaw's will made in 1482 was of lasting importance to the town, it was copied in English into Richard Percyvale's Great Domesday Book of about 1520, which is just as well as the original is lost.[5] Though Felaw also endowed almshouses, this, in modern English, is what he provided for the School:

> I will that my mees (messuage or house) opposite the Friars Preachers in Ipswich be used for ever as a common Schoolhouse and dwelling with a yard to the North for a convenient School Master, to be appointed by the Bishop of Norwich, on the nomination of the current Bailiffs of Ipswich. They (the masters) will pay no rent, but receive the rents

5   SROI C/4/1/4, fols 144r–145r.

from other property in Whitton and Brokes Hall. They will charge no fees for children born and living in Ipswich unless the parents have incomes of twenty shillings per annum or over or goods worth £20 and will keep the properties in good repair. And every morning at 6.00 a.m. the Master will take the pupils to sing the Mass of Our Lady at the north altar of the Blackfriars Church...

Felaw's charitable wish was that the school should be free to the sons of poorer burgesses, and that only those who could afford it should pay fees. It was certainly Squyer who saw to the establishment of the school in its new home opposite the Blackfriars church.

The strong links over many years between Howard, Felaw and Squyer led Irvine Gray to argue that Thomas Howard, son and successor of John as second duke, and eventually Victor of Flodden, is likely to have boarded at the school around 1460. An inscription seen over his tomb at Thetford 'after he had been a sufficient season at the gramer scole, ...' has misled historians into thinking that he was at the school there, but the family home was in south Suffolk, at Tendryng Hall. That Thomas came to Ipswich from Stoke-by-Nayland is implied by the fact that after the 'sufficient season', he took an Ipswich boy home with him, for further study under his father's chaplain. The Howard steward's accounts for 1465 include a debt by John Lopham, the leading Ipswich glazier who succeeded Felaw as burgess to Parliament in 1462 and 1463, 'for the bord of hys son when he went to scole here (at Stoke, at my master's place)'. Unfortunately, we lack the name of the two boys' grammar schoolmaster in the 1450s and 60s but they probably learnt to sing under William Godyng.

In September 1488, there is another ambiguous entry in the General Court Book: 'It is allowed Master [Thomas] Head, Master of Grammar (NB not 'of the Grammar School'), ten marks (£6 13s

4d) to celebrate for the Guild of Corpus Christi from Michaelmas to Michaelmas, that is for a whole year, at Cambridge, on condition that he be at Ipswich for the four quarter days and at the feast of Corpus Christi.'[6] Thomas Head MA (in 1496 made DD) had just been elected a fellow of Pembroke and would in future have to reside there. The most likely explanation of the order is that Head had been Squyer's nominee as master and guild chaplain but now needed permission to hold only the chaplaincy, mainly *in absentia*. Had he done any teaching while resident in Ipswich, this would have been the beginning of the school's long and close connection with Pembroke College. That Squyer had been elected town treasurer, in 1483, only shows that he was more widely useful and influential than most mere schoolmasters would be. He was trusted by several wealthy members of the Quay parish when they needed a supervisor or witness to their wills.[7] Felaw's patron John Howard, now duke of Norfolk, presented him to the rectory of Eyke near Woodbridge in 1484, a living next vacant in 1524, perhaps the date of Squyre's death. He was presented as non-resident at Eyke, found neglecting his cure (pointing to his pluralism) at the Visitation of 1499, just at the time he was being granted two quays and other land in Ipswich, clearly moving into mercantile trade.

It was probably in January 1520 that Squyer decided to retire from the mastership, for it was then granted to WILLIAM STEPHENSON, clerk, to celebrate mass for the Guild and also to keep the Grammar School for the coming year, entering into the school at Easter.[8] The school was not expanding, for the

6 SROI C/2/10/3/1, 142.

7 For Henry Fulslo, will dated 1487, he was supervisor; Jasper Cornelius, 1494, witness; and William Gosse the younger, 1497, adviser to his widow, executrix. All were of the Quay parish.

8 British Library Add. MS 24435, fol. 153v.

tenement next door, part of Felaw's gift, was next year leased to one James Lilly for twenty years, at six shillings a year. He was certainly not another schoolmaster, for William Stephenson was still 'grammar master in Ipswich' when he witnessed a will in 1522.[9] There was a William Stephenson who held one of the half-rectories of Pakefield before 1520 and the same, or another, was presented to the vicarage of Aldringham-cum-Thorpe, in 1537, by Charles Brandon, duke of Suffolk. If Stephenson had not already departed by 1528, he had to hand his pupils over to the former head master of Eton, newly arrived to take charge of Wolsey's Cardinal's College of St Mary.

Felaw's house

Felaw's house, when demolished in 1963, consisted of five small slum dwellings each of two storeys, the northern pair added in the nineteenth century. The builder then made a thorough job of unifying old and new, adding two huge chimneys matching the earlier stacks. For the next twenty years the site was unde-  veloped. Demolition photographs and plans of the 1985

9 SROI IC/AA2/8/210: Will of Richard Oke of Brook Street in the Quay parish, who made his will in the presence of James Hill and Richard Percyvale, justices, the parish incumbent, William Stephenson, Robert Joyne, coroner, and two other burgesses.

archaeological excavation show that a cellar had been inserted later in the rear half of the core and that there had been a substantial stone south wing, probably the kitchen, made as fireproof as possible. The north and south gable walls of the core rectangular house were of stone, like the kitchen wing foundations, but the excavation suggests that the front and rear walls were timber-framed. The vernacular buildings specialist Philip Aitkens has studied all the available evidence, including the house as shown on maps and plans, beginning with John Ogilby's survey in 1674. His interesting conclusions are tentative, the most striking being the suggestion that only the foundations of the kitchen survive from Felaw's own time. If Felaw left a house of the quality one would expect for a man of his standing, little but the foundations of the kitchen wing survived the many subsequent alterations. Mid-fifteenth century town houses of the hall-house type were open to the roof with a central hearth. At one or both ends of such a hall, two-storeyed cross-wings would have given privacy to the family. The house bequeathed in 1483 may not have made a convenient school and, although the accounts do not survive, we must assume that, as soon as funds were available, the building was heavily remodelled or completely rebuilt, with a new first floor and a staircase to reach it and a new roof covering the entire rectangular front range. The wind-braced side-purlin roof, which came down in 1963, was of a type fashionable throughout East Anglia during the sixteenth century. In the Morfey Museum there are two highly-glazed ridge tiles, crowstepped, probably from the 'new' roof, and one darker and cruder example which may have come from Felaw's roof. Three of the side-purlins rescued at the demolition were fixed outside the museum in 1988. Unfortunately, the four-centred arched door frame probably from the head of the staircase disappeared from storage in 1972.

A puzzling and intriguing find in excavating the house was the lead bulla (seal) from a papal bull of Boniface VIIII, pope from 1389–1404. The four calendared papal letters sent to Ipswich during that papacy all came to the Augustinian priories, St Peter and St Paul, dissolved for Wolsey in the 1520s, and Holy Trinity in the greater closure of the late 1530s. Four late-medieval tokens, jettons, were probably lost by boys playing.

At the Dissolution, the church of the Blackfriars was immediately dismantled for the great value of its stone for building but Birkin Haward has drawn an elevation showing what until then lay immediately opposite Felaw's House, with the west door through which generations of bleary-eyed boys must have passed every morning.

Squyer settled the school in its new home and in June 1487 a 'parcel of the common soil under the walls of the Friars Preachers, paying to the commonalty 3s 4d yearly and a red rose and it is permitted that John Squyer shall erect a new building on the same land as a latrine for the Grammar School boys'. The extra plot was to the south of the house, the yard to the north having already been left to the school by Felaw.

South-west view of Felaw's House. In the foreground is the stone kitchen wing. The core of the house on the street faced the Blackfriars to the refectory of which the schoolroom moved in 1612, leaving Felaw's House to 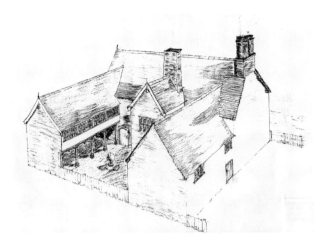 *accommodate the boarders and either the master or the usher. The galleried north wing added after 1600 probably served as the writing school in the 1660s. A conjectural reconstruction by Philip Aitkens, 2002.*

 *The west elevation of the Dominican Friary (Blackfriars) facing Felaw's House across Edmund Pountney Lane. On the left is the church with its main west entrance through which master and pupils passed 'to kepe ... the messe of our lady by note at the North Awter... at sex of the clokke on the morrow dayly'. The refectory is on the right. Reconstruction by the late Birkin Haward, January 1988.*

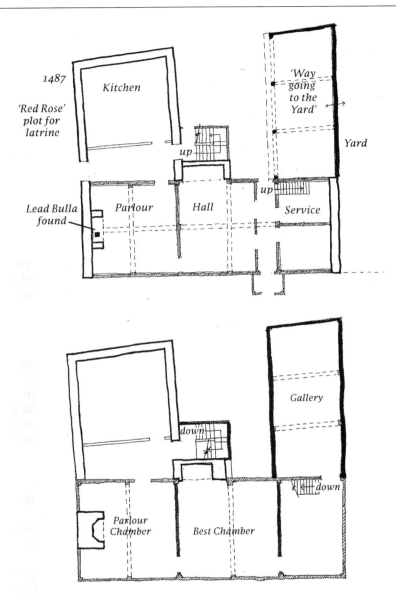

1487

'Red Rose' plot for latrine

Kitchen

'Way going to the Yard'

Yard

up

Lead Bulla found

Parlour   Hall   up   Service

Gallery

down

Parlour Chamber   Best Chamber   down

Felaw's House: Plans of ground floor (above) and first floor (below), based by Philip Aitkens on an inventory of 1663. The porch abuts on to Foundation Street, formerly Edmund Pountney Lane.

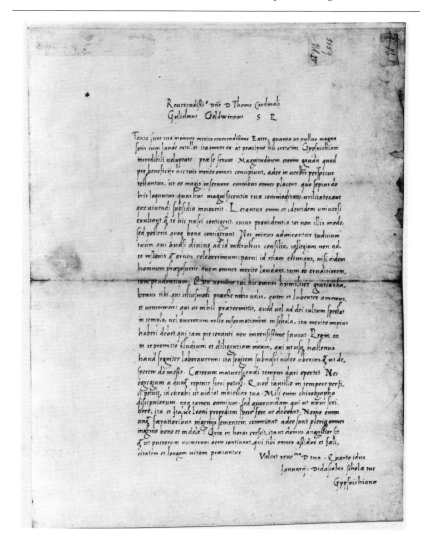

William Golding writes to Cardinal Wolsey 10 January
1529 reporting progress in the school
(PRO S.P. Henry 8, Vol. 52, No. 127)

III

Thomas Wolsey's Cardinal's College
of St Mary in Ipswich

Wolsey had plans for a double foundation: a school at his birthplace linked to a college at Oxford. It was to rival the great foundations of Henry VI (Eton and King's) and William of Wykeham (Winchester and New College). By September 1528 the school (called a college) was in session, but in 1530 its founder died in disgrace, and Henry VIII was glad to take over the Oxford college – Christ Church today – and to dismantle the Ipswich buildings for their materials. Much more is known about the running of the college (which took in the grammar school boys) than about the earlier and later school. The surviving Wolsey's Gate was only the riverside entrance, but much else remains of the College if one knows where to look.

THOMAS WOLSEY was born in Ipswich sometime between 1471 and 1475, and recent scholarship leans towards the earlier date. The infant soon began to astonish his none too law-abiding butcher father Robert Wolsey and his better-connected mother Joan, sister of Edmund Daundy. Daundy was an influential leader of Ipswich political and commercial life in the late fifteenth century. Wolsey's loyal secretary and biographer, George Cavendish, begins his account:

> And being but a child, he was very apt to learning; by means whereof his parents, or his good friends and masters, conveyed him to the University of Oxford, where he prospered so in learning that, as he told me in his own person, he was

called the boy-bachelor, forasmuch as he was made Bachelor
of Arts at fifteen years of age...[1]

If he was fifteen in 1486, the masters who prepared him for
Oxford and Magdalen College must have been Besett and Squyer and Thomas experienced the school's move to Felaw's house.
If Squyer had been an Oxford man (and a contemporary Laurence Squyer, perhaps a brother, was at Magdalen and, from
1486, master of the boys of the Chapel Royal) it might explain
why Wolsey travelled beyond Cambridge for his education.

After graduating, Wolsey became master of Magdalen College School and his experience of teaching there probably
brought benefits to Ipswich boys at the other end of his career,
when he devised the grandest plans for the school in his birthplace. The chronology below shows how rapidly this exotic
flower bloomed and faded. The most interesting and surprising
aspect of the story is the lively way in which he laid down the
curriculum and gave guidance to the masters about the way the
boys should be treated. His liberal humanist approach to education must reflect to some extent his own experiences at Ipswich and Oxford. Wolsey's address to his college and the curriculum to be followed in each of the eight forms was printed
in an edition of Dean Colet's Latin Grammar, published in
1529.[2] Wolsey wanted the youngest boys to speak and write
Latin, but then, in the third form, to begin to enjoy the Latin
authors. Only in the eighth form did grammar reappear and
then leavened with just a little Greek and the writing of English
essays:

1 Ed. R. Lockyer, *Thomas Wolsey, late Cardinal, his life and death*, London 1973,
31.
2 John Colet, founder of St Paul's School, and William Lily, first High Master,
were both Magdalen men, where Lily and Wolsey were contemporaries. Wolsey's
curriculum, in Latin, was published by Colet and an English translation appears in
Strype's *Ecclesiastical Memorials*, i, Part 2, 139.

I   Latin parts of speech and pronunciation

II   Translating Latin and speaking it, writing in an Italic hand

III, IV and V   Reading Latin authors:
Aesop 'Who can be more humorous?'
Terence 'Who more useful?'
Virgil 'the prince of poets, whose majestic verses should be read in a sonorous voice.'

VI   Latin historians; Lily's *Syntax* and irregular verbs

VII   *Horace* or *Ovid*, writing Latin prose and verse and learning by heart, for which the best time, Wolsey said, is just before going to bed

VIII   Advanced Latin grammar, a little Greek and writing English essays

Most surprisingly, and centuries ahead of his time, he stipulated:

> 'Pleasure is to mingle with study, that the boy may think learning rather an amusement than a toil. Tender youth is to suffer neither severe thrashings nor sour and threatening looks, nor any kind of tyranny, for by such usage the fire of genius is either extinguished or in great measure damped.'

The letter the first and only master, WILLIAM GOLDING (or Goldwyn), wrote to him in Latin in his fine Italic hand, as soon as the teaching had begun, shows that, in choosing him, Wolsey had successfully set the seal of success on his educational aims. Golding tells Wolsey how 'everybody, especially at Ipswich, vies in extolling his munificence and how they rejoice in his having been born there, who had bestowed such benefits, not only on them but on posterity. Especially, they admired his judgement not only in having established and adorned the college but in having set over it [in William Capon the dean] a man whose learning and wisdom they all praise and whom the inmates of the college love and venerate, who omits nothing which tends to the worship of God in chapel or the good instruction of the boys in school'. Golding promises renewed zeal and diligence on his own part and 'as he has laboured not sluggishly hitherto he already begins to see a more plentiful crop growing so that he does not despair of the harvest. But it must have time to ripen. What could be done in so short a time that I have done as your majesty[3] may see. For I have sent some writings of my pupils, not of all but of some, who as they now write so I hope they will soon be able to speak Latin as they ought, for no one ever employed a sower on more fertile soil, so full are they all of good intelligence and disposition. The flock hourly increases so that the house is too small to hold the number of boys comfortably'. [4]

The college seal, entirely renaissance in design, shows the Assumption of the BVM. She ascends between cherubs and angels standing in a crescent moon overlapped by Wolsey's cardinal's hat and with his arms below; she is crowned by Christ and God the Father, with the dove of the Holy Spirit above. The inscription runs: SIGILLVM · CO'IE · COLLEGII · THOME · WVLCY · CARDINALIS · OPIDO · GIPSWICI ·

3 In his enthusiasm Golding uses an expression which would amount to treason should the letter fall into the wrong hands. Henry VIII, usually 'your grace', became the first king to be so addressed.

4 Translated from letter from Golding to Wolsey, 10 January 1529, illustrated on p. 26. PRO S.P. Henry 8, Vol. 52, No. 127.

An Outline Chronology of Wolsey's College

1526
6 May – Papal bull for the establishment of the Ipswich college sent from Rome to Wolsey by the Bishop of Worcester, auditor of the Apostolic Chamber there.

1527
November – Thomas Cromwell visits Ipswich about the building of the college.

Henricus VIII Angliæ Rex &c.

1528
March – Duke of Norfolk writes to tell Wolsey that he has visited the site and ordered a plan of SS Peter and Paul priory. He can advise the Cardinal how to 'save large monie in buildyng there', presumably by using some of the buildings, particularly by modifying the church for the chapel.

14 May – Pope Clement VII issues a bull authorising the suppression of five small priories: Rumburgh, Felixstowe, Blythburgh (all Suffolk) and Mountjoy and Bromehill in Norfolk.

26 May – The king ratifies a bull for the suppression of the Augustinian priory of SS Peter and Paul in Ipswich.

31 May – The king ratifies a bull for the transfer, from Wolsey's Oxford College, of Snape and Dodnash, (both Suffolk) and Wix, Horkesley and Tiptree Priories (all Essex).

15 June – The foundation stone (above, with transcription and translation, right) of the college is laid by John Holte, titular bishop of Lydda and a suffragan of London. In the eighteenth century the stone was found built into a wall in Friars Road and presented to Christ Church, Oxford by the Revd Richard Canning where it is fixed mural in the chapter house.

AN·CHRISTI·M
DXXVII·ET
REGNI·HENRICI
OCTAVI·REGIS
ANGLIÆ·XX·MENSIS
VERO·IVNII·XV
POSITVM
p·IOHEM·EPN͞·LIDEM ͞

The Year of our Lord 1528 and the 20th year of the Reign of King Henry VIII of England and the 15th of June [this stone] laid by John, Bishop of Lydda

21 June – Building work is begun by 37 freemasons working under local master masons John Barbour and Richard Lee using Caen stone. Mr Daundy, Wolsey's cousin, has imported 121 tons, and promises 1,000 more before the following Easter.

26 June – The king grants the rectory of St Matthew's, Ipswich to the college, a living held at the time by Wolsey's natural son Thomas Winter.

29 June – The king's letters patent for the foundation of the college issued. It could be built in St Matthew's parish ('where the said Cardinal was born') or elsewhere.

30 June – Cromwell to Thomas Arundel: He must delay the erection of the college at Ipswich until 21 July, as the offices in Chancery will not expire till then.[5]

3 July – Wolsey commissions six eminent clerics, including Stephen Gardiner, later bishop of Winchester, to prepare statutes for the college.

28 July – Wolsey executes his foundation deed, based on the king's letters patent, converting SS Peter and Paul Priory to 'Saint Mary, Cardynall College of Ipswich'. William Capon STP, master of Jesus College, Cambridge appointed dean of the college, presiding over 12 priest fellows, 8 clerks, 8 children (choristers), a grammar-school master and usher, 50 grammar

5 There was a need to wait for certain formalities to be completed.

scholars and '12 poure men to pray dayly to God for the good astate of our Graces King & the said Cardinall, ther frends souls and all cristen soulls'. Later Thomas Cromwell makes draft lists of stipends (the dean and master both to have £13 6s 8d) and adds a second usher, who is also 'keeper of the schole-house'.

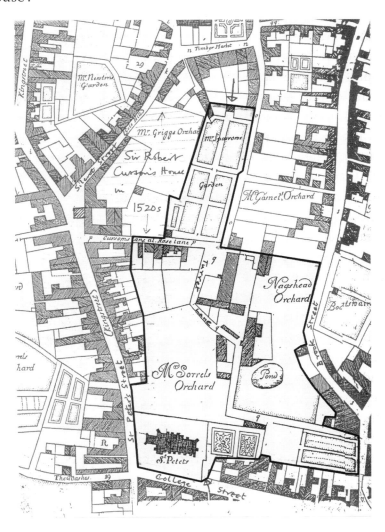

7 August – Wolsey, from Hampton Court, instructs Dean Capon to assemble the parishioners of St Peter's and offer them the choice of St Nicholas or St Mary Quay for their future worship. Dame Elizabeth Gelget leaves money for the purchase of a roof from Capon should the churchwardens of St Mary Quay choose to cover the chancel there with it.[6] The congregation there, about to be swelled by about half the parishioners of St

Peter's, would need a church in good order. St Mary Quay chancel roof shows every sign of being roughly re-assembled, probably from St Peter's.

Wolsey wanted his chapel to resemble those of Eton and King's, squarer and better for grand ceremonial. The Tournai marble font basin, lacking its large central pillar and four slender ones at the corners, is given an incongruous Tudor base. The west doorway of St Peter's was embellished with

heads, shields and fleurons in the jambs and two large vaulted

6 NRO will NCC 295 Palgrave 1528.

canopied niches to north and south probably for statues of SS Peter and Paul. This is Tudor rather than medieval work.

10 August – Dean Capon publishes the acquisition of many smaller properties given by Wolsey with the king's approval. Deed dated from 'the chapel of our said college', that is, the refurbished St Peter's.[7]

20 August – The king inspects and confirms a papal bull dated 12 June exempting the college from all ecclesiastical jurisdiction but that of the pope, the two archbishops being guardians of its liberties.

Capon rebus within letter C.

1 September – The college in session under William Goldwin, master. Wolsey sends his *Rudimenta Grammatices*, 'dedicated not only to Ipswich School, most happily founded by the most reverend Lord Thomas, Cardinal of York, but to all other schools in England'.[8]

8 September – Feast of the nativity of the BVM. Capon writes at length describing to Wolsey (who could not be present) the first

7 PRO E24/23/15 with college seal (illustrated on page 30) appended.
8 Title-page illustrated on page 42.

annual celebration of the foundation. After solemn mass the planned procession to Gracechurch in Lady Lane is interrupted by rain, but a lavish feast is enjoyed nevertheless.

Wednesday after Christmas – The Great Court grants the college the interest in all the property, in Ipswich and at Whitton, with which Felaw endowed the grammar school. Against 'Concessio' [granted] in the margin is written 'Vacat' [void], showing that the corporation managed to reverse the grant after the fall of the college.

1529
10 January – William Goldwin writes to Wolsey reporting progress and, presumably by the same messenger, the bailiffs reply to Wolsey's request that they grant the college the former endowments of the grammar school.

12 April – Capon writes to Cromwell: they have begun to set the freestone; there are troubles with the choir ('in our quere standith the honnor of your graces collage', as Capon wrote to the founder); but the school is so well attended that it must be enlarged; schoolmaster and usher take great pains.

30 April – Sir Robert Curson, Lord Curson agrees to Wolsey's request to be given Curson's house adjoining the college as his 'provost's residence' in the manner of the provosts of Eton and Winchester. Robert cannily asks for three years' grace to move out – thus avoiding the need ever to do so. A copy of a detailed survey of the property is all that remains today.[9]

9   British Library MS Aug. I, vol 2, no 48.

July – Cromwell's agent Brabazon reports that the college is going on prosperously 'and much of it above ground, which is very curious work'. Working day and night, more has been done in the last three weeks than for some time before.

July to September – Gifts of plate, vestments, books and other furnishings for the chapel arrive from many sources including Wolsey's York Place in London.

8 August – Bailiffs and portmen write to thank Wolsey for setting up the college to the honour and use of their town.

8 September – It is not known whether the second Lady Day procession was held.

13 November – Royal commissioners visit to make an inventory of all valuables and building materials. They estimate that the college had £10,000 worth of Wolsey's 'treasure' and take away with them the best plate and vestments.

1 December – Wolsey impeached.

1530
9 July and 20 July Dean Capon writes twice to Wolsey, in his first expressing pessimism about the future, the second telling him that the king was resolved to dissolve the college by Michaelmas.

19 September Commissioners sitting at Woodbridge rule that all the college lands were forfeit to the king.

4 October – Capon tells Wolsey that the Duke of Norfolk has ordered the dissolution of the college retaining only the dean, sub-dean, schoolmaster, usher and six grammar children pending the king's pleasure. The king orders the demolition of the college and the materials – 'Caen stone, harde stone of Kente, Rygate stone, chimneys ready wrought,... wainscot, smith's work, glass, the making of the kings armes, and badges in glasse, bullyons & buddes of tymbre turned & carved togedre with leaves and antique works imploied to the garnysshing of the rofe of the newe galerie... painting and gildyng... to be shipped to Galye Key in London' where they are to be used to enlarge what was formerly Wolsey's York Place, to become the royal palace of Whitehall.[10] Only Wolsey's gate, the waterside entrance to the college next to the chapel remains today.[11]

From the Cornhill and the Buttermarket, visitors passed under an impressive tower and walked through a long formal

10 PRO E351/3322.
11 The St Peter's parishioners successfully petitioned Cromwell for the return of their church in 1536.

garden. The Turret House, as it was latterly called, was pulled down in 1843.[12] It was probably a remnant of the Dean's house,

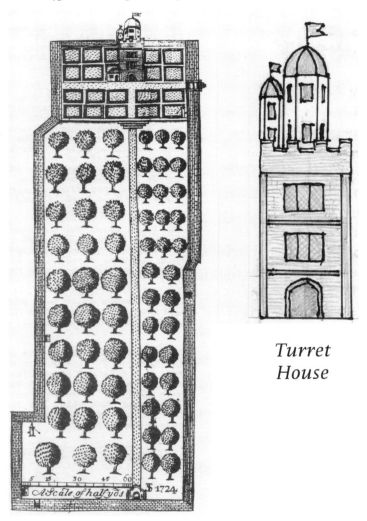

Turret House

12   There is a unique etching of the Turret House and orchard (above left), dated 1724, in SROI HD 480/30 fol. 200. It is called 'Mr Sparrows Garden' on John Ogilby's map of Ipswich, 1674. There were, according to Daphne Hart's reconstruction drawing, eight pepperpot turrets on Wolsey's Oxford college, so the two on the Turret House were in keeping.

well-situated, at some remove from the boys, for entertaining guests.

29 November – Wolsey dies at Leicester Abbey on his way to London.

Early 1531

Ipswich college property bringing in income of £2,234 a year assigned to the Oxford college (now to be known as the King's College of Christ Church), St George's, Windsor, the king and various other persons. Thomas Alvard, agent of Cromwell, is given the college site. Most importantly, the 'college or school' of Ipswich is assigned £60 a year, in another document only £43, to cover the stipends of master and usher and to be paid out of the profits of crown lands in the county, but Felaw's bequests not mentioned as probably already recovered by the corporation. Thomas Cromwell is still credited with ensuring that the school was not forgotten in the dissolution of the short-lived college.

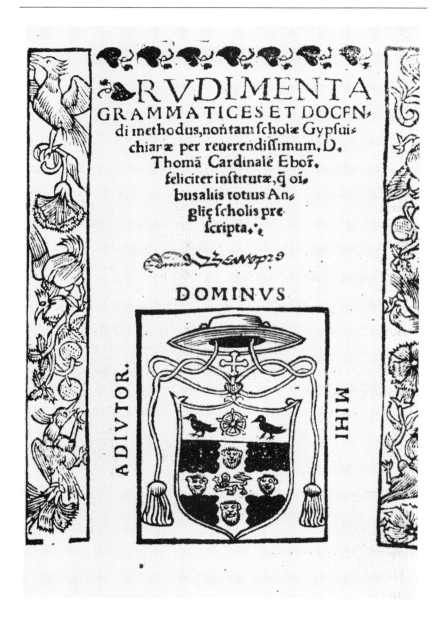

Wolsey's Rudimenta Grammatices *(British Library shelfmark C.40.c.39) to be used in his college and elsewhere (see page 36).*

IV

Six Tudor Headmasters

---

*William Golding, the first and only master of Wolsey's College,
stayed on for a total of ten years as master of the grammar
school, which Thomas Cromwell, Lord Chancellor persuaded
the king to re-endow. He and his successors who ran the school
for the remainder of the sixteenth century were an unusually
interesting and varied group of men. After the turncoat
Argentine they were all scholarly Protestants, some of them
published authors.*

THE CARDINAL'S COLLEGE had only one master and,
although he made a very bad career move when he accepted
the post, he ensured continuity in the education of his Ipswich
boys by staying on as master of the refounded grammar school
and standing by his decision for ten whole years. WILLIAM
GOLDING, who was born at Dorney near Windsor, entered
King's College, Cambridge as an Eton scholar in August 1515.
He took his BA early in 1520, proceeded MA three years later
and for seven years held a fellowship at King's, until he
returned to Eton as head master for three years from 1525. By
an error in the Eton Audit Books, his name appears there as
John Golding but no contemporary graduate of that name is
known.

Thus far, William's rise was rapid but it was a time when
young and able men could take charge of their schools – Thomas Wolsey had become master of Magdalen College School in
his mid-twenties. Wolsey invited Golding from Eton to be the
first master of his Ipswich College, which he intended should

outdo Henry VI's Eton and King's and William of Wykeham's Winchester and New Colleges. Golding served under William Capon, the college dean, from its opening in September 1528 until its closure after Wolsey's fall at Michaelmas 1530. We have read how, in January 1529, Golding so far forget himself as to address Wolsey as 'your Majesty', when sending him a progress report in ornate Latin prose, enclosing specimens of the first pupils' writing. In slightly patronising tone he praised the quality of worship provided by the dean in the chapel, formerly St Peter's church, but since dean and master enjoyed the same stipend, £13 6s 8d, perhaps that was not surprising. The main textbook used in the school had been Wolsey's own *Rudimenta grammatices et docendi methodus* which he dedicated 'not only to Ipswich School but to all other schools in England'.[1] In April, Golding was warning Wolsey of the need to enlarge the college as the pupils were 'all of good intelligence and the flock increased hourly, so that the house was too small to hold them properly'.

When the blow fell, the local boys had no school to go to, since they and their grammar school's endowments had been swallowed up in the college. Thomas Cromwell, Lord Chancellor, however, persuaded the king to refound the town school, reinstating the stipends for the master of £24 6s 8d (with £14 6s 8d for his usher), raised from the profits of crown lands in Suffolk, and Golding, £11 per annum better off, stayed on as master, only returning to a fellowship at Eton in 1539.[2] There

---

1 Quoted in translation from the title page of *Rudimenta* (STC.25944)

2 According to Appendix L in A.M. Stowe, *English Grammar Schools in the reign of Queen Elizabeth*, New York 1908, only six other schools received the schoolmasters' stipends from the crown: Leicester, Lichfield, St Saviour in Southwark, Tamworth, Whalley and Pontefract.

are two signs that, back in Felaw's House, he still adhered to the curriculum laid down by Wolsey.

One of the books Wolsey listed for use in his college was Juvencus' *Historia Evangelica*, a history of the Gospels with the Passion of Christ. This book, printed at Antwerp in 1534 by Johannes Gryphaeus, states on its last page (below) that the stationer Reginald Oliver was offering it for sale at his shop in the Fish Market – then the eastern half of the Buttermarket. Second-

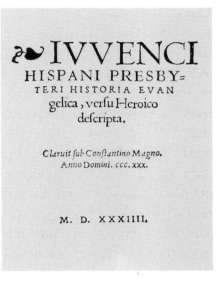

ly, Wolsey's *Rudimenta* was reprinted in 1535 and 1536, also in Antwerp.

We have other interesting glimpses of Golding at this time. He had already leased a dwelling known as Lady Daundy's Lodgings from the Blackfriars, and in October 1537, he and William Lawrence, a weaver, took a lease of 'Le Frayter House, with upper chamber', which can only mean their refectory, evidently already redundant for its proper use, but which did not become the school room until 1614. Perhaps Golding was the first to realise the use to the school of such a large well-lit building standing just across Foundation Street.[3]

3 PRO Ministers' Accounts, 30-31 H.8, No. 139.

Golding later held several Eton college livings with memorable names: Mapledurham from 1544-46, Stogursey from 1554-56 and, after vacating his fellowship in 1550, the rectory of Piddlehinton, Dorset. There he served until his death on 15 May 1562. It is ironic, for one who had been master of a college endowed by the suppression of religious houses, that his modest locally-engraved inscription brass at Piddlehinton is itself a piece of monastic spoil; it is palimpsest (engraved on both sides), for its reverse shows the lower half of the figure of a prior with his staff.

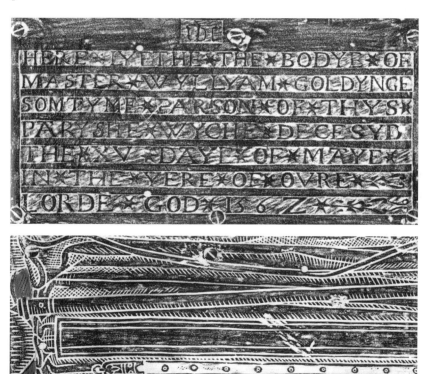

❀

In RICHARD ARGENTINE the school certainly had one of its most colourful and versatile heads. His story is a long and strange one and towards its end one can only conclude that he had become thoroughly unpleasant and troublesome. Born in 1511, he entered Winchester College as Richard Sexton, of Milton, Dorset in 1524. A fellow of New College for ten years from 1528, he proceeded BA in 1532 and MA in 1536. At Cambridge he was accepted as a bachelor of medicine, of Oxford, when he was made a doctor of physick in 1541.

It was probably in 1537 that he became usher at Ipswich, a year before succeeding William Golding as master on the latter's retirement to Eton. John Foxe gives a colourful account of Argentine's exploits in Ipswich in his celebrated *Actes and Monuments,* all from the testimony of Peter Moone, the tailor poet and Protestant activist of the town.[4] 'At his first coming to Ipswich, Argentine] came in a serving man's coat. And then he would accustomably use the reading of the lectures himself, in which he was well commended.' The perfect Protestant, he may have tutored the children and practised physick in households of the gentry and, as Foxe continues – 'being married to a very honest woman, remained there [throughout] the days of King Edward.' The bailiffs writing to the Lord Privy Seal in March 1538, recommending Argentine's promotion from usher to master, were most impressed with him: he had 'redde t[w]o days in the wyke sinse Cristmas last paste a lectorne of Pauls [e]pistills ad Romanos in open audiens not only to the glorie & laude of god ... but also to the gret lernyng, comfort & rejoising of the clargie & temporalte of this Borowgh and of the other the

4 John Foxe, *Actes and Monuments,* ed. S.R.C. Cattley and G. Townsend, 8 vols. (1837–41) vol. 8, 219–22.

kings lovyng subiects of other Tounes... that doth dayly repaire
to the seid lectorne...'[5] His usher would be Richard Pykering,
an Eton and King's College graduate. In a flurry of literary
activity and printing, which probably owed much to Argentine's energy and influence, more than two dozen books were
published over Ipswich imprints in 1548. Three of those printed by Anthony Scoloker were translations by Argentine from
writings of the Protestant reformers: *A ryght notable Sermon
made by Docter Martyn Luther ... uppon the twenteth chapter of
Johan, Sermons of the ryghte famous and excellente clerke Master Barnadine Ochine* and *Certayne Preceptes, gathered by Hulri-
cus Zuingleies, declaring howe the ingenious youth ought to be
instructed and brought into Christ.*[6] .In the preface to the last,
addressed to Edward Grimston, comptroller of Calais and after-

5 *Letters & Papers, Henry VIII*, v. 12, 688.
6 The three works are respectively STC.16992, 18764 and 26136.

wards M.P. for Ipswich, whose son was his pupil, Argentine appears in a more thoughtful light than we otherwise see him. 'Where(as) therefore God hath given unto you a Childe of great towardness [promise], furnished also with the gifts of nature as muche as maie be, Unto whome (for your sake) I am bounde to owe my service in all that I am able to do, I have translated this litle boke...'. In 1552 the master was paid forty shillings for the not very arduous task of making an English translation of the Latin borough charter. Thus far he had Peter Moone's approval.

When Catholic Mary succeeded her brother, however, Argentine was quick to change his religious allegiance. As Foxe wrote, now there was 'none more hot in papistry and superstition than he, painting the posts of the town with *Vivat Regina Maria* and in every corner'. The queen's visit to Sir Humphrey Wingfield's mansion in the town in July 1553 on her triumphal way from Framlingham to her proclamation in London was the turning point for him.

The next year, Argentine received a crown grant of the mastership for life but, finding himself a widower, accepted ordination as deacon and priest on 3 April 1556 by John Hopton, bishop of Norwich, and was immediately instituted to the livings of St Clement and St Helen, Ipswich, both parishes where Protestants were resisting the re-establishment of Catholicism. So scarce were suitable priests, that he was also the next year presented to Whitton and to Brantham with East Bergholt. At Brantham it was soon alleged that, as a pastor he was grossly negligent 'to the great peryll of the inhabitantes'; he quarrelled with his staunchly Catholic patron, Robert Wingfield, and with a London claimant to a lease of the benefice.

Prayere in the morninge
I beleve in god the father &c
Thou shalt have none other god &c

O god our heavenly father &c ...

Prayse at Nyght

O eternall god whiche wonderfully didst make ...

The now ordained master was also neglecting his school duties, if we are to believe Foxe, who tells how he was 'taking upon himself to preach divers times (but never without his white minever hood), such doctrine as was shameful to hear, saying mass and carrying about the pyx in high processions. Furthermore, leading the boy St Nicholas [a pupil no doubt acting as boy-bishop from December 6, St Nicholas day, to Holy Innocents on the 28th] with his miniver hood about the streets, for apples and bellie-cheer. And whoso would not receive him [acknowledge the boy], he made them [accused them of being] heretics, and such as would not give his faggot to the bonfire for Queen Mary's Child' [another name for the boy-bishop]. The boy-bishop tradition was well-established locally, for boys of Colchester grammar school were already taking the part in 1422. The chosen boy even had to deliver a sermon in church and he and his attendants were rewarded with lead alloy tokens, of the kind illustrated here, and probably had others to distribute to others.[7] That July, Argentine with his 'mates', chief of whom was Matthew Butler the constable, 'apothecarie, a curious singing man, a fine plaier of organs and a perfect Papist', were involved in an abortive attempt to arrest one Agnes Wardall, driven from her home in St Clement's parish for her beliefs, her husband Robert (despite a club foot) forced on board ship as a sailor. Returning to see her children but warned of the danger, she first hid in a nettle-filled ditch behind her house, then had a maid lock her in a cupboard.

7 Archaeologists have found four boy-bishop tokens in Ipswich, two in the Blackfriars area. The example from the corner of Bond Street and Rope Walk is Ipswich Museum R1975-22.

na Maria, and in enerp co2ner.

Furthermo2e, after the death of his wife (which was an ho-
neff woman)was made a p2ieff:taking vpon him diuers times
to p2each (but neuer without his white mineuer hœde)fuch doctrine as was fhamefull to heare,faping maffe,⁊ carping about
the pire in high p2oceffions. Furthermo2e,leading the bop S.
Picholas with his mineuer hœde, about the ffreets fo2 apples
and bellie chære. And whofo would not receiue him, he made
them heretickes, and fuch alfo as would not giue his fagot to
the Bonfire fo2 quæne Paries child. And thus continued he at
Ipfwich the moff part of quæne Paries daies,moleffing there
gœd men, fome fo2 not going to the church, fome fo2 not being
confeffed, fome fo2 not receiuing, ⁊c. till at length, toward the
end of quæne Parp hee came to London, and in this quænes
time began to fhew himfelfe againe a perfit p2oteffant. And
thus much of Argentine. Ex teftimon. Petri Moonæi.

Probably at Argentine's suggestion, Peter Moone was taken
before Hopton for examination, with the 'perillous woman' his
wife, as next described by Foxe. Argentine must have been
involved in drawing up lists by parish of 'such as favoured the
Gospell', by fleeing the town or refusing the sacrament, for
they were delivered to special royal commissioners sitting at
Beccles by the same Butler and others of Argentine's confeder-
ates.

Towards the close of Mary's reign, Argentine, foreseeing,
under a restored Protestant government, unpopularity in Ipswich with those he had persecuted, resigned the mastership he
had held for twenty years. At only at six other schools in the
land would he have been entitled to a higher stipend,[8] and he
had done much to raise the school's status, for example persuading Laurence Mopted to endow the first scholarships to
support Ipswich boys to Cambridge. Mopted, a Suffolk man
who was master of Corpus Christi college, was one of Argentine's dedicatees in a strange manuscript, dated 1555, pleading

8 In A.M. Stowe, *op.cit.*, Appendix L: the only masters paid more than at Ipswich
were those at Lincoln, Norwich, Salisbury, Shrewsbury, Southampton and Thame.

for the teaching of Arabic in the universities. Another was John Christopherson, bishop of Chichester, who had been educated at Humphrey Wingfield's Brantham house by the young Elizabeth's tutor Roger Ascham. Leaving Ipswich for London in May 1558, Argentine soon 'began to show himself again [now that Elizabeth was queen] as a perfect Protestant'. The rewards were plentiful.

On 12 March 1561 he became a prebendary with the rectories of Stockleigh Pomeroy and Stoke Fleming in Exeter diocese but by the following November was prohibited from preaching, for spreading seditious libels: his bishop was complaining to Archbishop Parker, that Argentine had 'vilely handled me and my chancellor' and 'hathe played the very knave agaynst [us]'. Lord Keeper Bacon had been 'sent his hole doyngs', for 'the whole citie hathe sent uppe letters agaynst hym' and he was in prison.[9] Ordered to be sent up, bound, to Parker and Grindal as ecclesiastical commissioners, he pleaded poverty and sickness when refusing. His last work, published in Basle (1568) but dated from Exeter in 1563, was no work of devotion: the Latin title *De Praestigiis et Incantionibus Daemonum et Necromanticorum* means 'Concerning tricks and spells of devils and necromancers'. By some means he regained his standing, for in March 1564 he was collated to the prebendal estates at Combe St Nicholas in Bath and Wells diocese. He resigned his Exeter prebend and livings in 1567 but still held Greatford in Lincolnshire and St Helen's at Ipswich, where he was only succeeded on his death in 1568, having survived a summons for non-residence earlier that year by the Norwich diocesan authorities. Robert Wardall, the reluctant sailor of St Clement's parish, by then ordained, replaced him as incumbent there in 1560 and,

9 C.C.C.C., Parker MS 114, No 166.

reciting the pastoral succession in the parish in a lawsuit in 1586,[10] refused to name Argentine, referring merely to 'another', a dignified and understated insult which the former Ipswich schoolmaster richly deserved.

Of the layman JOHN SCOTT we know far less but one of that name proceeded MA at Cambridge in 1537. Scott was granted the post for life with the same stipend as Argentyne enjoyed from Lady Day, 25 March 1558. He was probably only about 55 when he was buried at St Mary Quay on 22 August 1567. The highlight of his tenure must have been the receipt, after application by John Hawys the town clerk, of Queen Elizabeth's Letters Patent dated 18 March 1566,[11] confirming both the 'foundation' by her father Henry VIII, after the failure of the Cardinal's College, and the royal annuity for the master's and usher's stipends. Masters, but not ushers, were in future to be nominated by the borough for approval by the bishop of Norwich. As no statutes for the government of the school were included, the corporation was empowered to draw them up for the bishop's approval but this took five years. Just a week after this refoundation, on New Year's Eve (until 1752 the year ended 24 March 1566), there was a celebration in which 'Mr Scotts lads' entertained the corporation with a play for which the borough chamberlains paid ten shillings

JOHN DAWES (or Daus) was born about 1516, quite probably in Ipswich. A Protestant minister and a good scholar, he led a

---

10 PRO, E.134/28 Elizabeth/Easter, 29.
11 PRO, Patent Rolls, 18 March 7 Eliz.

full and eventful life before settling in Suffolk. He took his BA at St John's College, Cambridge, in 1537 but proceeded MA as a fellow of Christ's in 1541. As chaplain to Thomas, 2nd baron Wentworth of Nettlestead, he accompanied him in 1551 on his appointment as the last English deputy to Calais. At the fall of that city in 1558 (causing Queen Mary to make that sad remark about her heart having 'Calais' carved upon it), he 'lost all his goodes and one of his sonnes'. From thence he 'wente into Germanye to keepe his conscience free from Idolatrie', living there in poverty until Elizabeth succeeded her sister.

Returning home, he ran a private grammar school in Ipswich where he taught Adam Winthrop of Groton. Adam (1548-1623), father of the first Governor of Massachusetts, remembered his schoolmaster with such affection that he wrote a 'true narration of the lyfe and deathe of Mr John Daus' on the fly-leaf of his own copy of one of Dawes' published transla-

tions: Bullinger's *Hundred Sermons upo' the Apocalips of Jesu Christe*, London 1561, dedicated to his patron Wentworth.[12]

It is from Winthrop that we learn most about Dawes. He could not 'shewe where or when [Dawes] was borne, or of what parentage he came', but testified to his being 'very well learned in the latine and greeke tounges and also in the true knowledge of the holy scriptures'. Dawes dedicated another published translation from London the previous year, *A famouse cronicle of oure time, called Sleidanes Commentaries*, to Francis, 2nd earl of Bedford, whom he probably met in exile. Both books were printed by the Suffolk man, John Daye. Winthrop credits Dawes also with 'the Institutions of Mr Calvin in the largest volume, though Mr [Thomas] Norton afterwardes reviewed the same' and the book appeared over Norton's name only. Dawes' translation of 'the Ecclesiasticall storie of Eusebius out of Greeke into Englishe' was 'amongst other thinges he lost at the taking of Calice'.

In 1567, on the death of John Scott, Dawes was appointed master of the grammar school for life and through Roger Kelke, master of Magdalene and town preacher of Ipswich from 1560 to 1576, sent many pupils to that college, including Adam Winthrop and his own sons Joseph and Abraham. He also sent two future ushers there, Robert Inglish in 1567 and James Leman, later ill-fated as master, the year before. The future master, John Smith, went up to Magdalen, Oxford, in 1571, and would also have been a Dawes pupil.

---

12 I am grateful to Francis Bremner for alerting me to the existence of Winthrop's annotated copy of Dawes' book (STC.4061) in Harvard University Library.

The original letter Inglish[13] wrote applying for borough support during his studies survives:

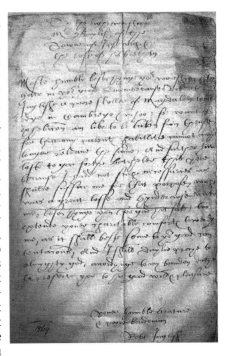

To the ryght worshippf[u]l M[aste]r Bayliff of the Towne of Ipsewich & the rest of his brethren. Moste humbly beseechyng yo'r worshipps to have in yo[u]r good remembreance Robert Inglish a poore skoller of Magdalen Colledge in Cambrege (whoo) for want of exhebic[i]on am like to be taken from thence for that my parents abillitie cannot any longer releave the same, and further have lost to goo forthe batcheler this yere because I hadd not such necessaries as shulde suffice me for that purpose, wich was a great losse and hynderance unto me, besechynge you (for god jhis sake) too extende youer charitable comfort towards me, as it shall best seme to yo[u]r good contentac[i]ons, and I shall daylie praye to almyghty god, accordyng to my bounden duty to preserve yow to his good will & pleasure. Your humble orature & poor beadesman,   Rob[er]t Inglish

Inglish was supported with 53s. 4d. annually out of the foundation (income from the Felaw lands) and served Dawes as usher for about three years from September 1573 but he had

13 Robert, son of Robert Inglish, weaver, of Great Waldingfield was christened there on 22 May 1554. If he was born as late as that year he was a precocious entrant at Magdalene. His letter is tipped into William Batley's Collections in SROI C/3/10/1/1/5.

grown up in Mary's reign and hankered after the old religion. He travelled to Douai, the English college founded in 1568 but forced to move to Rheims a decade later, to study for the Catholic secular priesthood. He was ordained at Chalons in April 1580 and sent straight back to England, to Norfolk, where, using the name More, he was harrassed by protestant spies but evidently escaped betrayal. He was last heard of as an inmate of the hospice in Rome in April 1586.[14]

In 1570, one of Dawes' pupils, John, second son of Sir John Jermy of Brightwell, presented him to the living of Stutton in 1570, a parish in the Stour valley, a hotbed of Puritanism, and for the next twelve years Dawes held the mastership and the living. It was in July 1571 that the borough Great Court published statutes and ordinances for the government of the school to supplement the queen's letters patent[15] and they give us much information about the way the school was run. The following January, John Pytman was paid 6s 8d 'for a frame to the orders' so that they could be hung up in the school.[16] There was nothing in them which made ours greatly different from other town grammar schools and no doubt they confirmed existing practice; new statutes would not automatically involve radical change. Surprisingly, the number of scholars in the school was then over a hundred and the master and usher were to 'forbear to receive ... any more' until the total dropped below this limit. It is hard to visualise so many boys crammed into Felaw's House at one time, especially as they had to sit in (perhaps on) seven forms to receive as 'many distinct degrees of learning'. Sons of local burgesses were to have preference and only

14 I owe these interesting details of Inglish's later life to Mrs Joy Rowe.
15 The only slightly abridged text of the Letters Patent and the Statutes are to be found in Gray and Potter at pages 166 and 39 respectively.
16 Treasurer's accounts C/3/2/1/1, f. 41r.

if there were vacancies could those living nearby be considered. The master could charge fees for eight boarders and the usher four, even if that took the total above the hundred.

> The hours of school throughout the year were six to eleven in the morning and one to four in the afternoon but, if the usher was in by six, the master could begin an hour later. During school hours, the boys were to speak to each other only in Latin, with a Praepositor in each form watching for defaulters. In an enlightened touch, Thursday afternoons were for recreation. The governance of the school and all difficult decisions were in the hands of the bailiffs, the town preacher, the master, the usher and for expulsions any three of them and the town clerk. If he chose, the preacher could wield great power in the school, and all boys had to attend at least one of his weekly sermons in the Tower church, 'making report' of it in whole or part when they returned to school. On Speech day, to be held on New Year's Day (Lady Day, March 25th), the six best scholars were to declaim Latin verses in front of the bailiffs. The parents or friends of scholars had to promise the bailiffs to keep them in school for four years from entry, unless there arose acceptable reasons for withdrawal. Attendance at church on Sundays was compulsory, under penalty of a fine, which could also be imposed for failure to speak Latin.   Masters and boys should, 'kneeling upon their knees, devoutly every day, say or sing such godly morning and evening prayers or psalms, as shall be written in a table to be hanged up in the upper part of the said School'.

In 1574, a new benefaction to the school arrived through the strange will of Roger Barney, merchant of Ipswich.[17] It was written in the form of a letter to 'his welbeloved frende' Agnes Herne from Birdus, perhaps Bordeaux. He hoped that his ships, the *Primrose* and the *Good Grace*, would return with valuable cargoes of wine and the blue dye woad. Barney left £300, 'to be in redynes to be dispersed amongst thirtie poore mens

---

17   The will, PCC 4 Pyckering 1574, was declared null and void 14 May 1575.

children whiche are not able to be helped by their frendes for the maynetenaunce of learninge'. Dr Kelke and the bailiffs were to choose the boys, who on entering the school would have 'a blewe coate and tenne pounds in sterling money a pece', apparently overspending the bequest immediately. Barney died at sea and his brother John had the will declared invalid but some pupils were helped at university from the proceeds of sale of stock still to be sold in 1577.

After Inglish left, probably in 1576, Dawes chose his own son Joseph as usher, and leaving him to look after the boarders in Felaw's house, moved to the tenement next door (also part of Felaw's bequest and probably to the north). This presumably cost him more in rent, but he and his wife Alice gained some privacy. In December 1577 the Great Court ordered the repair of this tenement, otherwise it was 'very likely to fall downe'; a new roof and much else was needed at a total cost of over £18.[18] In September 1579, there was plague in the town and Dawes was ordered to discharge the scholars from attendance at school until further orders from the bailiffs. Similar precautions were taken in the 1586 outbreak. In 1580, a new pump was housed under a tiled roof at the school, and his son Joseph resigned as usher in favour of a living in Bucks. This cast more of the burden of the school on the master, who, two years later, parted with his life interest in return for handsome compensation from his successor for loss of salary. One of Dawes' last actions was to replace an unsatisfactory usher, John Sterne, with Robert Browne, approved 'for his learning and religion' by the joint town preachers, Norton and Pemberton, and Dawes himself. Thus thoroughly vetted, Browne performed well for over ten years before being blamed for a decline in numbers in

18 Great Court Book C/2/2/2/1, f. 48v and Treasurer's accounts C/3/4/1/11, f.6v

1594. At Dawes' departure, the corporation paid him ten shillings for his dictionary, which he left for the use of the school.

For twenty years more Dawes lived and served at Stutton, 'preaching the worde of God and teachinge of his flocke'. He died 'above fowrescore yeres olde' and was buried there in May 1602. The following December, his widow Alice's will[19] showed how comfortably provided they were: she left money, plate, sheep and cereal crops when she died, like the great queen, early in 1603.

What is chiefly interesting about the next master JOHN SMITH, or Smythe, is the manner of his acquiring the mastership, in which his predecessor held a life tenure. Son of John Smyth the elder, of Ipswich, he was presumably educated at the school, matriculated at Magdalen College, Oxford, in 1571, was a fellow of the college from 1575–79 and held a number of west Suffolk livings before coming to the school. His uncle, another Magdalen man, was John Foxe, the author of *Actes and Monuments* quoted extensively in the account of Richard Argentyne. The letter Foxe wrote to Sir Christopher Wray, Lord Chief Justice of England, in November 1581, makes good reading as an example of nepotism in action.[20] It also shows how, through close kin, Foxe could be so knowledgeable about Ipswich in Marian times.

> Forasmuch as thys yong man, for whom I wryte, ys not so well known to your honour, peradventure, as he is to me, by long acquaintance and continuance, to signifie therfore to your lordshyp, not only upon privat affection, but upon treuth and knowlege, in his behalf: thys ys breifly to testifie

19 SROI IC/AA1/38/50.
20 British Library Harl.MS 416, f. 157. His letter to the corporation is at f. 135.

to your good L. that if the town of Ypsewych stand in neede of a worthy godly and lerned scholmaster, for all such indewments and ornaments requisite in such a function, as trew religion, lernyng, diligence and practise, for these and such other gyftes of abilitie, I know not how nor where they may be better spedd than in receavyng thys Mr J Smythe, beyng himself born in the same town of Ypeswych: whom both present occasion of tyme and the good vocation of Christ, I trust, offereth now unto them. Certifiyng moreover your goode Lorshyp, and not only you but also the whole town of Ypeswych, that who so ever shall receave hym for guydyng of theire schole, shall doo no such pleasure to hym as profyte to them selves, and commiddite to their yougth. D. Jesus tibi benedicat, et tuis. Amen.

Lond. Novemb. 23   Yours in Christ Jesu Joh. Foxe

He wrote a similarly fullsome letter to the corporation and, the following September, Wray requested that Smith should be appointed to the next vacancy, stipulating that he should come to the town and make his suit within two months of the mastership becoming void and 'so that in the meantime he do not enter into the ministry or otherwise behave himself than hitherto...' – strange conditions to impose on a man in orders already. Dawes retired and Smith took over but it cost Smith ten pounds down and about one quarter of his salary for the remainder of Dawes' life. As part of this arrangement, Dawes had to undertake that, should Smith default on the annuity, he would resume his duties and the full stipend. On Smith's arrival, a table was set up 'in the myddes of the Gramar Scole for the children to wryte uppon' and as 'a deske for the Dyxsonarye' which Dawes had left behind. The carpenter Robert Dawbny[21] was paid one shilling to make it, but the materials cost more.

---

21   John Webb points out in the introduction to his *Town Finances of Elizabethan Ipswich*, SRS 38, 1996, that Dawbny made the town's stout Cucking Stool the same year for 3s 4d.

Thomas Eldred, father of the Thomas who circumnavigated with Thomas Cavendish four years later, was paid 7s. 4d. for three deal boards to make the table and four trestles. On 17 November in his first year Smith was granted forty shillings 'for his paines and charges in presenting certaine publique pageants in joy of the Queenes Coronation' but this was in fact the anniversary of her accession. In successive years he was rewarded for 'frameing [composing] an oration on the Quenes dayes' and for 'speeches on the Guild days'. By then the Corpus Christi had reverted to being an entirely secular Guild Merchant. Sir Robert Hitcham, who had entered Pembroke Hall, Cambridge, in 1587 and later became the principal benefactor of Framlingham and Coggeshall was presumably one of Smith's pupils.

JOHN BARKLEY (or Berkeley), master from April 1586 until his death in 1604, was described by Irvine Gray in the 1950 *History* as 'something of a mystery'. This was partly because his name was so variably spelt, but Gray solved John's identity in time to publish it in the Suffolk Institute's *Proceedings* of 1983.[22] Described as 'gentleman' in the borough archives and in his will of 1602, he lived at Stoke Hall and his wife Elizabeth was the widow of Philip, a younger son of the first Lord Wentworth. Their son Edward, baptised at St Mary, Stoke, in 1586, graduated BA at Trinity, Cambridge, in 1605, presumably prepared for matriculation by his father at the school. The mention in John's will of a brother Rowland, a first name common among the Worcestershire Berkeleys, sent Gray looking there and in Gloucestershire, where the family seat is Berkeley Cas-

---

22 'An Early Headmaster of Ipswich School' in *PSIAH*, vol. 35, 227–28.

tle. The family steward, John Smith of Nibley collected manuscript 'Lives of the Berkeleys' around 1600, and, in Sir John Maclean's printed edition of 1883–85, Gray found the schoolmaster without difficulty. He was one of fifteen children of William Berkeley, mayor of Hereford, the sixth son of eight, of whom Smith says he was 'a fellow of New Colledge in Oxford, from whence he went to Ipswich where hee dyed'. His brother Edward, a wealthy mercer and benefactor to that company, left John £400 when he died in 1601, with another £600 divided amongst John's children Edward, William, Edmund and Mary. Thus we learn the names of three more likely early pupils at the school. John was certainly well-connected, a direct descendant of Lord Berkeley and Thomas Mowbray, duke of Norfolk. Perhaps the William Barkeley, gent., who was master of Colchester grammar school from 1574 to 1584, was John's brother.

Very little is known of Barkley's time at the school and the impression gained is of an elderly man ending his career here. He was certainly a layman, as was Leman his usher. There was a certain advantage in appointing lay schoolmasters, as they could not neglect their post for church livings. Barkley seems not to have involved himself with the arrangements for borough celebrations, for in 1595 it was his usher James Leman and in 1599 the private schoolmaster George Downing (later master) who received the payments for arranging pageants on the anniversary of the queen's accession. It was in 1599, during Barkley's tenure, that William Smarte (above), portman and burgess to parliament for the town, died leaving books and manuscripts to form the nucleus of what became the preacher's library under Samuel Ward. With a farm called Diggers at Wyverstone, this wealthy and generous man endowed a fellowship and two scholarships at Pembroke Hall, to be called Smarte's. His widow, Alice, next married Ralph Scrivener of Belstead and they provided for more awards at Pembroke with preference for their own kin.

The amazing survival, loose in the pages of a borough court book,[23] of a single sheet of paper with manuscript 'Prayers in the Mornynge' and 'Prayse at Nyght' obviously used in the school, might be thought to be a draft for or, more likely, a boy's copy of what was ordered for the table 'hanged up' in the ordinances of 1571. However, the mention of 'the Kinges hyght' dates the prayers firmly before the death of Edward VI in 1553. Diarmaid MacCulloch, Professor of Church History at Oxford, who has studied their content and style, notes with satisfaction that it was Cranmer rather than the anonymous Ipswich author who drafted the *Book of Common Prayer* of 1549. After full consideration he concludes that the date is likely to be about 1550, so that the only master who could have drafted the original was Argentine while still an evangelical. It would be most interesting to know how the prayers were modified for use in the school in Mary's reign and again in Elizabethan times. The prayers are illustrated on page 50.

---

23 SROI C/2/10/3/8 Petty and General Courts 1508-13, on dorse of agreement between John Balles and William Bemonde for payment of £4 13s 4d.

Samuel 'Watch' Ward in his 43rd year in 1620. He was, as town preacher from 1605 to his death in 1640, the most influential man in Ipswich, as Leman found to his cost.

V

James Leman

'The poore, and sore wronged Schoolemaster of his
Majesties more wronged Schoole in Ipswhich'

---

*Leman was, like several other masters and ushers, educated at
the school himself. His misfortune was to be appointed just
when the corporation, backed by the powerful Puritan town
preacher Samuel Ward, had ideas of using Felaw's bequest for a
charity school. He fought hard and successfully for the survival
of the grammar school which had prepared him for Cambridge.
Another layman replaced him, George Downing, but he was
elderly and ailing and the strain soon killed him. However, his
Ipswichian son joined the emigration to Massachusetts and a
great-grandson founded Downing College, Cambridge.*

JAMES LEMAN or Leaman was one of several Ipswichians to
be usher or master and he was both. Although he seems to
have flourished in the junior post under Barkley, he could
hardly have taken charge at a worse time, for, four years later,
he was dismissed, allegedly 'for his evil behaviour and unproffitable teaching', but that is by no means the whole story.

His father James was, from 1542, tenant of a small farm at
Whitton and young James was probably born there in the year
the young Queen Elizabeth came to the throne. He entered the
school under John Dawes at the age of ten and left for
Magdalene College in 1576, the year that Roger Kelke, master

there and town preacher of Ipswich, gave up the latter post. By March 1580, Leman, 'a poore young man', was ready to graduate but lacked the required fees, and the Great Court agreed to support him with five pounds from Roger Barney's gift.[1] For three more years, Leman had four pounds from the same fund. He was thus enabled to proceed from BA to MA and at Michaelmas 1594 was well placed, temporarily in the first instance, to succeed Robert Browne as usher, discharged for 'negligence in teaching the scholars'.[2] Browne seems to have taken the blame for the fact that the school 'is lately decayed and the nomber of the schollers there verie much decresed'. He had apparently 'followed other trades' but, one might ask, what was the master, Barkley, doing about this? In Browne's place, it was decided that James Leman 'shalbe tolerated to teache in the same schole untill a newe usher shalbe chosen'.[3] Two terms later Leman was elected usher 'duringe the townes pleasure, he behavinge him selfe diligentlie and peynefullie in teachinge the children', enjoying the same salary as former ushers.[4] The following Christmas, for 'A speache his schollers made upon Coronacion daye [the accession anniversary] & for other charges', he was given four pounds.[5]

When John Barkley died in February 1604 and was buried at St Mary's across Stoke Bridge, the corporation looked no further than their usher for a successor. In March Leman was elected for 'so long as he shall behave himself well in that place' and 'his *presentatio* therto ... was granted under the Common seale'.[6] Thomas Laster junior, not a graduate but son of an Ips-

1 SROI C/2/2/2/1 Great Court Book (GCB 1), 24 March 1580.
2 SROI C/4/3/1/3 Assembly Book (AB 3), 6 Sept. 1594.
3 GCB 1, 29 Sept. 1594.
4 GCB 1, 11 April 1595.
5 GCB 1, 20 Dec. 1595.
6 GCB 1, 12 March 1604.

wich scrivener, joined him as usher with the brief to teach the children committed to his charge to 'write, cipher, and cast accompt', the elementary skills Ipswich children had traditionally to demonstrate in order to make legal property transactions under-age. This is the first mention of mathematics.

Leman's troubles began when, in September 1605, the corporation ruled that Felaw's House and endowments were no longer to be used for the grammar school as had surely been that benefactor's intention. In fact, some of Felaw's endowments had been diverted since the refoundation of the school after Wolsey's College failed. Ever since the charitable Christ's Hospital had been established in 1572, it had been on the collective conscience of the borough hierarchy that provision had still to be made there for educating poor boys. Revising their view of Felaw's intentions retrospectively, the corporation would found a charity school, without dipping into town finances or their own pockets. Grammar school places were free to the sons of the town's burgesses, who entered as foundation scholars, but that was not something which needed to be changed. Leman was to leave Felaw's House as soon as possible, finding another place in which to teach his grammar pupils. Leman naturally protested but his chances of winning the argument were doomed when a new and powerful town preacher was appointed at All Saints-tide (1 November) 1605.

Samuel Ward (see page 66), a founder fellow of Sidney Sussex College and a thorough-going Puritan and radical beyond his times, soon took responsibility for the town's charities, particularly schools, and proved fully in sympathy with the corporation's revisionist policy over Felaw's gift. Leman obviously stood in the way of the proposed reform, so that, in September 1606, Ward and two other senior clergymen, Dr Millicent and Dr William Jones of East Bergholt, were sent to examine

Leman to establish 'whether he be worthy and sufficient for the place'.[7] Much else written in the Assembly Book at this date was heavily scored out, perhaps because it too clearly exposed the current prejudice against the loyal master. Leman sat tight, so that, when William Auder, MA, was appointed to run the new school (confusingly called Mr Felaw's School) from March 1607, he was allowed the Shearmen's Hall (whose roof is now on Cholderton church in Wiltshire) and the Felaw estate income, but the grammar school remained in Felaw's House. Because it was intended that Auder should eventually run his school there, promises were made, in October 1607, that a new King's Majesty's Grammar School would be built. However, that would be expensive and it was decided meanwhile to repair 'John Hobbes the pynner's house in Christ's Hospital' for the purpose. The corporation was in considerable turmoil over the two schools, because in March 1608 it was decided that 'the money laid out to be bestowed about the erection and finishing of a Grammar School, in the Hospital, shall be paid out of the revenues belonging to the Hospital'. It would have been far simpler to leave Leman (or preferably, from Ward's point of view, a reliable Puritan master) in Felaw's House and build Auder a new charity school in the Hospital using its own funds.

But Leman had to go. The following June he was discharged from his place for 'his evill behaviour and unproffitable teaching of the scholars committed to his charge, and other causes'[8] and, desperate for evidence which might support the corporation's actions over Felaw's intents, orders were given that 'the iron chest and Danske chest be broken open in the presence of the

7 AB 3, 5 Sept. 1606.
8 GCB 1, 6 June 1608.

clavigers and search made for records concerning the Grammar School'.[9] That October, Leman was allowed his last quarter's wages and twenty shillings from 'Mr Smart's revenewes' but he did not give up the struggle, refused to move out of the school house and appealed to Bishop Jegon of Norwich. Four members of the Assembly were summoned to Norwich to give the bishop an account of the affair. In March 1609 Edmund Day, a prominent dyer, had to ride 'to Bury [to see] about the trial of the title of the schoolhouse with Mr Leman'.[10] A petition was raised in his support by one of the common council men, John Warde, (certainly no connection of Samuel Ward's), who was fined five pounds when an attempt to turn him out of office failed. Letters arrived from the Master of Requests by the King's command the next month, and, the following August, a committee was set up 'to debate and conclude with Leman of all causes in controversy between the town and him'.[11] Three days later, the corporation presented George Downing for appointment but the bishop withheld his approval. Downing, probably because he was a sound Puritan layman, had been allowed to teach at his own house near the former Whitefriars. Two years later, the Privy Council became involved and the corporation was alarmed at the 'imputacon layde uppon the towne'. In January 1610, the elderly George Downing had to ride to Lambeth 'to answer for holding the place of schoolmaster, before the archbishop' at the town's expense.[12] These journeys to Norwich and Lambeth were too much for him and, that December, poor Downing died after only two and a half years in charge. In a tacit admission that Leman

9 A chest made of Danish spruce-wood. The clavigers were the official corporation keyholders.
10 GCB 1, March 1609.
11 GCB 1, 14 Aug. 1609.
12 It is surprising that the Lambeth archives contain nothing about the Leman case.

had been in the right, the assembly ruled that 'Mr Fellowe's School shall still continue a Grammerschool "as it hathe been of antient tyme"' and the revenues of Felaw's bequest were again to be applied to it.[13] No more was heard of the charity school but the Leman dispute rolled on. In November 1611, the town had to send Edmund Day to the Privy Council to explain Leman's dismissal and he and Robert Snelling were summoned to Lambeth the following April on the same business.

Leman's persistent intransigence brought benefits. The question of the school's endowment was settled for at least a century and it was not long before it moved across the road to the former Blackfriars refectory. Leman's story ended on 3 June 1622, when the archbishop of Canterbury and the bishop of London ordered the corporation to pay him an annuity of ten pounds for the remainder of his life. Leman's loyalty to church and crown was rewarded, while Ward and the Ipswich corporation, long before the era of party politics, already displayed what would long after be called radical tendencies. Care would be taken in future to appoint Puritan masters loyal to the borough hierarchy. The undated broadside addressed 'To the High Court of Parliament', refers to 'the expense of these seventeene last yeeres of his life' and states that 'he hath [at last] obteined a judiciall sentence'.[14] These phrases confirm that the sheet was published earlier that summer to force the hand of a reluctant corporation to make the payment ordered. The phrase 'the violent withholding [of] the onely mainteinance of his life' supports this suggestion. Leman dared to say that the founder's will had been disregarded 'onely to spare the Common purse of many rich men;

13 SROI C/4/3/1/4 (AB 4), 11 Dec. 1610.
14 The only known surviving copy of the broadside is here reproduced by kind permission of the Society of Antiquaries of London.

To the High Court of Parliament, or any Worthy
Member, or Members thereof.

Humbly sheweth Iames Leman, *the poore, and sore wronged Schoolemaster of his Maiesties more wronged Schoole in Ipswhich, That*

HIs Maieſtie hauing very oft moſt Graciouſly granted his humble, iuſt, and needfull requeſt, concerning the aforeſaid Schoole, *a famous antient feed-plot of Learning, lately removed without licence from the originall, and onely seat thereof, and now left to popular transposition, dayly alteration, and finall diſſolution: The Founders charitable Will, alſo vncharitably diſanulled, onely to ſpare the Common purſe of many rich men; And that (which is worst of all) this iniquitie is masked vnder a faire viſor, or cunning pretext of Pietie, and Conſcionable performing the ſaid Will.* And although with the expenſe of theſe ſeuenteene laſt yeeres of his life, of all his worldly meanes, and of very great ſummes disburſed by his friends, he hath obteined a iudiciall ſentence, according to the euidence of the cauſe : yet finding that ſentence, and all his *Maieſties* references ſtill ſtrangly fruſtrate, & vtterly of no effect holdeth himſelfe bound in all dutie of *Conſcience, Loyalty, and ciuill Honeſtie,* and is farther conſtrained by the violent withholding the onely mainteinance of his life, but moſt of all is vrged, by ingratefull requitall of his good deſert, to ſpend the ſmall relique of his moſt woefull, and weary life :

    Humbly crauing that by authoritie of this *High Court,* firſt and chiefely, the ſeate of the Schoole may bee refixed, in perpetuall honour of his *Maieſties Philomathie,* and the good Founders Will inuiolably ratified, for the generall, and perpetuall benefit of both *Church, and Common Wealth,* without any queſtion of the Petitioners wrongs, vnleſſe that great fauour ſhall voluntarily ſhine on him, to whoſe contemptible profeſſion all this moſt *Honourable Senat* is beholding.

and that (which is worst of all) this iniquitie is masked under a faire visor, or cunning pretext of Pietie'. It was seventeen years since the trouble first began in September 1605, and, for Leman, life had been 'most woefull, and weary', but in the end, by his persistence, he won. Where and how he passed the remainder of his time is not known, but, by 1622, he would have been in his mid-sixties; had he been in orders no doubt he would have taken a living somewhere, but he was not. The annuity was still being paid in 1631. One James Leman was buried at St Andrew's, Newcastle-upon-Tyne in December 1642, but it would be difficult to prove that he was the former schoolmaster.

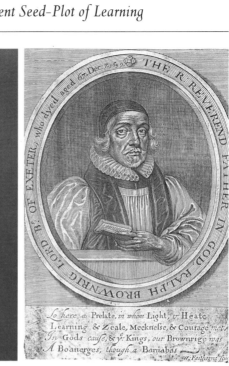

Lo here, a Prelate, in whom Light, & Heate
Learning & Zeale, Meeknesse, & Courage met.
In Gods cause, & y.e Kings, our Brownrige was
A Boanerges, though a Barnabas

W. Faithorne sculp.

Two Ipswichians, who were prepared by Leman for Cambridge, later became bishops but not in time to help him in his troubles. Benjamin Lany (1591–1675), left, was the son of John Lany, recorder of Ipswich and moved from Christ's College to Pembroke where he became master in 1630 and vice-chancellor two years later. A royalist and high churchman, he became chaplain to the king, which led to his ejection from Cambridge in 1644. At the Restoration he was rewarded with the mastership once more, and three bishoprics in succession: Peterborough, Lincoln and Ely. His portrait hangs in the hall at Pembroke College. Ralph Brownrigg (1592–1659), right, had humbler origins. Son of an Ipswich merchant, he was brought up by his pious widowed mother. He was successively a fellow of Pembroke, master of Catharine Hall and, in 1642, bishop of Exeter. Though no high churchman he was loyal to the king, for which he suffered during the Interregnum.

VI

Masters and ushers come and go and the school moves

After Leman, masters and ushers arrived and departed with unseemly haste and this was not the best time to move the school to new premises just across the road. Those chosen had to satisfy Samuel Ward that they would be godly mentors of their pupils and careful custodians of his preacher's library, to which most had the good sense to donate books. Three masters stayed rather longer than average, but very little is known of the school in their time, which may be a good sign. The last was considered a great loss when he moved back to his own school, Felsted; there he continued in charge for forty years.

When GEORGE DOWNING (often spelt Downynge) died in 1611 he was living in a leasehold house called the Whitefriars, no doubt a domestic building of the former Carmelite Priory just to the west of St Stephen's church. Presumably this is where he held his own school before becoming master. His three daughters Susan, Nahomie and Abigall were well provided for in his will and sons Emmanuel and Joseph had passed through the school to Cambridge. Joseph was to have 'all my bookes at home and at Cambridge'. Another son, Nathaniel, was left 'my Danske deske which standeth in the sommer parler uppon the Danske chest'. Emmanuel, already well established as a merchant in London and Dublin, married Lucy, sister of John Winthrop, the founder and first governor of Massachusetts, and helped to organise the transatlantic migration.

The Downings joined Lucy's brother there in 1638 but returned to old England later; their son was the diplomat Sir George and his grandson founded Downing College, Cambridge. As late as December 1614, Nathaniel Downing asked the town for a year's salary due to his late father, from the time that he held the mastership in dispute with Leman.

After Downynge's brief tenure, masters and ushers came and went with alarming frequency, perhaps because Ward, seeking men who shared his political and religious views, was too intimidating. Some candidates may have been far-sighted enough to see that they could well be found wanting. The school in the short term depended on loyal ushers and stop-gap masters, for there are indications that Leman was stubbornly refusing to leave Felaw's House, making the recruitment of a permanent master very difficult. A Mr Paddie or Puddie served the half year from January to June 1611, when three men travelled from London to interview at considerable cost to the borough, and Mr Cowper was appointed on 12 June.[1] The Assembly, still smarting from Leman troubles, laid down clear guidelines: 'if any dislike shall happen to be on the town's part, that Mr Cowper shall have three months' notice of that dislike and depart'. Incredibly, in only ten weeks, Cowper had already 'neglected the execution of the place by his long absence, to the utter decay of the said school'. He could have read sarcasm into his written notice: 'he doe not furder troble himselfe for the same'.[2] Thomas Laster, Leman's non-graduate usher, must have been providing continuity for nearly four years, and his leaving settlement reflected corporation gratitude. Perhaps the lack of permanent masters in 1610 and 1611 made it neces-

---

1 SROI AB 4, 12 June 1611.
2 AB 4, 20 Aug. 1611.

sary for a small committee of ministers chosen and led by Samuel Ward, to 'examine the schollers, whether there be any fitt to be sent to Cambridge or not, and certify which of them whose parents shall be willing to sende thither [those] they shall find to be fittest to be sent for the obteyning of a schollersheppe in Pembroke Hall, according to Mr Smarte his gifte'.[3] The expense, without an award, was beyond the means of most townsmen. The same committee inspected the condition of the master's house and chose the northern half of Taylors' Hall, the former dormitory of the Blackfriars, for the preacher's library.

JOHN COTTISFORD, MA, of St John's College, Cambridge, next served for five years, one as master and part of the next as usher to Read. Then, because Samuel Ward had failed to recruit 'some other sufficient man for a master' in Cambridge, he spent three years as master again with John Coney his usher, most disruptive for the school. ALEXANDER READ, a fellow

Augu$t 161$ The gift of Alex: Read Fellowe of Pembrook hall in Camb:

of Pembroke Hall since 1605, was given cramped quarters at the north end of the former Blackfriars refectory which he put up with for about a term. The Paris edition of the works of Seneca he left for the town library on his departure was generous in the circumstances. Cottisford's salary was augmented with four pounds a quarter 'for catechising the poor people in the foundation', showing Ward's concern for inmates' souls. For the same purpose, a pulpit was built in the hospital in 1614 – it is visible on Kirby's engraving on the first floor of the colonnaded south east courtyard. Sometime early in Cottisford's

---

3   AB 4, 11 Oct. 1610 and 19 Feb. 1611.

time at the school, the school moved over the road to new premises.

John Coney, a Norfolk man, whose father Robert had been a fellow of King's College, Cambridge and Lady Margaret Preacher in 1577, was himself ordained after King's, in 1607, aged 24. He was a conscientious librarian to Ward, accessioning and arranging books and inscribing donors' names, in good imitation of print, in the books of those for whom typeset labels were not afforded. In one of his own gifts, he styled himself 'in Ludo Regio Paedagogi & Librarii Gyppenvicensis'. To

take account of his extra work in the library, Coney's salary was increased to £20 per annum, and when he died in the spring of 1618, his widow received forty shillings from the corporation 'for her husband's paynestaking in his lyfetyme about the settling of the bokes in the librarie'.

When, in January 1616, the corporation found another suitable master, Cottisford obligingly agreed to relinquish his post once more, temporarily taking on the reading of prayers on Sundays in the Tower church for ten shillings a quarter. NICHOLAS EASTON, MA, another Pembroke Hall man, had been master of Beeston School in north Norfolk and agreed to move to Ipswich at Easter for £30 per annum, with Cottisford as his usher (paid only two pounds less) for his first two years.[4] Clearly the Assembly felt grateful to the easygoing Cottisford,

---

4   Easton's salary was made up of the Royal stipend of £24 6s 8d, £4 from Smarte's and £1 13s 4d from Christ's Hospital revenues. Cottisford's consisted of the usual £14 6s 8d, augmented by £13 13s 4d from Felaw's revenues.

and some reservations about Easton's stamina, for they ruled that: 'if afterwards Mr Easton shall die or leave his said mastership, then John Cottesford shall be master of the school again'. From 1622, the obliging master-cum-usher took the vicarage of Bedingfield, where he died and was buried in 1632.[5] Easton brought his wife Dorothy (née Rude, whom he married at Trunch in 1598) but they refused to accept the house offered. The corporation agreed to hire another and to bring 'a load of stuff' of theirs from Beccles. Presumably at Easton's request, as many of the 36-strong Assembly as thought fit visited the new schoolroom at one o'clock on a Friday in December 1617, to 'view and consider of some course to be taken for the helping of noise in the same Grammar School' – understandable with over one hundred boys in one room. The next summer, after only two years in post, Easton took his wife back to Beccles and the two Ipswichian fellows of Pembroke, Ralph Brownrigg and Benjamin Lany (see page 74), were asked to suggest a successor. Perhaps Cottisford's departure left Easton too heavily burdened. A month later the defecting master was coaxed back, with the promise of a salary of forty pounds (and the usher to have only half that). If he should wish to depart again, he was to give a year's notice; he could chose his own usher (Robert Cadey for two years, then Eleazar Holt, MA, of Caius, covered the remainder of his time) and the town would now bring *two* loads of his household stuff from Beccles. In his absence, the teaching was undertaken by two local clergymen, Alexander Rainold of Tattingstone and Nathaniel Smart of St Nicholas. Both were paid generously and the latter was also given the remunerative catechising work at the Hospital.

5   John Cottisford senior, citizen and goldsmith of London was buried at Bedingfield in 1629. The father's occupation may perhaps explain why John junior could be flexible about his appointments and emoluments.

After all the uncertainties of Easton's early years, the borough records fall almost silent for the remainder of his mastership. In 1622, Richard Martin, portman, endowed scholarships at Cambridge with the revenues of Swan's Nest farm, Westerfield; his or his wife's kin, if any suitable, were to benefit. One of his pupils was Edmund Boldero, fellow of Pembroke until ejected as a Royalist. With others, Boldero confronted the Puritan iconoclast William Dowsing when he came to cleanse Pembroke chapel of superstitition. He served under Montrose as a captain, narrowly escaped hanging, and at the Restoration became master of Jesus College, Cambridge. Easton presented two books to the town library, both likely to have been useful in the school: Calepini's Dictionary in eleven languages, 1609, and Scapula's Greek and Latin Lexicon, 1619. There is just one entry in 1625 about Easton 'appointing a youth' to make a formal speech of welcome to visiting Colchester townsmen, then nothing more until July 1630 when his successor, WILLIAM CLARKE, educated at Westminster and an MA of Trinity College, Cambridge, was 'to be sent for'. Easton had taken the mastership of the grammar school of Sir Nicholas Bacon's foundation at Botesdale near Diss. The salary was only twenty pounds per annum but a country school held in a former chantry chapel suited him for the rest of his life. He was buried at Redgrave (in which parish Botesdale lay), on August 16th 1638, and his wife Dorothy, aged about 60, only three days later.

William Clarke asked that 'a Dyall and other things thereunto belonging be set up' in the school, a clock to tick away the long hours of the narrow diet of subjects studied. He chose Robert Woodside MA (1604–58), who served as usher for eleven years and returned to spend the last months of his life as master. Son of Robert Woodside, gentleman, of Bury St Edmunds, he was prepared at the grammar school there for

Caius College, Cambridge. His wife Ann bore him a son and daughter, both christened at St Mary Quay church during their first period at the school. For the Woodsides, Felaw's House was renovated in September 1636; 22 foot square of the hall floor was 'replanchered', the windows of the chamber and closet were reglazed, the chamber over the way going to the yard was refloored and the chamber ceiled. Only one story from the time of Clarke and Woodside survives: it dates from 1635-38 when Matthew Wren was bishop of Norwich.[6]

> The schoolmaster of Ipswich being a precise man, some had informd Bish: Wrenne that he never taught his Boyes the Optative Moode, least they should take Gods name in vaine; the Bish: sent for him and questions him, he answers, that he converst not with the Moodes, for they were as many formes under him, as such a Question was beneath the dignitie of his Lordshippe; and what his Usher did, he knew not; then the Usher was cited; and he to cleere himselfe, proou'd that he taught, *O utinam &c*: [Oh would that, or Oh that] *Obrutus insanis esset adulter aquis*. or *Regulus esset equis*.

This story only confirms that the school day held little variety and few delights: just two men, hardly communicating, wrestling with boys in seven forms. Clarke worked for Ward in the library, to which he was a donor himself, and his hand is to be found in the benefactors' book. The preacher was silenced for life in 1635, for repeated failure to conform to the instructions of Wren and Laud, and died early in 1640. His successor as town preacher was Nathaniel Smart junior, married to Clarke's

6 Anecdote number 335 collected by Sir Nicholas L'Estrange in Harleian MS 6395 fol.53. Puritans believed it sinful to wish for other than what God willed. Laud's ally Wren would despise such fundamentalism. The first quotation must come from a popular textbook. It is from Ovid's *Heroides* 1.1: 'would that the adulterer [Paris] had been overwhelmed by raging waters'. The second, from Martial, has no wish element.

daughter Ruth. The first Civil War was moving towards a climax, when Clarke retired from the school in December 1644, and the Puritan corporation lent several thousand pounds from the hospital funds towards the costs of the Parliamentary army. Clarke took on the perpetual curacy of St Nicholas, in succession to his son-in-law Smart, and had more time for the library, for which he ordered a splendid refurbishment in April 1651. When he died, in 1653, he left two houses; besides land in Lincolnshire, a legacy of forty shillings to the poor of his parish and desired 'my Lattin books may be kept for my son John, if God give him abillity to make use of them'. John left the school, in 1655, but not for the university.

In September 1644, before Clarke retired, the bailiffs wrote to CHRISTOPHER GLASCOCK, master of the school at Chipping Ongar, 'desiring him to accept the place of master... and to come over and treat concerning the same'. Glascock, born at Great Waltham in 1613, was educated at Felsted and Catharine Hall, Cambridge, taking his MA in 1638. His strong Essex roots, with perhaps hopes of the mastership of his own school, made him a difficult fish to hook. The powerful Ipswich figure Peter Fisher handled the negotiations and the bailiffs wrote on Christmas Eve confirming the appointment and pressing for Glascock's 'speedy and convenient removall'. The master's house could not be available 'the week after Xrmas' [the current abbreviation] but on 8 January, a 'drugg' would be sent for their household and the family could join the coach at Chelmsford the next day. His reply dated 'Dec. last' explained how he had 'met with so much importunity from my Friends, that I could scarce be as good as my Word, meeting so many difficulties in Parting with them'. He preferred to employ the wagon and coach he had organised. The salary was to be forty pounds, with free tenure of the house Clarke was occupying, on which twenty pounds could be 'expended upon a buttery and such other things as are necessary'. The house was not good enough for Mrs Glascock, however, which 'neither when shee was ther, nor since, never liked, and Mr Fisher did engage himselfe to procure us another more Convenient, which wee desire might be done'. He could hire another, with an extra forty shillings towards its rent, letting the former master's house to his best advantage. There is no doubt that the corporation wanted his services very badly but, after only five years, he left to take the Felsted headship, which he then held for forty years, dying in post at the advanced age of 77 but apparently effective to the last.[7] There is little recorded about his mastership, save that there were difficulties over retaining ushers, and in 1648 the borough treasurer was 'to make a door to the doorway [entrance arch] of the School House, to keep the yard private, and make up a shed in the yard for the hearing of scholars in the summer time'. Judith Glascock bore her husband a son, Christopher, and a daughter, Joan, during their stay. Ipswich certainly had some of his best years and efforts were made to 'intreat him to continue', but to no avail. In 1658, after Beck had retired and Robert Woodside (Clarke's usher) died after only a year in the post, application was made to Glascock to return to Ipswich. Even had he wished to do so, his powerful patron, the third earl of Warwick, related by marriage to Oliver Cromwell, had no intention of releasing him at Felsted. Warwick gave the Felsted churchwardens their instructions on 23 February 1659:

---

7   According to Michael Craze's *History of Felsted School* that school 'became more aristocratic and more scholarly' under Glascock than under his distinguished predecessor.

Gentlemen
I am given to understand that the towne of Ipswiche have lately endeavoured to draw Mr Glascocke yo'r School-master from yo'r Towne upon proffer of as good allowance and expectatc'on of better profitt then he hath at Felsted, wherein if they should prevaile I beleve it would turne yo'r Towne and the adjacent parte of the Country to prejudice; which I haveing taken into considerac'on togeither with his great charge of children [There were now seven children in the family.] have thought fit to grant him a Lease of One and twenty yeares of the Farme called Moreton farm... the better to incourage him to continue comfortably amongst you. [More details follow.] And so I rest
Yo'r very Loving friend
Warwicke

Five years later Glascock was again wanted at Ipswich; his letter to the bailiffs dated 11 May 1663 is a masterpiece of tact:

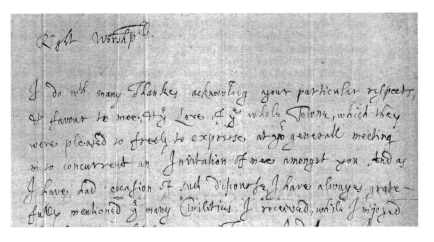

Right Worshipfulls
I do w'th many Thankes acknowledg your particular respects & favour to mee, & the Love of the whole Towne, which they were pleased so freely to expresse at yo'r general meeting in so concurrent an Invitation of mee amongst you. And as I have occasion of such discourse, I have always gratefully mentioned the many Civilities I received, while I injoyed the benefit of living in yo'r Towne. And were I in a

condition so free, as that I could do it, I should testify my reciprocall repects in a complyance, w'th what you desire in yo'r Letter. But I beg leave to mention to you the convenien-cy of my present place, that I enjoy, & that it is a thing to be considered of, a removall to no appearing advantage. I do believe I should enjoy the Society of many loving freinds at Ipsw'ch, yet I must also do those that right, amongst whom I live at present, that many of them do professe a very mis-fortunate desire of my stay here with them. Besides I am under the Patronage of my Noble Lord of Warwick [by now the fourth earl, brother of the third] to whom, & to whose relations I am so far obliged, as that I must not precipitately resolve w'thout his allowance. Had he been in the Countrey, I would have comunicated it to his Lordship, before the return of your Messenger, but he is expected to come downe this week, till when I must crave your patience, & before that, a journey to Ipsw'ch would be ineffectuall. I would not willingly be guilty of prejudicing you by delay, but hope to give an account of it, this next week. In the meane time be pleased to accept the tender of a thankfull acknowledgment from, R. Worp'lls Yours very much obliged, Chr. Glascocke

Glascock's immediate intended successor, John Mereweather,[8] a fellow of Magdalene, Cambridge, arrived on Lady Day 1650 (25 March) and 'left the town before Easter leaving the school unprovided for; it is conceived by the Assembly that he hath no interest to return again, whereby the school and the schol-ars are likely to suffer much. Enquiries are to be made for other fit person for the place if Mr Mereweather does not sud-denlie give notice of his return'. William Clarke covered the vacancy and it was not until September that the Great Court formally retained 'Mr Beck of Brentwood... to perform such articles concerning the said school as Mr Glascocke did or should have done...'. The town clerk must here have been employing legal caution in the wording; surely there can be no

8 At the Restoration, despite having a wife and six children to support, he refused to subscribe to the Act of Uniformity and lost his Norfolk livings of Tasburgh and Stratton St Michael. See Blomefield v. 202.

85

implied criticism of the man the burgesses worked so hard to keep. However, if Cave Beck was not a breath of fresh air after all his painful Puritan predecessors, it will only have been the limits set by those 'articles' which prevented his broadening the curriculum greatly. As for fresh air, his first request to the Assembly was for 'a house of office near the Free School for the use of the scholars'.

The Refectory Great Schoolroom

On the plan of Ipswich inset on Speed's map of Suffolk, 1610, the school is clearly marked on the west (*i.e.* Felaw's House) side of Edmund Pountney Lane but, by 1614, perhaps as early as 1612, it had moved across the road. For the school to have to move at such a time of crisis must have been disruptive but, if Leman's intransigence was the indirect cause, he did the school much good in the long run.

Too often the building portrayed in the left foreground of Joshua Kirby's 1748 engraving of 'The West View of Christ's Hospital in Ipswich' has been mistaken for the former *church* of the Dominican friars but that, like most churches, ran east-west to the left of the cloistral buildings in the print.

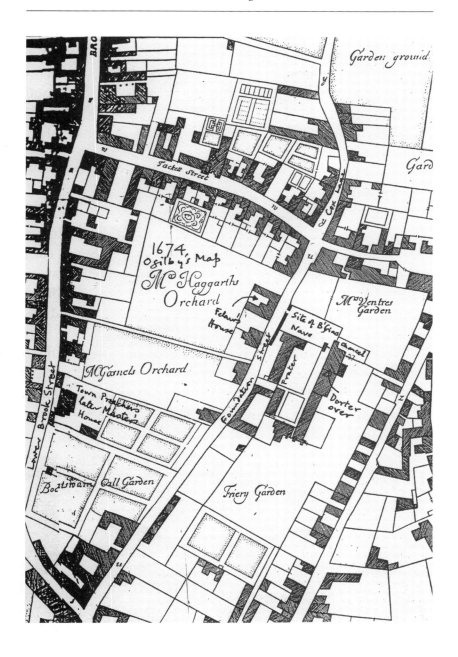

At the Dissolution of the friary, in 1538, the church was soon demolished for its valuable building stone and the wall on the left of the engraving is its south wall. The north-south building, with gothic windows, is the former *frater* and a fine light building it made for the school for a century and a half, with west light coming in through the large window of the pulpitum  (from it, the friars were read to during meals). When the Blackfriars' site was excavated, two pieces of stone tracery from this window were found; enough, with Kirby's engraving, to enable Birkin Haward to draw a reconstruction of the whole window.

Orders were given in August 1612 for the new schoolroom to be 'planchered' [floored], locks to be provided for the doors and seats at both ends; a 'lover [louvre] shall be made in the roof'. It is odd that a pitched-roofed medieval building should need ventilation but, with over a hundred boys in a room 65 by 23 feet, there was a problem, which in July 1614 was unsolved.

The first order was for a 'lover to be made... by letting down some part of the ceiling upon the spars and riveing the tiles of the housetop'. Three weeks later, perhaps after consulting a builder, something more practical was proposed: 'three pentices to be made over the holes now made in the roof... instead of the lover'. They are clearly shown on the print. How the seven forms were laid out originally, we can only conjecture, but, allowing for inertia over a century and half, there are seven lines around the perimeter of the schoolroom in the 1748 ground plan, as well as seats at each end for master and usher.

There is also in the school library today a tall schoolmaster's desk of the early seventeenth century, perhaps made for the new schoolroom.

Between the refectory and the church south wall can be seen one window and the pitched roof of Alexander Read's cramped one-term accommodation, the 'backhouse' the usher John Coney and his wife took over when he left. 'J' on the plan confirms how small it was (see over).

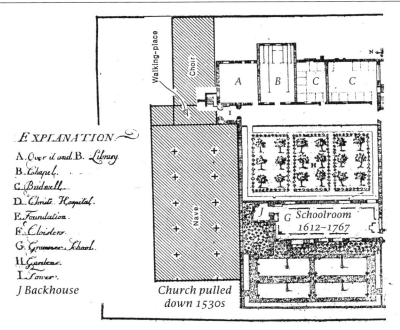

EXPLANATION.
A. Over it and B. Library.
B. Chapel.
C. Bridwell.
D. Christ. Hospital.
E. Foundation.
F. Cloisters.
G. Grammer School.
H. Gardens.
I. Tower.
J Backhouse

*Church pulled
down 1530s*

Foundation Street

90

VII

Cave Beck: A Royalist Master during the Interregnum

'A divine of steddy reckonings, shrewd fetches, narrow serchings, mathematically given.'

Of all the unlikely things, Cave Beck, the master during the Commonwealth, was a Royalist who had served the king at Oxford; about this he will presumably have been discreet. Although in holy orders, he was ready for the intellectual challenges of new disciplines and particularly excited by the formation of the Royal Society. Unless he was constrained otherwise, he will have taught a broader curriculum than his Puritan predecessors and was working on an early version of a universal language. After his time at the school, it went through another unsettled period and his successors, during the next fifty years, may have resented his influential presence in the town.

CAVE BECK (1622-1706) came to the school as master from Brentwood very soon after the execution of Charles I, whom he had served at Oxford during the siege. When that city surrendered in June 1646, the king was already a fugitive and Beck was wise to seek other employment. If, as seems likely, he had been usher to the Puritan master of Brentwood,[1] he would

---

1 Provision was made for ushers at Brentwood in the statutes of 1626, but the earliest usher whose name is known for certain was appointed in 1674. The master at the time was John Latham, a lay member of the local classical presbytery.

have had to hide his Royalist instincts there, good preparation for securing and retaining the mastership at Ipswich, where he seems never to have been without friends and influence. He was certainly the most versatile and gifted of the early masters and the one the writer would be most intrigued to meet; at least we have an engraved portrait.

He was the second son of John Beck and Anne Flecher (probably née Cave, and widow of Adam Flecher), christened at St Mary's, Whitechapel in Stepney, on 6 October 1622. His parents were married at St Margaret's, Westminster, on 12 April 1618. John Beck described himself as 'pandoxator' when entering his son at St John's College, Cambridge, in June 1638, which could mean baker, brewer or innkeeper. Cave had been prepared for Cambridge for five years at William Braithwayte's private school in Leadenhall; his master's work on musical notation, published in 1639, is likely to have been an early inspiration to Beck for his language ideas. At Cambridge, his tutor was John Cleveland, the poet who wrote witty verses in support of the king's cause. Graduating BA in 1642, Beck enrolled at Gray's Inn that August but, either he did not take to the law, or the outbreak of the Civil War that autumn distracted him, for he took the study no further. Cleveland joined the king at Christ Church, Oxford; the indication that Beck probably followed him there is that his name occurs in a list of those upon whom the king conferred MAs, one of only two without citation. Knowing of Beck's later achievements, the likely inference is that he was engaged in undercover cypher work. Certainly, there were at Oxford in the 1640s several others interested in codes and universal languages, the most eminent John Wilkins, warden of Wadham from 1648; it was from him that Beck later received harsh criticism of the manuscript he planned to publish.

Beck arrived at the school in September 1650. His predecessor was a staunch Puritan and Beck must have smothered his
Royalist feelings to obtain the acceptance of the borough lead-
ers, particularly the brothers, Nathaniel and Francis Bacon. The
Bacons were both active on the parliamentary side and influential throughout the region; at least all three men had Gray's Inn
in common. As master, he took seriously his responsibility for
the library in the former Blackfriars dormitory, not far from
the school in the refectory. So that several hundred volumes of
theology could be checked and ordered without expert help, he
devised a unique system of shelf marks, lines painted obliquely
across the fore-edges of sets of books, with the same distin-
guishing astronomical or alchemical symbol on each book in a

*Five complete sets
of books with Beck's
lines and symbols.*

*Shelf D4 with white
spots above and below
a black line.*

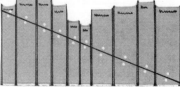

set. Basil Breame was paid three shillings on 12 April 1651 'for making the lines on the bookes'.

In 1657, Beck resigned from the school and published his *Universal Character* in English and French editions. The dedication was to the Bacon brothers, 'patronis suis colendissimis', and four friends, two certainly Puritan ministers, added verses in praise of this early attempt at universal language. One of them, Joseph Waite of Sproughton, addressing his 'intimate

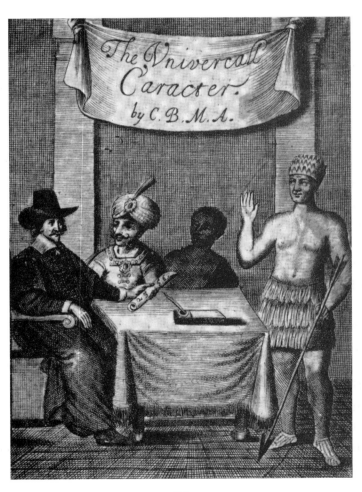

and ingenious friend' in gentle jest, wrote: 'let me be dead before this see the shop'. Beck's language, which he had doubt-less tried out on his pupils, uses the Arabic numbers 1 to 9 and 0, to be pronounced 'aun, too, tray, for, fai, sic, sen, at, nin and o' respectively. About 4,000 words in general use are listed in alphabetical order. For example, 'a floor' is 652, written thus and pronounced 'sicfaitoo'. Prefixed letters indicate parts of speech derived from the same word. The title page claim that 'the practice whereof may be attained in two hours space' was optimistic, if that involved learning the numerical dictionary by heart. Faithorne's engraved frontispiece shows Beck hand-ing a scroll bearing numbers to an Indian, an African and an American indian. The latter, armed with a large arrow, raises his hand in recognition that 2356 represents the verb 'to hunt'.

After his time at the school, Cave Beck must have proved a considerable trial to the five masters who followed him during almost fifty years until his death. If anything, he seems to have filled the vacuum left by Samuel Ward in the town, though Ward and Beck would have struggled to find much in common. Active in many fields, he was available for advice and to fill gaps in the mastership and the lectureship and his continued interest in, and hold over, the town library forced the school to build up its own collection, something which was overdue. It would be good to be able to associate him with the Royalist Oak Apple Day tradition that lasted into the 1950s but no-one knows when it began. Boys who failed to wear oak leaves on the 29th of May risked being stung with nettles, a greater hazard for those wearing short trousers.

There is no record of Beck's ordination; as schoolmaster he was lay but, with Nathaniel Bacon's influence, he became per-petual curate at St Margaret's, Ipswich, on leaving the school, signing the registers annually for the next twenty years as 'curate' or 'minister'. He became resident tutor to the children of Leicester Devereux, 5th viscount Hereford at Christchurch, the Tudor mansion still in the park next to the church. He was later chaplain there and, with others, guardian to the children when their parents died. In 1660, Hereford was one of the six peers who journeyed to Holland to bring back Charles II and Beck was one of his attendant gentlemen. While there, Beck was sent to see Dr John Earle, translator of *Eikon Basilike* into

After I had finished the Defence of the King's Book, I received this Letter from a Reverend Minister of *Ipswich* in *Suffolk*, which deserves to be taken Notice of.

SIR,

SOME years after the Kings Tryal, Major Huntington at Ipswich assured me, That so much of the said Book as contained His Majesties Meditations before Naseby Fight, was taken in the Kings Cabinet, and that Sir Thomas Fairfax delivered the said Papers unto him, and ordered him to carry them to the King; and the Major affirmed, that he read them over before he delivered them, and that they were the same for Matter and Form, with those Meditations in the Printed Book, and that he was much affected with them, and from that time became a Proselyte to the Royal Cause: He also told me, That when he delivered them to the King, His Majesty appeared very joyful at the receiving of them, and said he esteemed them more than all the Jewels he had lost in the Cabinet. Also I remember, when I waited upon my Lord Vicount Hereford into Holland, (who was sent by the Parliament with other Lords, to bring home King Charles II.) my Lord sent me to Dr. Earl then at the Hague, to request his Knowledge, whether the King was Author of the said Book, the Dr. told me, as sure as he knew himself to be the Translator of it into Latin; so certain he was King Charles was the Author of the Original in English.

For my part, I am apt to believe no Person was able to frame that Book, but a Suffering King, and no Suffering King, but King Charles the Martyr.

Your Humble Servant,

Cave Becke.

F I N I S.

Latin. When Richard Hollingsworth published his case for the work having been written by the king himself, Beck gave assurances he had received at Ipswich, from the officer who read the manuscript after Naseby, and his opinion that: 'For my part, I am apt to believe no person was able to frame that book, but a suffering King, and no suffering King, but King Charles the Martyr.' The living of St Helen's, whose church had been used by independents during the Interregnum, reverted to the Crown and was given to Beck. When the former town preacher refused to conform, Beck was one of three ministers who shared the duty for a time. He now held the two Ipswich livings, from 1674 Monk Soham (15 miles north) and another in Worcestershire. He had two wives called Sarah; the first, who gave him a son, John, at the school in 1666 but dead by 1701, died in the plague year 1665, and the second outlived him.

In his charge of the town library, Beck added very few religious works; new donors were encouraged to give books on mathematics, history, law, topography and science, including a good set of Boyle's works and the earliest publications of the Royal Society. Dr Nathaniel Fairfax, ejected for nonconformity from his Willisham living and practising medicine in Woodbridge, advised secretary Oldenburg to accept Beck as Suffolk correspondent on scientific matters, describing him as 'a divine of steddy reasonings, shrewd fetches, narrow serchings, mathematically given'. In a reminder Fairfax added that Beck was 'of a genius made for new works'. Once appointed, Beck bombarded Oldenburg with such things as his 'art of memory' and his account of witches (in fact, monsters) in Suffolk. How much, but in vain, Beck coveted fellowship of the new Society can be seen through his enthusiasm for the task.

Beck's last surviving achievement is an elaborate display of fifty painted panels between the rafters of the medieval double

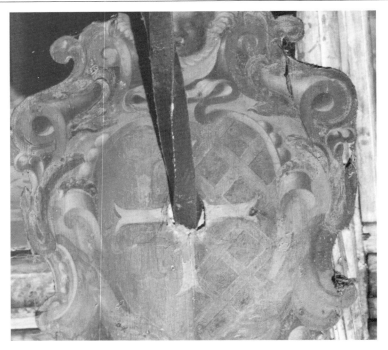

hammerbeam roof at his church of St Margaret's. This he planned with Devereux Edgar, the wealthy Tory Ipswich magistrate who paid for it, whose father Thomas had been Recorder of the town. The two central panels are an unusual form of the Royal arms of William and Mary. Put up between November 1694 and March 1695, the whole celebrates the satisfactory settlement of the religious troubles of the century and struggles between crown and parliament; an element of mourning for Mary, who died that December, was inserted. Five years later, a series of heraldic shields was fixed to the ends of the hammers where, before William Dowsing's visit in 1644, wooden angels had spread their wings, and the local worthies honoured in this way were an eclectic group crossing all religious and political divides. Cave Beck awarded himself unlikely arms, since he could hardly have been descended from two medieval bishops Bek. Painted over, but showing through the top coat, is the same Bek impaling Cave of London, imaginatively representing his parents' marriage. John Gibbon, cousin of the same Devereux Edgar, was probably referring to Beck in his *Introductio ad Blasoniam*, 1682, when he wrote: 'I know a private school-master in Suffolk that instructs his scholars in this science', meaning heraldry. Beck was still chaplain (and had been tutor) to the 8th viscount Hereford when the latter died in 1700, leaving him £10. In August 1706, Beck made his own short will leaving his wife, Sarah, three houses in St Nicholas parish, one tenanted by a Basil Breame, perhaps painter of the lines on the books (or a son). The will was not proved until the following July but successors at St Helen's and Monk Soham were inducted in 1706. Sarah was buried at St Margaret's on 4 October 1708, but the register is deficient at the time of his burial two years earlier.[2]

When Beck gave up the mastership, there was, as usual, difficulty in recruiting a successor[3] but when the choice fell on ROBERT WOODSIDE, who had been usher to William Clarke for over ten years, the new master was no stranger to the school and the town. It is not known how he had filled the intervening years; as a layman, church livings were not an option. Evidently William Dixon, MA, the Caius man who had served Beck as usher since 1651, was not thought well of by the

2   This account of Beck and the revised article for the *Oxford DNB*, 2004, owes much to the published work of the linguistics scholar and author Vivien Salmon (whose OI husband Paul was professor of German at London University). Her article 'Cave Beck, a Seventeenth century Ipswich Schoolmaster' in *PSIA*, 33, 285–98, increased our knowledge of the man and his *Universal Character*.
3   David Cressy in 'A Drudgery of Schoolmasters' shows a dramatic fall in the number of schoolmasters in Norwich diocese between a peak for the century of 80 in 1636 to 46 in 1662, and this trend continued, the percentage of graduates dropping from 76 in 1662 to 19 in 1677. No wonder there were difficulties in Ipswich.

corporation; he should 'provide himself as soon as he please of some other place for that this towne intende to Choose Another Usher as soone as they can with Convenience'. Woodside was 'to be aidinge to the towne in the findinge & procuringe of a Fitt Usher to serve in the Schoole'. Dixon was not to be hustled off and, in the event, outlasted the master. At the first Assembly (26 May 1657) after Woodside's appointment, it was agreed 'that thes bookes Followinge That is to saie, Scapula, Erasmus Adagies, twoe Dictionaries & a Bible shallbe bought at the Charge of the Towne & sent to the schoole to be used As Common bookes and that the Master be desired to buy the Same'. For these books, some duplicating works in the town library, the chamberlains paid £2 17s. In April, the Assembly ordered a chimney to be built in the Great Chamber in Felaw's House, the master's residence. When Robert Woodside died in November 1658, Beck returned for six months as master and Ann Woodside was allowed £16, 'monies laid out about the schoolhouse and for presses [bookcases] and things there by her left'. The next man chosen defected to Thetford grammar school without ever arriving.

HENRY WICKHAM, an MA and fellow of Trinity from 1651-55, served as master from June 1659 until 1662 when he took the living of Wilby, Norfolk. Bringing his wife and goods to Ipswich cost over four pounds, for which he was reimbursed. At the beginning of his short mastership, he dismissed Dixon and had three more ushers, falling out with the second so seriously that Nathaniel Bacon, Cave Beck and Matthias Candler, vicar of Coddenham, were asked to intervene. Two abortive appointments later, JEREMY COLLIER, MA, another Trinity man who was an intruded fellow at St John's in 1644 and who had been usher at Boston, Lincs, and master of Aldenham 1649–53, took the post. This fiery character's tenure was brief but eventful and again a committee had to sort out master–usher differences, finding against the latter and appointing Thomas Page usher the following day. In November 1663, an extra member of staff was added in 'Mr Youngs, Writing School master for the boys that go to the Grammar School'. He used 'a chamber at Lettice's house', made fit for the purpose. Later a room in Felaw's house was used and successive ushers were paid rent for making part of their residence available for a writing school. It was made a condition of Youngs' appointment, that he should 'come to church with his schollars on Fridays'. Where were the master and usher?

The authorities, alarmed by the unsettled state of the school, asked the three ministers sharing the lectureship 'to examine the schollers in the Free School and to see how they profitt in learnyng'. It was hoped 'that they would be pleased to agree among themselves to visit the school once a weeke to see the scholars lattine, and to do what they think fitt for the Improvement of the said school'. The result was that Collier was given notice in April 1664 that he would be replaced that Michaelmas, to which he evidently reacted badly, and was discharged on 24 May. Page was put in charge temporarily and another master elected in July was dismissed in November. If Collier was not a success, his son and namesake, prepared at the school for Caius in 1666, is interesting.[4] He became the third Ipswichian bishop that century, albeit a Jacobite and so non-juring, and a controversial author of considerable note. His *Short View of the Immorality and Profaneness of the English Stage* was, perhaps for the wrong reasons, a best seller.

4 Apparently Jeremy junior stayed on after his father left.

A SHORT

VIEW

OF THE
Immorality and Profaneneſs
OF THE

English Stage :

Together with
The Senſe of Antiquity
upon this
𝒜 𝓡 𝒢 𝒰 𝑀 𝐸 𝒩 𝒯.

By *JEREMY COLLIER*, M.A.

The Second Edition.

London, Printed for S. Keble at the *Turk's-Head*
in *Fleetstreet*, R. Sare at *Gray's-Inn-Gate*,
in *Holborn*, and P. Hindmarsh against the
Exchange in *Cornhil*. 1698.

JEREMY COLLIER A.M.

VIII

Stephenson, Coningsby and Leeds 1664–1737

Between Stephenson's arrival, in 1664, and King's retirement, in 1798, six masters averaged 22 years in office each. Very little is known of Stephenson's 30-year headship. Robert Coningsby brought his love of books from Merchant Taylors' school. Edward Leeds, who had served his father at Bury school as usher, had to contest an election for the mastership which was run on party lines. He too did much for the school's library.

ROBERT STEPHENSON, MA, went from Sudbury grammar school to Magdalene in 1655. He took his MA in 1662 and obtained his first teaching experience as founder master of Woodbridge School. There for only a year or two, he instituted a Liber Admissionum, a useful source for that school's history. He may have instituted or continued one at Ipswich,[1] but, if so, it was consumed, with so much else, in the bonfires the Revd John King lit when retiring at the end of the next century. On his arrival Stephenson found a somewhat bruised usher holding the fort. Thomas Page, MA, a fellow Magdalene man, had coped bravely with Jeremy Collier until the abrupt departure of the latter. Nine more ushers, several of them Ipswichians, were appointed during Stevenson's 31-year headship until he, like Woodside, died in office on 10 June 1695, aged only 61. The inscription on his grave slab in St Mary Quay church exag-

---

1 He arrived in late 1664 or early 1665. The house he occupied as master was, in 1674, assessed for tax on six hearths; only a few dwellings in the Quay parish were twice the size.

gerates his tenure by four years. At the Great Court, which appointed him 'to continue master duringe the townes plesure', the orders for regulating the school and its scholars were read aloud. It was next ordered that they 'shalbe faierly Ingrossed and sent to the Bishopp for his Confirmacion and if M[aste]r Bailiffs or the Assembly shall thincke fitt to alter any article in the same to be done before they be sent'.

It would have helped Stephenson to have long-serving ushers but three of the nine are particularly interesting. George Raymond, MA, served from 1673

GEORGE RAYMOND,
Of *Catharine - Hall* in *Cambridge*.
May 12. 1669.

to 1679, later holding livings in Norfolk, as well as at St Nicholas and St Lawrence, Ipswich, Westerfield and Shotley. He was almost certainly born and educated in Ipswich, going up to Catherine Hall, Cambridge, as a sizar in 1670.[2] It was during his time that his college offered to settle two scholarships upon 'five eminent schools in the nation, namely, Paul's, Merchant Taylors', Eton, Ipswich and Bury', provided that those concerned would match their candidates' scholarships, something the Ipswich corporation clearly failed to do.[3] Another Ipswich and Catharine Hall man, John Camplin, was the next usher to serve for long (1680–86). Thomas Johnson, MA, usher 1689-91, was a scholar of Eton and King's and a fellow there, a classical author and translator, but led a colourful later life, teaching briefly at Eton and then becoming master of Chigwell, from which office he was dismissed. This 'man of companionable

2   He died in 1725, having published several sermons, some preached at Bury Assizes.

3   It is interesting that the next two masters appointed, Coningsby and Leeds had been ushers at two of the schools listed.

facetiousness and lively conversation' made a disastrous marriage and bankruptcy and tippling were blamed for his failure.

At least Stephenson was a fixture and under him the school should have prospered.[4] The obsequious but beautifully penned petition of John Rackham[5] shows how coveted foundation places were:

> To the Right Wor'ppful the Ba'liffs and the rest of their bretheren
>
> The humble peticion of John Rackham, Taylor, of Ipswich, being a free-man
>
> Humbly sheweth that yo'r peticioner understanding of the benefit given to such schollers of the grammer schole as are intended to be brought up for Cambridg and that there is one of the number in which the benefitt was bestowed lately gon out of the schoole which is Goodman Smith's sonne

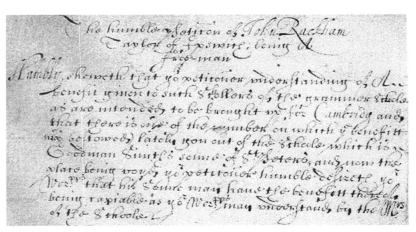

4 From 1670 the grammar school should have been safe at last from those who might wish to divert its endowments to a charity school. The will made that year by Nicholas Phillips, portman, enabled the foundation of a school in Christ's Hospital, adding education to the other provisions of Tooley's and Smarte's Foundation, a century after the 1572 Letters Patent had by implication required it. It was not a grammar school, because the blue coat boys there were never more than about twenty in number, and, at fourteen, they were usually sent to sea as apprentices.

5 SROI C/3/10/1/1/5.

of St Peters and now the place being voyd yo'r peticoner humble desireth yo'r Wor'pps that his sonne may have the benefitt thereof being capiable as yo'r Wor'pps may understand by the M'rs of the Schoole

Wich if yo'r Wor'pps will be please to bestow on yo'r peticoner yor peticoner shall acknowledg himself greatly obliged to yo'r Wor'pps & shall daily pray for yo'r Wor'pps p'servations

The lad was admitted as a scholar, in January 1665, but like many another did not fulfil his father's higher ambitions.

Only two years into Stephenson's time, in October 1667, a new committee of the Assembly (of eleven men, five were to serve) was charged 'to consider of the schoole & what course may be taken to advance the same & to make report thereof to some assemblie'. Two months later, two members of the Assembly were sent to Philip Candler's house, threatening him with canon law if he continued to teach grammar there, and this despite his late father's efforts with Beck and the Recorder to sort out differences between Henry Wickham and his usher. In 1670, Candler took on the mastership of Woodbridge School for the next nineteen years; when he applied to be usher at Ipswich in 1686 he came third in the field of three.

Treasurer's accounts show that it cost the corporation as much as £15 a year to keep the school fabric in order; much of it on locks, keys, bars and shutters. Could it be that boys were not to be trusted? New locks had last been provided throughout the premises in 1663. The bill for just under one pound, submitted in November 1672 and paid exactly a year later, is mainly for locks: for the schoole doore, a chest and double cross ward chest locks with screws for Mr Stephenson's and [the usher] Mr Butler's desks. More door locks were required again in January 1675 and was it boys who had broken the 218 quarrys of glass required at the 'Free School house of office' in 1683? It is strange to note that Robert Stephenson was among those fined threepence in 1685 for 'suffering muck and filth to lie before their several houses or ground... to the great annoyance of the streets and ways there'.

In 1676, Christopher Wase, a former master of Dedham school, but now Esquire Bedell of Law at Oxford, conducted a national survey of free grammar schools on whose behalf he was concerned. After the Restoration it was realised that these schools had been responsible for educating such men as Cromwell, Milton and Hampden and they could not therefore expect much official support. In common with the masters of Dedham, Hadleigh and Sudbury, questionnaires issued to them by Stephen Newcomen of Ipswich had not been returned. Glascock, still at Felsted, had replied fully.[6] Wase need not have feared for the future of Ipswich school, for the corporation of the day was consistently working for its good.

In 1681, Stephenson married Susan, daughter of Robert Chenery, a prosperous linen draper of Needham Market, and they had a son and two daughters, of whom only Suzan survived her parents.[7]

6   The Wase MSS are Corpus Christi College Oxford MS 390/1-4. The archivist Dr Michael Stansfield kindly abstracted these failures of communication. Stephen Newcomen, born in 1645, was the son of Matthew Newcomen the celebrated Puritan minister, lecturer at Dedham.

7   When Robert made his will in 1691 he was a widower in excellent health and most concerned to provide for Suzan, who was only about eight years old. He left property at Layham, Suffolk and other possessions which came from his late wife: lands at Little Bromley in Essex, in Suffolk and part-ownership of merchant ships, the *George* and the *Sea Adventure*, of which latter a cousin was the master. Having no son to use his library he left his books to a nephew and namesake, son of his brother Samuel. To see that she was properly educated and cared for, he chose as Suzan's guardian the celebrated Dr John Fairfax, ejected from his living at Barking in 1662, and instead running a house church in Needham and ministering to Presbyterian congregations in Ipswich.

In the early 1680s, a linen manufactory was set up in the town for the employment of Huguenot refugees from France; sailcloth was an important product. They used St Mary Elms church for worship and the boys were taught, first by a M. Caesar de Beaulieu in a room in Felaw's house, then by the Revd Balthazar Gardemau in the southern half of the Blackfriars dormitory (next to the town library). How, one wonders, did the two groups of boys in such close proximity get on? Perhaps it was to avoid them coinciding in the playground that the assembly in August 1682 reminded the master that 'no remedyes or playdays be given, but on Thursdays in the afternoon, and then for all the afternoon if the master see cause'. By 1689, the master may have been tiring of his burdens, for the town clerk was ordered 'to draw up orders for better regulating of the grammar school and to have the lecturers and some of the ministers of the town their approbation therein'.

From shortly after 1605 until 1771 (when the 13 year-old William Batley remembered hearing the last), a Latin oration was delivered by the head boy in St Mary-le-Tower church each November 5th, in celebration of the nation's deliverance from Gunpowder Plot. In 1615, the churchwardens paid fivepence for the order of service to be followed and mustered it annually with the church's ornaments. A manuscript notebook containing two such orations, colourfully entitled 'Conjuratio Nitro-Sulphurea',[8] survives. They were written by Robert Pupplett of Ipswich, then of Catharine Hall, for declamation in Great St Mary's in 1695 and 1697. These sermons were surely based on

---

8   Literally 'Gunpowder Conspiracy'. Nitre and sulphur, with charcoal, make gunpowder. I am grateful to Miss Barbara Pratt for drawing my attention to the notebook in SRO Ipswich (FN400/6/1) which contains the orations. Terry Bird kindly translated several passages, and cracked the optative mood conundrum in Chapter VI. After the first oration Pupplett's rooms in college were whitewashed, for his second he was given a capon.

those he heard or gave at Ipswich for, as town clerk, his mercer father Richard was entitled to educate sons at the school. Pupplett's orations are festal, stirring and stylish, reminding his listeners (whose ready understanding of spoken Latin must be assumed) of every defeat of the old religion and every victory for the reformed church in England that century. He was particularly condemnatory of Jesuits. One short passage, here in translation, gives the flavour:

> Fawkes, you most dreadful of all people; did the most illustrious order of senators, did the revered heads of the bishops, did the dignity and splendour of a great king strike the eyes of your soul not even a little?

There is no doubt that new heads bring useful experience from their previous schools and the men they served there. ROBERT CONINGSBY (1661–1712), the first Oxford man to head the school for well over a century, had been boy and under-master at Merchant Taylors' School. After St John's College, he learnt his profession under Matthias Shortyng, the master there for five years. In 1693, he published *Mythologia* –

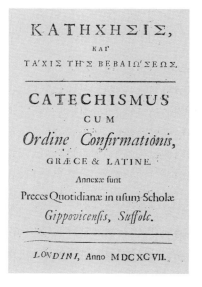

Greek fables explained – over an imprint including a Christopher Coningsby, surely a relation. His belongings followed him from London by sea 'in the hands of some hoyman' in October 1695. At Merchant Taylors', a Greek and Latin Catechism, with the Order for Confirmation, had been used since its publication in 1683 to advance boys' knowledge of the classical languages while reinforcing their spiritual training. Coningsby needed a similar text book at Ipswich and, in 1697, had a new edition printed in London, including orders for morning and evening prayers (as prescribed in the 1571 ordinances), with midday prayers for good measure.[9]

Coningsby was certainly a book man and Woodside's first steps towards a school library in the late 1650s became bold strides. Fewer than thirty volumes of this collection survived the 1940s when the rest were sent to be pulped for the war effort but, at least, headmaster Holden's son Edward catalogued 157 works he found in 1877.[10] In about 1800, there had been twice as many, the donor inscriptions showing that most were given in Coningsby's time. From 1697, the new master established a tradition of leavers and other former pupils presenting books to the school. Each gift is inscribed in Coningsby's hand: 'Ex Libb: Scholae publicae Gippovicensis'. Devereux Edgar, whose joint exploits with Cave Beck in beautifying St Margaret's church have been mentioned, sent his sons to Coningsby and saw to it that they gave books on leaving. After Beck's death in 1706, Coningsby took over the town library and made a complete manuscript catalogue. New acquisitions there also bear his hand: 'Ex Libb: Bibl: Ipsvic:' On the last pages of Coningsby's manuscript town library catalogue are several geometrical constructions, most of them totally fallacious, a reminder that you can only teach what you know.

9 British Library shelfmark 3503 b.39.
10 Two or three missing books reappeared in the time of Tom Cook at his College Gateway Bookshop in Silent Street.

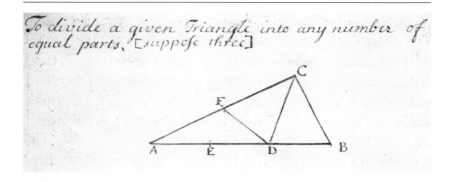

It seems surprising that, in 1702, the school needed a Turkey carpet costing seventeen shillings; it must have been for occasional use only, since a 'box to put it in' cost half-a-crown more. That year, Edward Hubbard, cabinet maker, entered his sons Edward and Henry 'upon Mr Snow and Mr Tyler's gifts'. Father carved the pulpit for the Tower church well enough to suggest the hand of Grinling Gibbons on it. Edward became master of St Catharine's and Vice-Chancellor and Henry sat for his portrait to Gainsborough when Registrary at Cambridge and a fellow of Emmanuel College.

Amazingly enough, in 1705 the Great Court, dissatisfied with the existing provision for Christ's Hospital, took over Felaw's House, 'commonly called the Usher's house' for the Christ's Hospital master's dwelling 'and the room that has usually been a schoolroom shall be for the same use'. The grammar school was not affected by these changes of use for buildings as Gaudy, just chosen usher, had his own house in St Mary Elms. However, the loss of income from Felaw's lands was severe.

Amongst Coningsby's pupils were two sons of Peter Hingeston (pronounced 'Hinkston'), borough organist for 55 years. The younger, Robert, became a long-serving usher and master but of the elder, Peter (1694–1749), who went up to Pembroke in 1711, there remains a small manuscript poetry book, bound in full calf, in which he started writing when he was fourteen. The flyleaf is inscribed 'Ex libris Pet. Hingeston Scho: Gipp: Alumn' Maij 10mo 1708'. He was no great poet but it is worth placing a few verses alongside the geometry already exposed to ridicule.[11]

A Valentine

When that the Shepherds sound their pipes
And swains begin to sing
When pretty warblers tune their throats
To Usher in the Spring
Choosing their mates they chirping dance along
And spend the new come year in everlasting song
Then pardon me if I do choose
You for my Valentine
Since if we see with ev'ry Swain
An Amarillis shine.

On the Word PERPENDICULAR

Of old as Records tell us, every Nation
Had its peculiar Words in fashion,
So we to show what learned folk we were
made choice of this word Perpendicular.
With us the World is perpendic'lar grown
And Independent spread all o'er the town:
For now a man can't buy a Wig that's good
Without two dangling fardles to his face
For perpendicular is all the Mode
Nay we're so modish, that the rogues we see
All hang in Perpendicularity
Thus said the Country Squire with's foaming bottle
When's pockets were as empty as his noddle
E'Dad I'll tell thee friend I shot a Hare
And who would think if 'twas perpendiculare

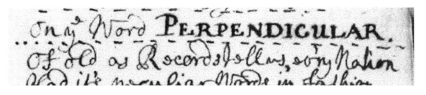

11 SROI HD 379/8., fol. 15 recto.

Coningsby died, still master and aged only 51, holding also the rectories of Woolverstone and Trimley. He penned his own will in his confident and elegant hand, naming Devereux Edgar one of his executors. He had provided a press for the school, which he now left to it, adding five books 'at my study': Ptolomeus Bertij, Constantini *Lex. graec*; Hesychij *Lex graec*; *Spelmanni glossarum*, and Leigh's *Critica Sacra*. The latter bears his inscription. He seems to have felt that the school had more need for books than the town but left an orderly town library with an up-to-date author catalogue in his own hand, as well as a useful collection of texts, ancient and modern, for the use of his successors in the school. Without his encouragement, it is doubtful whether works like Moxon *On the Use of Globes*, 1674; Cluver's *Introductio in Universam Geographicum*, 1682, and an Arabic grammar would have been donated; they are among the works which the school still has.

As for ushers, in 17 years he had four and it is the last of them about which we know most. John Gaudy, usher from 1705 to 1713, was born in 1670, eldest son of Cressingham and Rebecca Gaudy *alias* Crosby, entered Ipswich school as a foundation scholar in 1682 but, four years later, inherited his milliner uncle  John's whole estate. This included a sizeable house in St Lawrence parish (four hearths) and meant that he could continue his education, though his name is unaccountably absent from the Cambridge or Oxford lists. By contrast, his brother Cressingham had to stick to his shoemaker's last, earning an extra five pounds a year as one of the four serjeants who carried the corporation mace before the bailiffs in procession and generally kept the peace.

While usher to Coningsby, Gaudy could afford to present fine books to the school library regularly: *On the Psalms of David and the Prophets* [1614] in 1705, Leybourn's *Mathematical Sciences* [1690] in 1707 and *Opera Horatii* [1580] in 1710, but, in 1712, Coningsby died and Gaudy was not chosen to succeed him.

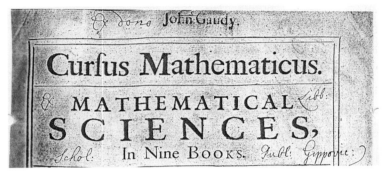

❧

Until the Municipal Reform Act of 1836, a poll of all the free-men could be held for a vacancy to any office in the borough, and such elections were conducted on party lines. Polls were conducted in public, each freeman declaring his preference aloud to the presiding bailiffs at the hustings. There had been little point, however, in holding elections for the mastership when, as has been shown, it was difficult to persuade good candidates to accept the post. Party feeling was running high in the borough in 1712 and there were now two contenders; one of them, the Revd Thomas Bishop, minister of St Mary-le-Tower, had the support of the Blue party. Gaudy and his true Blue brother incautiously put their weight behind Bishop, who lost by 166 to 196 votes to the Yellow candidate.

It was a time of Whig ascendancy in the town and the Yellow winner, with low church and nonconformist support, was EDWARD LEEDS, son and namesake of a celebrated master of Bury School, for the last five years his usher.[12] Coningsby was a Tory, so why was Leeds a Whig? Sir Thomas Hervey of Ickworth and Bury was a Whig politician who accepted the principles of the 1688 Revolution and the Hanoverian succession. His son and heir John, who became successively 1st baron Hervey and 1st earl of Bristol, was educated under the elder Leeds at Bury school. In 1704, on Leeds senior's recommendation, Leeds junior became tutor to the Hervey children, and, of course, nothing augments political leanings more than patronage.[13] At Ipswich, the new Whig master and old Tory usher co-existed for only one term.

Gaudy did not resign voluntarily, for he had many allies in the town and was a married man, described as 'Gentleman' when he married Elizabeth Stiles at Hintlesham in 1707. In January 1713, he was dismissed by the two Whig bailiffs who had supervised the election on the grounds that he had been elected 'during the pleasure' of their Tory predecessors. The Great Court promptly indemnified the bailiffs 'in suits of law threatened to be commenced and prosecuted... for and about the profits or place of usher and he [Gaudy] being discharged therefrom', but nothing more was heard of the matter. John Gaudy probably continued teaching boys privately at his house in St Mary Elms and was for a year incumbent at St Margaret's. His

12 Edward Leeds senior was renowned for keeping a pack of hounds, and rewarding his scholars by mounting his black mare and taking them out hunting on foot.

13 Lists of those voting for each candidate in this hotly contested mastership election were recorded by that assiduous recorder of borough events, Devereux Edgar, in his commonplace book SROI K15/2. Edgar was a prime mover in establishing another charity school in 1709 with high church and Tory support based on the Tower church: Grey Coat Boys and Blue Coat Girls. Boys in blue coats belonged to Christ's Hospital school. The low church Whig equivalent based on St Lawrence followed eventually, for Redsleeve Boys and Greensleeve Girls. Supporters of the two schools insisted on the correct colours being worn in the town so that they could judge behaviour.

son William, born to his second wife Elizabeth Gosnold in 1711, was prepared by Leeds for Catharine Hall in 1728; by then, therefore, Gaudy and Leeds had settled their differences.[14]

Edward Leeds was the first master to live in what is now called The Master's House, 19–21 Lower Brook Street. Previously known as the Preacher's House, it had been built by Samuel Ward's predecessor as town preacher, Dr John Burges, in the 1590s and acquired by the borough for Ward. From 1712, lecturers had to be compensated for the loss of their accommodation, which now housed successive masters' families with all the boarders until 1852.[15] This left the corporation free to sell

14 In 1735 Gaudy became vicar of Tuddenham St Martin but, on William's death in 1749, made a will in favour of his daughter Elizabeth, recommending her to remember the charity school for Grey Coat Boys and Blue Coat Girls. He then moved to Lincolnshire to be Vicar of Long Sutton and died there in 1751, survived for only a year by his daughter Elizabeth, since 1749 a lunatic in the London Bethlem Hospital.

15 Today the house is marked by an Ipswich Society blue plaque commemorating William King, son of the Revd John King, master and the founder of the Co-operative Movement.

the schoolmaster's house in the school yard (somewhere near the refectory great schoolroom) to pay for repairs to the schoolroom and the walls of the yard, and, of all things, to repair the town's 'dirt boat'. Leeds, a Peterhouse man, came to Ipswich as a layman but, four years later, he was ordained and held the living of Wherstead, from 1718, and St Matthew's, Ipswich, from 1727, both for life.

Leeds' first attempt to replace Gaudy as usher failed, because Charles Porter, BA, the first to be chosen, 'in a public manner declared himself incapacitated to supply the said place', taking the Crown living of St Matthew's instead. Richard Golty, son and namesake of the rector of Dennington was a better prospect and served until succeeded by the future master, Robert Hingeston, in 1721.

The printer John Bagnall came to Ipswich after a London apprenticeship and set up the weekly *Ipswich Journal* in 1720. Leeds commissioned two books from Bagnall two years later (the first from an Ipswich press since Argentine's activities in 1548), a slim *Catechesis* with thrice-daily prayers, all in Latin (the 1571 ordinance made no mention of Greek), and *Epigrammatum et Poematum Sacrorum et Psalmorum Delectus*,[16] both *In Usum Scholae Regis Henrici Ejus Nominis Octavi* – 'for King Henry VIII's School'. For printing the two books Bagnall was paid 17s 6d by the borough chamberlains. The Catechism was not based on Coningsby's Latin and Greek edition of 1697 but on Leeds' father's Bury school version, printed at Cambridge in 1673. Like his predecessor, Leeds cared about books and manuscripts, rescuing for the town library the thirteenth-century vellum Vulgate used from 1584 to 1711 as the bible on which to

16 Extracts from the book with translations by R.C. Burnell, head of Classics for 34 years until 1997, were published in the *Old Ipswichian Magazine* 23 for 1975.

swear oaths in Ipswich courts. He was the first to recognise the value, as documentary evidence, of the puritan William Dowsing's manuscript journal of iconoclasm in Suffolk churches in 1643–44, and fortunately for future scholars, made a copy for himself in 1705 just before the original was sold and lost.

Leeds retired to his living at Wherstead in 1737, demanding £200 in compensation for the loss of £11 per annum from Felaw's revenues which had been diverted to Christ's Hospital since 1718. For 19 years he had been paid only the bare stipend of £24 6s 8d but the borough authorities, when considering his request, may have realised how much he added to that by charging fees for out-of-town pupils. For one boarder, admittedly from a wealthy background, Peter, son of Alderman Ralph Creffield of Colchester, he charged over £26 a year on average while preparing him for an undistinguished career at Cambridge. Peter, who was born in May 1719, boarded from 1728 until 1736, when he left for St John's. The extant accounts of his guardian, Charles Gray, later MP for Colchester, who settled the lad's bills both before and after the death of his mother Lady Creffield in October 1734, give colour to Peter's life at school.[17] Peter was nine on arrival, thirteen when he succeeded his grandfather Sir Ralph in estates at Mersea and elsewhere and seventeen when he left for Cambridge.

The Leeds enjoyed only two years together in retirement and Edward had five more as a widower. The large slab under which they both lie in the nave at Wherstead bears elaborate but scarcely decipherable Latin inscriptions to them both.

17   Essex Record Office Round MSS (D/DRc)

How Leeds could almost double his stipend with one boarder's fees

At Ipswich School

Date	Item	£	s	d
April 1728	To Mr Leeds	3	4	0
	Dancing Master	1	5	6
Jan. 1729	To Mr Leeds for his bill	13	5	6
June	To Mr Leeds for his bill	11	2	6
	Eringoes[18] for Mrs Leeds		7	0
	Coach hire and expenses, two journeys	1	5	0
	Dr [William] Beeston [M.D.][19]	1	1	0
	Nurse	6	8	6
	Dr Beeston	5	5	0
	Apothecary	3	7	0
	Coach hire to Ipswich		15	0
	Mrs Leeds	1	1	0
Jan.1730	Mr Leeds	13	10	0
	To Mrs Leeds for Christmas Gift		10	6
	A Chaise to Ipswich		17	0
Jan. 1731	Mr Leeds	25	3	10
Jan. 1732	Mr Leeds	13	18	6
May	Cloathes and a hatt	2	13	6
June	Mr Leeds	14	6	2
Sept.	Paid him (Peter Creffield) in cash		10	6
Jan. 1733	Mr Leeds etc.	16	13	1
June	Mr Leeds	12	5	0
	To the servants		7	6
Aug.	Cash to him		5	0
	Colours		3	6
Sept.	Paid John Blyth for a Wigg[20]	1	6	6
Oct.	A watch for him	3	15	0
Dec.	The bills at Ipswich	16	16	11
	To Mr Leeds for him [P.C.] in cash	2	2	0
June 1734	Mr Leeds	14	7	6
Jan. 1735	Paid Mr Leeds for him	13	8	6
	Servants and expenses		16	10
	To him in cash	1	1	0
	Paid Mr Reading his Writing Master[21]	1	1	0

18 Candied eringo roots were a Colchester delicacy
19 Peter was expensively ill
20 A wig for a fourteen-year-old
21 This skill he should surely have acquired already

Mar.	Paid John Blith for his wig and shaving[22]	1	3	6
Mar. to May	Paid him in cash	3	0	0
	For a Newmarket cap and carriage	1	12	0
	Pd John Smorthwait for mending his watch		6	6
	Pd Mr Peter in cash		10	6
	Carriage of his boxes		4	6
June	Cash	1	1	6
	Paid for a Hat, hose and gloves	1	1	0
	Cash	1	16	0
	Paid Mr Leeds' bill	15	10	0
	His servants as usual		7	6
July	Paid Mr Reading the writing master		5	0
	Paid Mr Bland for his Cloathes	4	3	4
	Paid S. Philips for making them	1	2	6
Aug.	To William Smith for Boots and Shoes	1	1	0
	Stockings		7	0
Oct	3 pair of stockings		6	6
	To two parcels to Ipswich and a Dog		2	6
Dec.	To Mr Leeds for him	26	0	11
	To servants		7	6

Preparations for Cambridge

Jan. 1736	To Field's Testament & Nelson's Festivals		10	0
	To Mr Blomfeild, taylor			
	for his two suits of Cloaths & lace	14	5	6
	A hat & lace	1	1	6
	A pound of Tea		8	0
	A surplice		9	0
	Mr [James] Tunstall [tutor] Caution money	25	0	0
	Charges for the journey and at Cambridge	5	3	0
	To John Kendall for an Escritoire	4	1	6
	Its carriage to Cambridge		8	6
	A pound of Tea	1	1	0
	A Tea Kettle		7	0
April	A Bill sent to Cambridge for Mr Peter	70	0	0
July	Remitted to Cambridge	85	0	0
Apr. 1737	Remitted to Cambridge	138	0	0
July	A Bill to Mr Tunstall	94	3	7

22 Shaving at Sixteen

IX

Bolton, Hingeston and King 1737–1798

Halfway through a period of long-serving masters, Thomas Bolton's six years seem no more than a stop-gap. Robert Hingeston spent his whole life at the school enjoying a cultured circle of friends including his neighbour Thomas Gainsborough. John King, bringing his experience as usher at Newcastle-upon-Tyne, stayed 31 years, but sent up much of the evidence for his greatness in the smoke of the bonfires he lit in retirement.

THOMAS BOLTON, a John's, Cambridge, man unusually skilled, for a schoolmaster, in oriental as well as classical languages, was appointed on the understanding that he would not expect the extra £11 from Felaw's land revenues. He stayed only six years, before retiring to livings he held already at Barham and Hollesley. His son Thomas, at the school under Hingeston, became his usher in 1763, the last to hold that office, which was abolished when he vacated it in 1771. Bolton, feeling his age, resigned on 1 October 1743 and a week later the Great Court voted overwhelmingly to look no further for the next master than the present usher. Elections to the mastership were now traditional, but this one was uncontested.

ROBERT HINGESTON gave his whole career to the school, first serving Leeds as usher for sixteen years, then Bolton for six. He was born in Ipswich on 8 March 1699, the younger son of Peter Hingeston and his wife Martha, daughter of Andrew Sorrell. For 55 years Peter (1667–1743) was organist to the borough, playing for corporation services in St Mary-le-Tower. He had been apprenticed to his uncle John at York, successively state organist and private musician to Oliver Cromwell and then court musician to Charles II.

Robert entered Ipswich School in the time of Robert Coningsby and John Gaudy. The single fraught term that Leeds and Gaudy were colleagues may have taught Hingeston something about personal relations and the need for diplomacy. Robert was the first of his family at Cambridge when he entered Pembroke Hall in 1716, probably holding a Smarte scholarship. Graduating BA in 1719, he proceeded MA in 1723. In 1721 he returned to Ipswich, to serve Leeds as usher, and at Westhall in December 1723 married Catherine, the 17 year-old daughter of the Revd Samuel Bull, rector there, and also a minor canon of Norwich Cathedral.

Hingeston's first act on appointment was to publish his gratitude in the *Ipswich Journal*. The promise 'with Regard to their Health, Morals, and Improvement in Learning', displaying an interesting order of priorities, he kept for the next 24 years

IPSWICH, October 21, 1743.

BY the Favour of the Bailiffs, Burgeſſes, and Commonalty, being appointed Maſter of the GRAMMAR-SCHOOL in this Town, with the uſual Privileges, and Aſſignment of a convenient Houſe for the Reception of Boarders, I think myſelf oblig'd in this publick Manner to return them my hearty Thanks ; and beg Leave to aſſure them of my conſtant Endeavours to promote the Intereſt of the ſaid School, by a diligent Attendance, and faithful Diſcharge of my Duty therein : And thoſe Gentlemen, who ſhall favour me with their Children, may depend upon my utmoſt Vigilance and Care, both at Home and at School, with Regard to their Health, Morals, and Improvement in Learning.

ROBERT HINGESTON,

until his death in 1767, when he was buried in St Helen's church, having set an unbeatable record of long service to the School.

Robert and Catherine Hingeston had nine sons and five daughters, not all of whom survived childhood, and the Master's House had also to accommodate the boarders of the school. At least three sons and two nephews, sons of his elder brother Peter, were educated at the school. To support this large family he held several livings: Creeting St Peter from 1724, Great Bealings 1726, Newbourne 1727 and, on his father's presentation, St Helen's in Ipswich from 1730 to 1739.

In July 1746, the Great Court invited seven ministers and laymen, five of whom were to form 'a committee to inspect all former rules and orders concerning the Grammar School and to draw up the necessary rules and regulations for the governing the said School in conformity with the charter and according to the present circumstance, and therein to have regard to settling limits of jurisdiction between the  master and usher; and that they have power to send for papers and records in the power of the corporation; and that they make their Report to some Great Court'. The group, yet another temporary governing body, reported in the November following. Titus Tweady was senior and took the chair, enthusiastically assisted by the Revd Richard Canning, perpetual curate of St Lawrence (shown above in a portrait by Gainsborough), and Craighton, the proprietor and printer of the *Ipswich Journal*. Tweady and Craighton had both been at the school and then held Martin exhibitions at Cambridge and two of the parsons were also Ipswichians (*below). In 1747, Craighton published Canning's anonymous and highly critical account of the management of borough charities by previous corporations.[1] Many chapters gave offence, not least the one on the school which first castigated attempts to divert Felaw's original endowments, and then printed the new regulations in full. The town library chapter relates how, in a small way, the corporation had their own back on Canning for his public criticism.

Served on the committee

Revd Titus Tweady,* 1684–1749, Pembroke, rector of Trimley

Revd Richard Canning, 1708-75, minister of St Lawrence
Revd William Cornwallis,* Catharine Hall, vicar of Chelmondiston
Revd Charles Beaumont,* Peterhouse, rector of Witnesham, parent
Mr William Craighton,* Catharine Hall, printer and publisher, parent

Nominated but did not serve

Thomas Thurston Esq., of Dale Hall, Ipswich
Revd Richard Brome, St John's, minister at St Margaret's, parent

T. T W E A D Y.
AUL: PEMB:
1707.

The only committee member who was a freeman, and therefore entitled to attend and address the Great Court, was Cornwallis, so it was he who delivered the report. As Canning com-

---

1 The full title of the anonymous book is *An Account of the Gifts and Legacies that have been given and bequeathed to Charitable Uses in the Town of Ipswich; with some Account of the present State and Management, and some Proposals for the future Regulation of them, Ipswich*, Printed by W. Craighton, 1747.

124

mented, some points were wilfully misunderstood, but the most telling argument was probably accepted. In 1571 the master and usher had to teach 100 free scholars and, while their stipends were unchanged nearly two centuries later, the pound had only one-fifth of its Tudor purchasing power. In future, they should only have to take twenty free boys, with perhaps five more paid for from Smarte's and Tyler's charity. They could then charge for town or country boys admitted as fee-payers.

The master would take the upper three forms and the usher the lower four. The master had only to teach those with a grasp of Latin syntax and the ability to translate Latin into English and *vice versa*. Disputes between master and usher, over boys' suitability to go up, were to be settled by the bailiffs, town lecturer, town clerk and the local clergy.

There would be five school days each week, with morning and evening prayers read by a master, a senior pupil reading a third set at eleven. Friday lectures at the Tower church would be attended by the whole school.

The hours from 1 March to 1 October were seven to eleven and half past one to five. From 1 October to 1 March, they were eight to eleven and half past one to half past four. On Tuesdays and Thursdays, school ended half an hour earlier.

The Christmas holiday ran from O Sapientia (December 16) to the day after Plough Monday (the Monday after 6 January), Easter from the Friday before Passion week to the Monday fortnight following, Whitsuntide from the Friday before Whitsunday to the Monday fortnight following.

It was probably in January 1752 that young Thomas Gainsborough, his wife Margaret and their two small daughters moved from a rented house in Lower Brook Street to 34 Foundation Street. Gainsborough had come to Ipswich from Sud-

bury, perhaps in 1750, to try his hand at making a living painting the local gentry and landscape. The Gainsboroughs' garden
ran alongside the easternmost thirty yards of the Master's, and
the two men soon became good friends. It would have been natural for the artist to give lessons in the school, as well as private
tuition in people's homes. The Hingestons at one time owned
the delightful 'Daughters of the Artist' (the two little girls
chasing a butterfly, painted in about 1756) and Gainsborough
painted both Robert and Catherine Hingeston and other members of their family.

Considering his strong musical pedigree, it is unfortunate
that no record remains of Robert Hingeston's accomplish-
ments. We only know that he was a member of the circle of
friends who met weekly for music and other polite amuse-
ments during and after Gainsborough's time in Ipswich. Most
members of the group sat to Gainsborough: John Gibbs, the
borough organist; Samuel Kilderbee, town clerk; John
Sparowe, apothecary and thirteen times Bailiff; the clergyman
Richard Canning, scourge of the Whigs in their handling of
borough charities; William Hubbard (when not in Cambridge)
and the flautist William Wollaston, member for Ipswich,
present when his parliamentary duties permitted. Only a
sketchy description remains of the conversation piece of the
music club when it was in the collection of a Mr Strutt. John
Bensusan-Butt named more of the members,[2] some from the
description: Captain Abraham Clerke, John Wood, dancing
master, Joseph Eyre, John Kirby, brother of Joshua and William, and Sir Richard Lloyd of Hintlesham. The lost sketch was
unfinished and only five members were shown, just Gainsborough, Clerke, Wood, Gibbs (asleep) and a cellist named Mills.

---

2   John Bensusan-Butt, *Thomas Gainsborough in his Twenties*, Colchester 1989.

During the 1950s, the late Wallace Morfey, OI and long-serving governor of Ipswich School, successfully collected portraits of the twelve most recent headmasters (and one earlier – Beck) and long reflected on the possibility that Gainsborough had painted his neighbour Hingeston. In 1961, he not only found the portrait but became its possessor. It had  until then been incorrectly identified as Revd James Hingeston, son of the master, and so listed thus by Waterhouse in 1958. When it was painted in the early 1750s, however, James was only about twenty. As it shows a cleric of between fifty and sixty years of age, it can be confidently identified as Robert.[3]

Towards the end of his mastership Hingeston may have lacked the energy for another change of schoolroom. In November 1763, the Assembly appointed a committee to dispose of the refectory which had housed it for 150 years but no new site had yet been chosen. Robert Hingeston died in office, in April 1766. He was buried in St Helen's church under a black marble slab, which also records the burial there of his widow in 1793, aged 86, and six of their children. It was finally the resting place of their longest surviving child John, a surgeon, who died at Eastcote Lodge, Ruislip, Middlesex in 1810, aged 73. He it was who recalled that Gainsborough was 'a great favourite of

---

3 Wallace Morfey told the whole story in an article in the *Old Ipswichian Magazine* 31 for 1983. In 2001 the portrait was purchased by Ipswich Museums and Galleries and it now hangs in Christchurch beside the Gainsborough portraits of Canning, Wollaston and Kilderbee.

my father; indeed his affable and agreeable manners endeared him to all with whom his profession brought him into contact, either at the cottage or the castle. My father's residence bears testimony, alike, to his skill as a painter and his kindness as a man; for the panels of some of the rooms are adorned with the productions of his genius'. Four months after Hingeston's death, his refectory schoolroom was demolished and the site let to John Gravenor, gent. Yet again, a move for the school seems to have come at a very bad time, with only the usher, Thomas Bolton junior, to oversee it.

JOHN KING shares, with Stephenson, the record for the longest serving master: thirty-one years, from 1767 to 1798. He has often been described as the most successful. Why then did he burn the entire records of the school when he came to retire to his vicarage at Witnesham? The catalogue of the town library[4] which he was commissioned by the corporation to compile in the first year of his retirement is a poor thing, even compared with the manuscript catalogue Robert Coningsby made nearly a century before on his own initiative.

The Revd John King was born at Richmond in Yorkshire in 1738 and, after graduating seventh wrangler at Peterhouse, became a fellow there. For seven years he was undermaster at Newcastle-upon-Tyne grammar school, teaching the future Lord Eldon, no doubt a useful patron in later years. There is no doubt that he was exactly the man the corporation wanted. The Assembly was told 'indeed, the application of such a gentleman has the appearance of a fortunate event for the Town'. For

---

4 *A Numerical Catalogue of the Books in the Town Library under the Public Grammar=School, Ipswich*, Printed by William Burrell, 1799. A second title-page halfway through the book has 'Alphabetical' in place of 'Numerical'.

King, the stipend laid down in 1746 (to which the Felaw £11 was added, to lure him) was soon more than doubled for him by the addition of the town lecturership worth £52 10s. Two years after his arrival, he married Elizabeth Sarah Bishop at St Margaret's church. She was granddaughter of the Thomas Bishop who lost the mastership election to Leeds in 1712. King's growing family will also have profited by his holding the Crown living of St Matthew's, for four years from 1772, when he exchanged it for Witnesham, a Peterhouse living carrying £450 a year for the rest of his life. The statutory 25 day-boy scholars were educated free (the one-penny fines of morning latecomers went straight to the master for good measure), but King also packed about 70 boarders into the Master's House, charging what the parents were prepared to pay. Altogether, he must have been one of the most highly-paid schoolmasters in the land. Many of his former pupils spoke highly of him and became eminent in later life, including his own sons. One of them, William King, the pioneer of the Co-operative movement, left an account of life in Ipswich and the school at the end of his father's mastership.[5]

A selection of King's pupils
William Kirby, FRS, the entomologist parson of Barham
George Henry Law, bishop of Chester, later Bath and Wells
Richard Hall Gower, captain, naval architect
Sir George Adam Wood, major-general commanding the RA at Waterloo
John Spencer Cobbold, Hebraist, dean of Caius College
John Davie, master, Sidney Sussex College and Vice-Chancellor

5   The manuscript, SRO Ipswich S92 Kin, was presented to the borough library by a greatgrandson of the master in 1923. Charles Partridge (OI) edited it in twelve instalments for the *East Anglian Daily Times* from 6 May 1922 to 6 Oct. 1923.

Sir Philip Vere Broke, Bart, rear admiral, 'Broke of the Shannon' after his victory over the Chesapeake
Sir Charles Broke Vere, MP, major-general, promoted at Waterloo
Sir John Thomas Jones, Bart, major-general, military engineer
George Rix Clarke, author of *The History and Description of Ipswich*, 1830
George Crabbe, son, namesake and biographer of the poet
William French, master of Jesus College, Cambridge

Today the Master's House is in full view from Lower Brook Street but in King's time it was hidden behind a brick wall. In the playground behind it, some 30 by 80 feet, boys played cricket and flew kites. Indian corn was grown in the beds along two sides of the playground and the 'great' boys used to send the juniors over neighbours' walls to steal fruit. The end of the playground opened on to Foundation Street opposite the Shire Hall, where the assizes were held,[6] and Christ's Hospital school. By turning left, crossing the road and going through an arched gate into the yard, boys arrived in front of the northeast range of the former Blackfriars, the upper floor of which was now the schoolroom. King's first task was to complete the settling the school there, since the move had come right at the end of Hingeston's tenure and his life.

From Joshua Kirby's plan of 1748 (see page 90), it is possible to compare the old and new rooms. The floor area of the friars' dormitory over A, B and both spaces C was 70 per cent larger than that of the frater (G) but it was almost four times as long as it was wide, whereas the frater was only three times longer

---

6   The Shire Hall was architecturally similar to and coeval with the Unitarian chapel in Friars Street.

than its width. There are plates by Henry Davy (page 157) and Jabez Hare OI (above) of the new interior and two exterior views by Russel (page 136) and Davy (page 142) of the yard which was a useful playground. The boys shown are dressed for the 1840s, not much different from the dress of King's time. The tower at the northern end of the range was formerly erected over the south end of the friars' walking place which had divided the nave and chancel of their church. Now truncated, it contained a staircase giving access to the first floor schoolroom. The displaced town library went down into the former sacristy (marked A on Kirby's plan), too damp to be suitable for storing valuable books. The furniture to be seen in the interiors probably came from the frater schoolroom, since only a chair costing sixteen shillings (probably for the master) was new.

William King describes the rather dangerous game which was played by opposing teams of three each with an anchor boy. Charles Partridge remembered it still popular in the school a century later, then called 'Highcockalawrum'. In the

1790s, 'Little Jack nine tails, one two three' was the signal for the first boy in the attacking team jumping onto the horizontal backs of the defenders in line. The aim was for all the jumpers to land on the same boy so that he gave way under their weight, when the jumpers won another turn. If the 'down' team stayed up, it would be their turn to jump next.[7] When boys were injured at play, Dr John Clubbe, a neighbouring surgeon, was sent for.

A stout good-looking Frenchman called D'Egville, with well-powdered hair and a pigtail, taught dancing in the 30 by 20 foot schoolroom in the Master's House. First he taught boys the correct way to bow before they progressed to the Cotillon and the Minuet de la Cour. Annual balls 'for the County' were held jointly with the young ladies of Miss Harrison's school, also in Brook Street, in a 'regular Ball Room in St Matthew's Street'. Money was saved up to treat partners to cakes and negus – a variety of punch. As the threat of a French invasion grew, the boys became highly patriotic volunteers, drilling regularly with wooden guns.

King states that there was no official fagging in the school but a good deal of bullying, some arising from the 'employment' of small boys as servants to their elders. He was only twelve years old when his father retired and sent him to Westminster. There he found that the reverse was the case. William was once caught by his father coming back from town with gunpowder he had bought for another boy. He was flogged but the other was not punished; this was to teach him 'not to be made the tool of others'. Boys were allowed a penny a day pocket-money which they usually spent with Brett, the man who stood

---

7   At the author's school in the 1940s it was called 'Highjimmynacker'. How youthful traditions persist.

in the school yard with baskets of fruit, cakes and nuts. John King employed his brother-in-law to assist him, the pious and mild-mannered clergyman John Sharpe, but even he carried a vine cane and hit boys from behind when they least expected it. Two other masters taught in the writing school, which was built in 1771 in the garden next door to the Master's House for £250. In 1777, presumably to fill a vacancy there, King advertised in the *Original Ipswich Journal* for 'a Third Assistant, a young Man of liberal Education... he must have a good Temper, and a clear distinct Voice and if he is capable of teaching Navigation etc. it will be an additional Recommendation.' Harmer, the senior writing master in William King's time, taught a steady firm hand, took snuff and had great difficult with his h's 'which he put in and left out in the wrong places'. His assistant was severe and a flogger.

Boarders had to share a bed, boys under ten with seniors, who bullied them but they did not dare to complain. Evidently John King came to realise that this was 'a great error in education' and William deplored all forms of corporal punishment in later life. Three great keys – to the school, the school-yard and the playground – hung on a leather strap in John King's parlour:

> When my father took them off the hook, on which they were hung, they made a considerable noise, which was heard in the large room where the boys were, and was the signal for his appearance. Sometimes the noise made by the boys was terrific – playing, jumping, quarrelling. By way of quieting them, we used sometimes to take down the keys and give them a good shake. The boys immediately became silent and looked to the door expecting to see my father. They waited for some minutes to satisfy themselves before they began again.

King first wore a wig when he went up to Peterhouse, having his head shaved for the first time then to accommodate it:

133

My father continued to wear a wig all his life... After he retired to Witnesham a barber came from Ipswich once a week to dress it. Of course, he had one for Sunday, special, dressed with more care. His wig was originally powdered but, when the tax on hair-powder came in,[8] it was a matter of great curiosity among the boys whether the wig would be powdered or not. There were two windows of the [Brook Street] school room looking into the front court, by which the barber entered. He was as punctual as the clock as to his time. The two windows were crowded with boys to solve this knotty question: would Mr King continue the powder? There was great difference of opinion. The bell rung, the gate opened, in walked the wig without powder. Great was the triumph of the true prophets. The question was partly economic, partly political. Many people left off powder to spite the Government... I do not know what my father's politics were then.[9]

King's engraved portrait, after a miniature by James Dunthorne, probably shows him at about the time he retired in poor health, Nevertheless, he lived on quietly in his Witnesham living until 1822, when he died, aged 83. The existing Suffolk white brick rectory bears the date 1823, so that King passed his last years in a more venerable house. Since a retiring head-

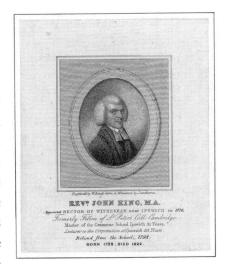

master's books are important to him, one last memory of the

8   From 1795, those who used hair-powder had to take out an annual certificate on which the stamp duty was one guinea.

9   The 1790 poll book of the election for County members of Parliament shows that John King cast his votes for both the Tory candidates. Like most of the masters, he was not a freeman, so had no votes in borough elections.

then twelve year-old William King deals with that aspect of the move to the country:

> Our first labour at Witnesham was arranging the library. We had a large Book-case about 12 feet wide. This was placed on one side of the parlour, leaving about four feet at each end. At one end was my father's bureau. At the other a small round table and the coal scuttle in winter. In the middle of the room was one table, or two of the same size, each four by three and half feet. Four could dine comfortable at one, or six crowded, and when both were put together eight could dine comfortably or ten crowded...
>
> The books were tied up in parcels of six or eight volumes each, so that it might seem easy to place them in the shelves. They were put into the waggon, and so carried to within twenty feet of the parsonage. The carters took them out and placed them promiscuously on the floor in a state of nice confusion. We were utterly perplexed to put them to rights, and, not being tall enough to reach the top shelves, we brought the garden steps into the room to help. These had been made, as in olden times, to help ladies on horseback. A rail passed up one side, and this, projecting upon the top step, thought proper when moved to push itself through the glass of one of the doors. Fortunately, large plate glass was not in fashion. So the damage was small; but it was a vexation. We laboured all day at our work without finishing it, so when the time of departure came, we put the books on the shelves pell-mell, and left the finishing till another day, and walked back to Ipswich. When, half-way through our walk, we recollected that we had a catalogue of the books in our pocket, which helped us much to restore order at the latter end.

After the demolition of the refectory schoolroom in August 1766 the school moved to the first floor former dormitory of the friars. This 100 by 25 foot room was lit by windows at each end and four more on the west side. Stairs led to it built in the stump of the south crossing tower, all that remained of the church. Doors from the left: 1. The former sacristy, now a very damp town library; 2. The pointed door with surrounding Gothic windows, former chapter house, now a small chapel; 3., 4. and 5.: stores and kitchens; 6. Norman door facing north: the front entrance to the town house given to the Dominicans on their arrival in 1263 and preserved to honour their benefactor.

Below: The school on two sites from King's time until Fenwick's.
Master, boarders and writing school in Lower Brook Street.
Dormitory great schoolroom with a large playground between it and
Foundation Street.

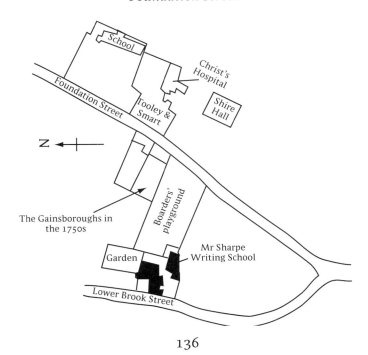

X

Ingram and Howorth
Bringing the School low

As successor to King, Ingram began well, but the offer of the headship of Giggleswick, in his native Yorkshire, was too tempting for him and his wife to resist. The next man appointed reneged when he realised how mean and makeshift were those who ran the town and the school. In desperation they appointed William Howorth, master of the school at Needham Market, and Ipswich was saddled with a non-graduate head for thirty-two years. Although in that time Howorth naturally made friends who would speak well of his efforts, the school was overtaken by others locally, including one run by an able and artistic schoolmaster who had probably one of his own pupils.

KING DID NOT begin his 24-year retirement at Witnesham in 1798 merely because he was sixty but because his health was failing. The corporation tried to find a worthy successor, but not hard enough. They were right to reject the Revd Joshua Hird whose application stipulated that he should hold the lectureship as well; when it was read to the Great Court 'no motion nor order was made thereon'. Here was the clue however, and it was ignored: the master's salary on its own was too small to recruit a first-rate scholar and teacher.

In July, the Rev ROWLAND INGRAM, BD, was nominated by a seven-man committee chaired by Philip Bowes Broke of Nacton 'as a person fully competent to discharge the duties of the mastership with the highest respectability, in learning, and morality'. Descended from the Ingrams of Temple Newsam, Yorkshire, he was educated at Dedham school, his father Robert, a former fellow of Corpus, being vicar of Wormingford and Boxted nearby. Ingram was successively fellow and tutor of Sidney Sussex college[1] and a private tutor at Eton; he had recently married Mary, daughter of Sir Cuthbert Shafto.

Wallace Morfey[2] wrote that Ingram 'started brilliantly at Ipswich but the corporation did not hurry itself to find for him the sort of perks King had enjoyed. Maybe his aristocratic young wife did not take kindly to having to run a boarding house of seventy boys to provide her husband's main source of income'. Within two years Ingram was attracted to the vacant headship of Giggleswick in his ancestral county. There was then no boarding house there but the spread of the nearby town of Settle over some of the farmlands of the school's original endowment brought in income that enabled the governors to offer a salary of £400. Ingram stayed at Giggleswick for a memorable forty years.

1   He was 7th wrangler in 1786 but his elder brother had been senior wrangler two years earlier.
2   Quotations are from Wallace Morfey's entertaining 'Troubles in getting Heads', covering the appointments of heads between King and Fenwick, in the *Old Ipswichian Magazine* No. 36 for 1988.

The corporation next chose the Revd Dr Samuel Watson, a King's scholar at both Westminster and Christ Church. Before he arrived, however, he learnt that it had been decided to take part of the Master's House for use as the schoolroom. King's great schoolroom could then be added to the nearby alms-houses. Watson immediately withdrew his acceptance.

The corporation dropped the idea of taking the Master's House as quickly as they had thought of it but now had to look elsewhere for a suitable master. Fatally, they chose the Revd WILLIAM HOWORTH who had for ten years from 1786 had been assistant to Dr Thomas Grimwood at Dedham grammar school, a school which had from time to time rivalled Ipswich. It used to be said of Dedham and Ipswich that  when one was up, the other was down and, perhaps with some justification, Dedham styled itself a Royal Grammar School in 1825. It was Grimwood who, in January 1798, conducted Howorth's marriage at Dedham to Hannah, daughter of the vicar there, the Revd Richard Fletcher. Tragically she died, aged only 23, giving birth to their son William later that year. Howorth seems to have married his deceased wife's sister Elizabeth at St George's, Hanover Square, two years later. Young William was educated under his father at Ipswich and became Rector of Whitton-cum-Thurleston, where father and son lie under a large ledger slab in front of the altar steps.

Since 1796, Howorth had been master of Needham Market grammar school but his insistence on numerous repairs to the buildings before he arrived there had forced the trustees to mortgage the whole of the school's income to pay for them. They could therefore offer him no stipend, leaving him to live on the fees of private pupils until their debts were paid off. In the circumstances, the vacancy at Ipswich must have seemed like manna from heaven and Howorth was suitably obsequious in his application of March 1800:

Being desirous to offer myself as a Candidate for the Mastership of the Grammar School upon the present Vacancy, I shall esteem myself much obliged, if you will notify the same to the worthy Electors assembled for that Purpose, & assure them that their Support & Countenance upon that Occasion will infinitely oblige me. I remain Sir, your most obliged & humble Ser[van]t
Wm. Howorth

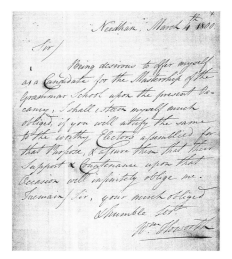

As the only non-graduate since the 1480s, Howorth was lucky to be appointed, and promised that 'It shall be the Study of my Life to approve myself deserving of the important Trust [the electors] have reposed in me, & the disinterested & flattering Manner in which they have conferred it'. Two years later the corporation added the lectureship and its salary to his offices and that sealed the school's fate for the next thirty years. In 1810 it was ruled that there should never be more than thirty free boys in the school at one time, leaving the master free to recruit fee-payers on his own terms.[3] In 1819 the Revd William Edge brought out a second edition of the *Gifts and Legacies* survey which had caused such a stir in Hingeston's time. He confirms that only thirty boys were on the school list at the last speech day (29 September 1818), so were there none paying Howorth directly? On speech day the master was required to give his report on the year to the bailiffs and they then filled any vacancies. Each scholar received a book exhibition of two pounds annually. Edge, himself an old pupil, added that the Eton Latin and Greek grammars were used and other books in rotation at the discretion of the master.

Howorth's headship was predictably undistinguished. Only half as many boys went up to Cambridge as had done so in King's time and the only record he beat was King's long service, by one year. In his last two decades, Howorth produced no one of distinction in any field and indeed the school was almost eclipsed by the St Nicholas Academy run from 1819 to 1835 by Robert Burcham Clamp. Clamp (1795–1875) was probably a Howorth pupil, with flair and an artistic temperament to make up for his own lack of a degree. His pupils included several eminent men who would surely have joined the school under livelier management: Edward Robert Smith – the artist E.R. Smythe, Orlando Whistlecraft the weather prophet, [Sir] Alfred Baring Garrod, physician and scientist (who did transfer to the school) and James Sowerby, of the great family of botanists, are just a few.

One less than reputable local worthy at the school between 1802 and 1805 was William Stevenson Fitch, son of a chemist in the Buttermarket. As postmaster of Ipswich and a chemist

---

3   Lord Brougham's committee in 1818 reviewed the provision of education nationally. In Ipswich there were 26 day schools with 1395 scholars. The grammar school was one of the four with endowments.

also, he became an avid and unscrupulous collector of original documents illuminating Suffolk history. The keeper of manuscripts in the British Museum said of him 'his name should be Filch'. Fitch's order of priorities was parchments, pills and post and for letters and parcels he could hardly be bothered to give change. In 1850 he took Dr Purland, a guest who was visiting the town, to see the buildings of his old school, then partly demolished, and Purland wrote down the story Fitch told him concerning one of the rooms (C) on Kirby's plan (page 90) below the dormitory schoolroom.

Fitch... when a student here used, in common with the rest of the lads, to abstract quantities of gunpowder below [the schoolroom] and which was used as a magazine, it was converted into fireworks, and the pyrotechnic display took place immediately in front of the door, to the imminent hazard of blowing the whole fabric – including the Master – into the air! The door was not fastened and there was one hundred barrels of powder!

Fitch was thirteen in Trafalgar year, when the fear of invasion from France was at its height. Howorth perhaps had no chance to dissent when the undercroft was taken over as an arsenal in time of national emergency.

One innovation occurred in Howorth's time. From September 1815, dinners were held annually at the Great White Horse and his former pupils were invited. The first invitation in the *Ipswich Journal* gives only the time of dinner – four o'clock – and states that tickets were to be had of William Brooks, the proprietor, who much later sued Charles Dickens for his libellous description of the house in *Pickwick Papers*. The report of dinner mentioned that 'forty gentleman enjoyed the elegant dinner and neat speech of the headmaster'. Six stewards were elected to arrange the dinner to be held the next year, the first named was the Revd William French who, by the time he presided over thirty others at the tenth dinner in 1824, was master of Jesus College, Cambridge. Tickets for the fifth dinner cost seventeen shillings. No steward acted on more than one occasion and no year was missed, but there were no more advertisements after those for the tenth dinner. Perhaps Dr French spoke for too long. They may have continued, because George Rix Clarke, an old boy himself, wrote of them in his 1830 *History of Ipswich* as though they continued, adding 'and there is generally a strong muster of the gentry, clergy and yeomanry of the county...'.

As he enjoyed the combined stipends for master and usher, it was up to Howorth to recruit and reward his own assistants. For New Year 1825, he advertised for 'a Gentleman ... to assist in Instructing Youth in the Classics and Mathematics'. What did that leave for Howorth to teach? When in January 1832, aged 71, he announced his retirement, the assembly made no attempt to disguise the general feeling that the school needed rescuing. They pointedly set out to find 'a Scholar of high reputation and attainments so that the Grammar School of this Town might be restored to its former high reputation'. Howorth consoled himself for this lack of appreciation by trying to extract as much money from his employers as he could. In April he applied to the bailiffs for 32 years' arrears of Felaw's gift to the master and Smarte's to the master and the usher, a total, by his calculation, of £266 13s 4d. He had no intention of relinquishing the lectureship, worth £70 p.a. at the time, for a weekly sermon on Sunday mornings in the Tower church.

The committee set up to put the school on a better footing for the future dismissed his claim, partly because he seemed only to have thought of it after his resignation. Even after the formal abolition of the lectureship at the municipal reform of 1835, Howorth hung on to the office and his stipend, only agreeing, three years later, to retire if he could enjoy a pension of £50 a year for life. Sam Read's drawing of him giving one of his last sermons in the Tower church pulpit, with Admiral Page in his high pew, spectacles on forehead, only possibly paying attention, is a fitting *envoi* to Howorth.

XI

Ebden and Fenwick
Struggling to recover the School's fortunes

Ebden prevailed in the last election struggle for the headship before Municipal Reform swept such irrelevances away. He immediately made a favourable impression in the town, but after a few years ran out of steam and numbers declined to an even lower point than under Howorth. Fenwick was energetic and effective, but had to subsidise the provision of essential facilities from his own pocket. The comforts of a Norfolk living and marriage beckoned.

THE EIGHT-MAN COMMITTEE that turned down Howorth's claim had been engaged from the moment he resigned in setting the school on a firmer footing for the future. They rightly tackled the thorny question of the master's emoluments, exploring various possible sources of income.

	£	s	d
The Royal stipends of the master and usher, since 1781 held together	38	13	4
From Smarte's will for master and usher	6	13	4
Original profits of Felaw's lands at Whitton	11	0	0
Income from letting Felaw's House (no longer in any school use)	21	0	0

For some reason they omitted the third item, and still considered the total of £66 6s 8d insufficient 'to induce a scholar of high reputation and attainments to undertake the vacant Mastership or for the labour and responsibility of the situation'. From the revenues of Snow's and Tyler's charities, boys had been allowed two pounds a year for books and those leaving for apprenticeships received five pounds. The committee believed that 'it would be of far more importance to the rising generation that they should be provided with eminent Masters than that they should have an allowance for books'. Printed books were now cheaper and parents, even of the free scholars, could afford them. These funds should therefore be diverted to the master and, furthermore, all boys should pay six pounds on entry to the school, and two pounds annually to the master, and that 'the number of free boys to be educated should be extended to fifty'. Only by rewarding masters well would the school 'be restored to its former high reputation as a seminary for learning and be an incalculable benefit to the Town and neighbourhood'.

Now that the salary was settled, the search was on for the best man available. To select eight candidates from the thirty who applied to succeed Howorth, the assembly chose four eminent academics: George Biddell Airy, shortly to become Astronomer Royal; Dr William French, master of Jesus, Cambridge, and only 34; the archdeacon of Sudbury and the rector of Hadleigh. That done, the assembly, determined to obtain the best advice, invited three different clerics and a layman to decide which candidate 'should be considered to have the greatest qualifications to fill the office'. One of those consulted was Dr Samuel Forster, rector of Shotley, who, at the end of his own 25 years as head of Norwich school, had reduced the number of boys to eight and another was the celebrated, but 72 year-old anti-slavery campaigner, Thomas Clarkson.

The two strongest candidates were the Revd William Church Totton and the Revd JAMES COLLETT EBDEN. Totton, of Westminster and Trinity, Cambridge, had, after graduating, returned to his old school, of which he had been second master for the past thirteen years. Ebden had himself not attended even an endowed school; nor had he any school experience. His surgeon father of Hethel, Norfolk, kept a private asylum at Stowupland. Stowmarket grammar school was in difficulties, so James had been sent to a private school in the town.

Ebden's strengths lay in his achievements at Cambridge. After graduating at Caius and a year as junior fellow, he was a don at Trinity Hall for eleven years and vice-master of the College when he applied. He was a founder member of the Athenaeum and of the British Association.

The four selectors declared themselves unable to choose between Totton and Ebden but, on being pressed, said that 'the weight of testimony seemed to be in Ebden's favour'. The assembly passed a resolution confirming their determination that the choice of head should be based solely on the testimonials and the advice given upon them by gentlemen 'influenced only on account of their respectability in the town'. Accordingly, they would be putting Ebden's name to the freemen, confident that he would be chosen without dissent.

The freemen had only twice previously exercised their right to a poll for the mastership or lectureship run on party lines. At the first, Leeds beat his rival in 1712, and, in 1791, there was a poll for the lectureship involving two former pupils. The Revd Thomas Hallum, for the Blues, beat the Yellow former usher Revd Thomas Bolton junior, by 322 votes to 315, the contest being 'carried on with great violence, uproar and confusion'. In the current acrimonious conflict over the Reform Bill it was perhaps inevitable that there would be another.

While Ebden was expressing satisfaction in the local press over the preference given to his testimonials, Totton drew attention to the great advantage he could bring from 'having acquired an experience of Thirteen Years as a master in one of the first Public Schools in the Kingdom'. He hoped that his friends would be nominating him to the freemen but, in the following week, the matter took an entirely new turn.

The surprise move was made by the Wellington Club, whose members were the extreme right-wing of the Ipswich Blues. Ebden was a Yellow, though not an active party man, and they were determined to thwart his hope of becoming master. One local applicant, who had not been shortlisted but who was known to be a sound Tory, was the Revd William Clarke. He was invited by some members of the Club to re-enter the field by publishing a direct appeal to the 'Worthy and Independent Freeburgesses of the Borough of Ipswich' in the *Ipswich Journal*. This appeared on 3 March, warning them to 'guard their rights, privileges and opinions, which certain influential persons were attempting to counteract by urging a slavish adoption of the committee's choice and not putting it to the burgesses at large'.

Clarke had been educated at Dedham and Jesus College, Cambridge. His father, master of the elementary school at East Bergholt, had been blind for his last eleven years and had relied on his son to manage the establishment. William, who had succeeded him, claimed that for the past sixteen years his 'principal and continual occupation had been the Education of Youth'. It was certainly not his only occupation for, after ordination, he held a succession of curacies, which he had been allowed to neglect for at least fifteen geological excursions in Europe.

There were only ten days between Clarke's announcement and the meeting of the freemen in Great Court but the Whigs undertook the contest with all the vigour that normally went with a parliamentary election, determined to uphold Ebden's selection. All voting at the time was public, so they knew who to canvas.

Some freemen lived at a distance, in London, Norwich, Bury St Edmunds and Harwich and they expected to come to vote at their candidate's expense. Ebden's father put up £600, to cover his son's costs, and his agent (a Blue, but opposed to the Wellington Club's action), postmaster Fitch and another went secretly to London to hire a steamer and three coaches to bring down Whig supporters. At this stage, the disgusted Totton withdrew, leaving the field to Ebden and Clarke.

Clarke sent his agent to London to find how the land lay there and to bring a steamer-load of Blues, if their opponents had *not* planned to do so, but on enquiry he found that the Yellows were bringing so many voters to Ipswich that his election was a forlorn hope. Accordingly, he sent word on Sunday, cancelling any arrangements to bring in supporters from London or the nearby towns, but embargoing any announcement until 3 o'clock on the next day.

Clarke left it until a quarter of an hour before the poll was due to open before informing Ebden that he was withdrawing. At 10 a.m. the doors of the Moot Hall were opened and a crowd surged in. 'Never,' reported the press, 'have we ever seen gloom and dismay so evidently depicted upon the countenances of the Free Burgesses. They had indulged in the expectation of revelling in the frolic of a contested election'.

Ebden was duly proposed, and seconded by an old boy cleric, the Revd William Harbur, incumbent at St Mary Quay, who had been taught by Ebden at Cambridge. 'He felt sympathy for Mr Clarke, whom he knew personally and respected, but never had a man been so badly advised or urged to pursue a course so injurious to himself'. The election was a formality. In expressing his thanks, Ebden declared his delight that many with political leanings opposite to his own had supported his appointment on academic grounds. This could have finished the business but for several hours speeches were made by both sets of protagonists, continually interrupted by the other side. Local papers gave full coverage to the proceedings. 'Men of education and clergymen ought to have something better to do than pelt each other with mud like infants' was their final comment.

Never again could such a contest arise. The Municipal Reform Act of 1835 swept away the ancient rights and privileges of the freemen and, shortly thereafter, the appointment became firmly vested in the new Town Council. Under the heading 'Patronage', the commissioners' report described the Wellington Club's actions as 'very disgraceful', dismissing Clarke as one 'whose testimonials were inferior to many of the other candidates'. He was, it was stated, a personal friend of the town clerk (John Eddowes Sparrowe), himself a member of the club. The assembly had been wholly right to try (unsuccessfully) to avoid a party fight over this crucial appointment. The new borough council and the trustees of the Ipswich charities took some time to work out who was running the grammar school (officially a borough charity). Both bodies claimed the right to appoint headmasters (from here on it is appropriate to use the more modern title), settle salaries and consider building developments, yet they were composed of many of the same people, aldermen and councillors, on the one hand, and trustees on the other. Boys at entry were to be between 8 and 12 and all but ten must leave at 15. The idea that each of the forty council members could nominate one free pupil appealed greatly and the mayor could chose an extra boy. Ebden sat with the other body and extended nomination rights to his fellow trustees. The school grew substantially, in a burst of patronage, but the tone of council discussions of the school during the later 1830s and 1840s had an air of desperation. Costs seemed to be spiralling out of control and the problems of the buildings seemed insurmountable.

The municipal commissioners found that the council was paying Ebden a salary of £150 and commended the fact that 'since his appointment, [he had] been laying out money [his own by implication] for the improvement of the school'. The handsome headmaster presided over a grand ball at the school before Christmas 1833, which was  attended by 'all the Beauty and Quality of the neighbourhood'. Howorth had allowed the new Ipswich Society of Professional and Amateur Artists to take over one of the rooms beneath the great schoolroom. Ebden joined and was soon elected Chairman. There were two young artists of promise in the school, the Keene brothers, Charles and Henry, but only Charles went on to national fame as 'C.K.' the *Punch* artist. The sketches with which young Charles decorated the margins of his *Iliad* include one of Ebden himself (see above).[1]

---

1 Keene's marginalia appear by kind permission of Michael Broadbent, owner of the Homer volume.

In a *Punch* cartoon of 1872 Keene set the scene of a very old schoolboy joke in the Lower Brook Street playground.

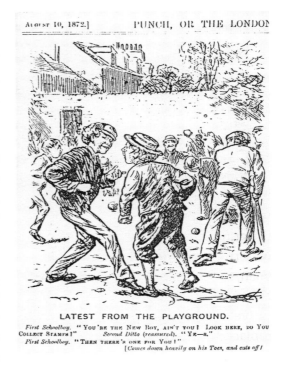

LATEST FROM THE PLAYGROUND.

First Schoolboy. " You're the New Boy, ain't you? Look here, do You Collect Stamps?" *Second Ditto (reassured).* "Ye—s." *First Schoolboy.* "Then there's one for You!"
[*Comes down heavily on his Toes, and cuts off!*]

Edward Byles Cowell joined the school in 1833, at the age of seven, and told his biographer that he was fortunate in his school fellows and masters, who taught him that most valuable lesson: *how to learn.* He became not only a fine classical scholar but skilled in many languages, as the most eminent Sanskrit scholar of his day and a professor at Cambridge. There he taught Edward FitzGerald and inspired him to write *The Rubaiyat of Omar Khayyam.* He was a gracious guest at Browne's Speech Day in 1884. George William Kitchin, a great friend of Cowell at school, was destined to be, successively, dean of Winchester and Durham. Sir John Sprigg, Prime Minister of Cape Colony, was also a Ebden pupil.

It was in August 1840 that the charity trustees appointed John Medland Clark, designer of the 1844 Custom House, as their architect to provide an improved Christ's Hospital school. In the event, Chenery's farmhouse in Great Whip Street was adapted for the purpose but Clark also showed them an imagi-

native refurbishment for the great schoolroom, the late thir-
teenth century dormitory of the friars preachers, still used by
the grammar school. Fred Russel's watercolour drawing above,
very romantic in feeling, shows how impressive it would have
been, the emphasis being on ornament and symmetry. Staircases would be lit by stepped lancets, chimneys would have decorative cowls, and the existing window openings would be
replaced by two-, three- and five-light windows in the decorated style, regular spaced, three of them gabled dormers.[2]

Ebden had begun most promisingly but, as time went on,
numbers declined – 21 in 1837, 30 in 1839 and 18 in 1841, nine
of them boarders – so that when he resigned in 1843 the school
was referred to in the council as being at a very low ebb. By
March 1841 Ebden reported that he rarely or never used the
dormitory great school, it being cold and its roof leaking. The
implication is that the largest room in the Master's House was
used for teaching, good enough reason for reducing numbers.
At the 1841 census that June he and his wife Eliza (née Wylde)
had five children under ten, and there were two resident school

2 The watercolour drawing is in Ipswich Museum and was reproduced in the
Ipswichian for 1979. At the time, it was suggested that it was a proposal to rehouse
the Grammar School, but the Charity trustees minutes SROI GA403/1 for August
1840 show that it was for Christ's Hospital.

assistants, a nurse and six other servants. Nevertheless, at his departure, there were expressions of high esteem and sincere regret. He who, of all Ipswich heads, had the costliest and most arduous experience in pursuing the appointment apparently found schoolmastering not greatly to his liking. In 1843, he took two livings near Huntingdon, and was aged ninety when he was buried at Great Stukeley in 1884.

Yet another committee had to find a new head and advertised the vacancy twice in the *Ipswich Journal*. The best of four candidates short-listed from 24 was the Revd JOHN FENWICK, MA, of Croydon (below). He had been fellow and tutor of Corpus Christi College, Cambridge, when appointed in May 1843. White's 1844 *Directory of Suffolk* mentions that 'a year ago, ...

IPSWICH

FREE GRAMMAR SCHOOL
Founded by Queen Elizabeth, A.D. 1565.

THE HEAD MASTERSHIP of this School will be Vacant at Midsummer next. The right of presentation is in the Mayor and Council of Ipswich, who are desirous to receive the applications of properly qualified Candidates for that office.

The Emoluments consist of an Endowment of 116£.6s.8d. annually, payable by the Corporation.

The Head Masters' Residence, which is well situated, will be free of rent, rates, and taxes; is capable of accommodating from 30 to 40 Boarders, and will be kept in repair at the expense of the Corporation.

The Head Master (independently of Boarders and Day Scholars) will be required to give a Free Classical Education to a limited number of Scholars, not exceeding 50, to be nominated by the Mayor and Council, and a good Commercial and General Education to such of the Free Scholars as may require it, at the rate of One Guinea a Quarter each. He must be a Graduate of one of the Universities, and in Holy Orders.

The applications of Candidates for the New Mastership, and Testimonials of Qualifications, are requested to be addressed, under cover, to the Town Clerk, Ipswich.

*** The Testimonials to be forwarded on or before Tuesday, the 2nd of May next.

Ipswich, March 18th, 1843.

a new school room was erected by the corporation' and 'a lending library (chiefly of Greek and Latin classics) has been attached to the school by various donations' – for the boys or the public? The new great schoolroom would be paid for largely by selling the site and materials of the old building. Our sole knowledge of the new room's appearance, which only served nine

years until the move to Henley Road in 1852, relies on a drawing by a pupil who was a most promising artist.

The 1843 great schoolroom was attached to the rear of the Master's House. Edward Poynter, a future president of the Royal Academy and knight bachelor, drew the interior twice about 1850, once in pencil and again in pen and wash, thoughtfully writing the names of some of his friends on their desks to show where they worked. The building of perhaps seven bays had 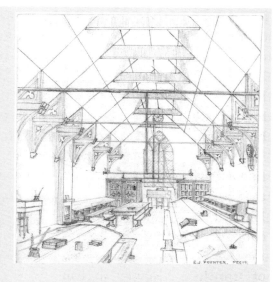 *mock hammerbeams and a three-light window with Y-tracery lit one end, probably the east. What look like tie-rods across the width may have carried gas down to flares below. Five of the tables at which forms worked are shown, a large headmaster's desk below the window and two smaller desks for assistants, one of them probably the surviving usher's desk of about 1620. An Act of Parliament clock (late eighteenth century) hangs on the right in the fourth bay; Phipson later drew this and the two bookcases at the far end (formerly presses A and B, and C and D, in the town library). One small fireplace can be seen but no other comforts, no pictures nor even maps to make the room a little brighter. One envies neither pupils nor masters of the time. Poynter's careful drawing demonstrates his instinctive grasp of perspective while giving no hint of his talent for the lightly draped female figures which would later bring him fame and fortune.*

This was not to be the last addition to the school before its move. Council minutes for 1846 mention a proposal for a cloister or covered way at the east of the playground abutting Foundation Street. There were serious drainage problems in the playground, with a pond of doubtful composition in all but drought conditions and upon which boys sailed their boats. At the next meeting, the less romantically named 'shed should be built for the reception of the Free Boys and Day Scholars'. Presumably this was a day room for their recreation. Mr Baldiston, council surveyor since 1845, had drawn the plans and Mr Pettit would build it for £63 15s. Bond and Co. would provide 'Iron Pillars for the Shed on the Playground' for an extra £15 17s. Dayboys came in from Foundation Street through a one-way turnstile designed, apparently, to prevent boarders getting out. A pupil of the time remembered it as a 'curious species of turnstile which existed at the top of the playground, by which entrance was effected but the possibility of exit effectually removed, and those who got into the machine were afflicted with an anxious impatience to get through before their limbs were mangled – a feat hardly to be accomplished by very little boys'. Next to this was 'the shed', which possessed few charms, and only those who were utterly regardless of personal appearance ever ventured into those realms of eternal chalk dust. Next, Fenwick's success in recruiting boarders led to a crisis in the available sleeping accommodation by May 1848. He could have extra bedrooms 'over the yard and gateway next Brook Street' if he paid half the £400 cost, not unreasonable since the boarders' fees were his to keep. They were erected even closer to the time of the great move out of town, about which the council was thinking already, but only tentatively.

The former playground in front of the now abandoned Blackfriars dormitory range was no longer available for boys' recreation. J. H. Josselyn recalled that 'when we wanted to play cricket we were marched to the Race Course (nearly two miles east) and we had not much of a "pitch" when we got there. When we wanted a swim we were trotted all the way to the bathing place (in the Gipping)'. The 'Old Grammar School Yard' was occasionally used for balloon ascents, coal gas from the main being the lifting agent. On 9 May 1846 Charles Green took off there on his 321st flight and landed in a barley field at Otley half an hour later. He was practising for a flight the next month to celebrate the completion of the Eastern Union Railway as far as Ipswich.

The deserted dormitory great schoolroom

William Collett, son of the headmaster of Woodbridge, was a small boy in Fenwick's last year and remembered him as 'quick in movement, somewhat harsh in voice, and very stern in manner, at least such he seemed to us little boys.' No boy was allowed to sit down in school until he knew the multiplication table perfectly. 'He was of middle height, broadly and strongly built. He had a remarkable voice, and a great power of speech, which he delighted to exercise. He was not married then, and did not entertain; nor did he take part in town affairs. On Sundays he appeared resplendent in glossy broadcloth, in cap and silk gown, or hat and a portentous neck-cloth.' Helping the vicar at the Tower, 'he, like no one else, could make the old church re-echo'. But Fenwick was tired of making do with inadequate buildings and returned to Cambridge as junior proctor in 1850, in 1858 taking the rectory of Thurning in north Norfolk for the remainder of his life; he died there in 1889. We can hardly blame him for not staying longer as he, like his predecessor, was working for people with no vision for the school, who barely concealed their distaste for what the establishment cost in maintenance. The council did express 'sincere regret' that Fenwick, held in 'great esteem' was leaving, for he had taken on the school at a low ebb and improved it beyond recognition. Two clergymen who had served him, successively, as

resident second masters, each published brochures in support
of their claims to succeed him. Fenwick gave John Hawkins, his
current assistant, strong support in a letter addressed to the
mayor and corporation, which was also printed. It was
Hawkins' bid which provoked an anonymous printed broadside
saying: 'Do not the interest of the Town require in a master of
a Grammar School, some knowledge of Accounts and Mathematics, an entire freedom from suspicions of holding Tractari-
an [high church] Opinions, and a good repute for consistency
and moral conduct? That these are no better than foolish puff-
ing and indiscreet canvassing is the opinion of Common
Sense'.[3] From the handwriting it was Fitch who added the last
sentence. Hawkins' cause was further supported by the written
and printed statements of ten parents, including the headmaster of Woodbridge School, but luckily there were another nineteen applicants from whom to choose one capable of transforming the school educationally and taking it to new buildings to
be built less than a mile to the north, but, in those days, sited in
virtually open country.

3 These rare printed items are preserved in the collections Thomas Baldock Ross
made to commemorate his year as mayor in 1849–50 (SROI qS 352, 3 vols). An
auctioneer and estate agent, he certainly realised that most of the printed and
manuscript items there preserved would otherwise be lost for ever.

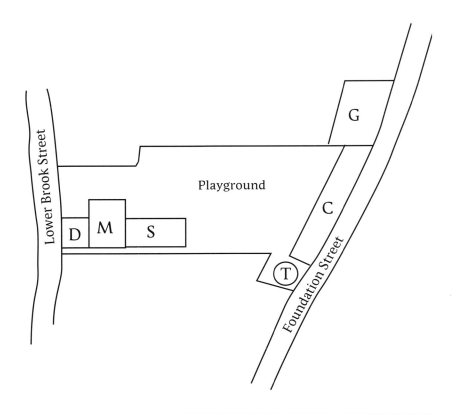

The School at the end of its time in the 'unhealthy hole' between Foundation Street and Lower Brook Street, extracted from Monson's map of Ipswich, 1848, to show the buildings Fenwick passed on to Rigaud.
M: The Master's House, still Nos 19-21 Lower Brook Street
D: Fenwick's new dormitories, built about 1849
S: The temporary schoolroom used from 1843–52
C: The cloister or covered way of 1846 'for the reception of the Free Boys and Day Scholars' and called 'The Shed'
T: The one-way turnstile by which they came in
That so much was built just years before the important move shows the paucity of the council's forward planning.
[G: House where Thomas Gainsborough lived in the 1750s]

XII
Stephen Jordan Rigaud
Founder of the modern School 1851–1858

Rigaud arrived from Westminster with tremendous drive and took the usually cautious Council by storm. At his urgent insistence a new school was built on the road to Henley. Prince Albert came to lay the foundation stone and a chapel was soon added by public subscription. The move forced many things to change, and Rigaud had founded the modern school. However, as with his predecessor, too many of the expenses came from Rigaud's own pocket and he threatened to take his pupils elsewhere. A parental complaint about a son's caning was heard before the local magistrates who were equally divided on their verdict. Rigaud had many loyal supporters, but the public humiliation was too much for him. He left with his family to become bishop in Antigua, but there succumbed to Yellow Fever within a year.

IT SEEMS QUITE REMARKA-
BLE that Rigaud applied to Ipswich, even more so that he
accepted the post when it was
offered to him. Having recently been runner-up at Rugby
and King Edward's, Birmingham, had he persisted he
would surely before long have
been chosen as head of a similarly renowned school. Perhaps

there was something about Ipswich and the plight of its school which appealed to him. The Rigauds were of Huguenot descent and his father and grandfather were mathematicians and astronomers; the latter had run George III's observatory at Kew. By the age of thirty-four, Rigaud had acquired much valuable experience, which many influential referees were ready to write about in glowing terms. His letter of application giving a commendably brief but comprehensive account of his career was accompanied by no fewer than 63 testimonials, all but six addressed to those other schools' governors in the Midlands. At Exeter College, Oxford, the highest honours in both Classics and mathematics had been conferred on him and he had become a fellow while still an undergraduate, teaching divinity as well as his main subjects. He forfeited his fellowship in 1841 on marrying Lucy Vulliamy, three years his junior and daughter of the Royal clockmaker, but the college appointed him to a tutorship rather than lose his services. At a time when university reform was in the air he had fallen out with many of his more reactionary colleagues by favouring change; otherwise, as he wrote, he could have produced even more testimonials from academics.

In 1846, he became senior assistant master at Westminster (senior usher was his title), teaching the top mathematicians and taking the form below the headmaster's. He also ran the house which, now in another building, still bears his name. According to the man who took them over and rapidly quelled them, Rigaud left him 'a most unruly set of boys'. Rigaud wrote that his 'very wish to succeed to the duties of the late Dr Arnold [at Rugby] and the present bishop of Manchester [at Birmingham] may show that I am sincerely attached to the principles of the Protestant Reformation [he was a low churchman] and in no way committed to party views'. He wished to make Ipswich

School, like Birmingham's equivalent, a centre of English as well as Classical education for the town and neighbourhood. The groups of letters after his name showed the breadth of his interests: FRAS (the Astronomical Society), MRSL (the Royal Society of Literature); for good measure he was an Associate of the Institution of Civil Engineers.

The committee sifting the applications spent eight hours reading the references, presumably not only Rigaud's, but his was the only name they presented to the full council. They must have been overwhelmed by encomiums from bishops, deans, college heads and head masters, all urging his appointment. One councillor asked, rather bluntly, whether if they appointed 'so eminent a man' there would be even 'a fair probability of his wishing to continue [long] in the office'. They did take the risk, but, to justify their choice, ordered the printing and distribution of their new headmaster's testimonials in a forty-page pamphlet. Fenwick's resignation was to have taken effect on 10 October but he handed over during the summer vacation. By 13 September Rigaud was addressing councillors about school numbers and fee income, a fortnight later pressing them to move the school altogether. He even offered to contribute his entire salary towards the cost in an attempt to persuade waverers that such a drastic step was essential.

The effect on the normally cautious and indecisive councillors must have been electrifying, for printed 'Instructions to Architects' were published on 15 October, offering a 25 guinea premium for the best scheme received by 18 November. Rigaud cheerfully accepted that, for a year or two, considerable difficulties would have to be endured. Then the Rigaud family could move into what the 'Instructions' described as the 'Residence for the Head Master attached [to the southern end of the building], providing accommodation for a Gentleman and his

IPSWICH GRAMMAR SCHOOL.

INSTRUCTIONS TO ARCHITECTS.

The proposed site of the New Grammar School is an Acre of Land at the south end of the Field situate between the Henley Road and the Field now used as a Cricket Field.

A Tracing of the Site and Locality is annexed hereto.

It is proposed to take the Cricket Field as a Play Ground,—at the same time it is desirable that a limited space should be reserved next the Cricket Field, and appropriated for the use of the Boys when the weather or other circumstances may render the Cricket Field less suitable.

The outlay proposed is not to exceed £3,000.

The accommodation required : —
School room for 200 Boys :
Library or Class Room : :
Dining Room for 150 Boys :
Housekeeper's Room :
Sleeping Accommodation for 70 Boys :
Suitable Rooms for Undermasters :
Kitchen, Outhouses and other usual Domestic Offices :
A Residence for the Head Master attached, affording accommodation for a Gentleman and his Family : .
Stoves and Fixtures of every kind, and all proper Provision for Drainage, to be included in the proposed outlay :

The Architect to specify the nature of the Materials throughout the building :

The character of the Building should be simple and imposing, but the chief object in view is a compact and convenient arrangement.

The Drawings to be made to a scale of 6 feet to an inch, and to include a Plan of each floor—a longitudinal and at least two transverse sections—the Elevations and Perspective Views to be tinted in Sepia or Indian Ink and not otherwise colored.

The Drawings, with such explanatory details as the Architect may consider necessary, are to be sent to my Office on or before the 18th of NOVEMBER next. Each Design to be distinguished by a Motto, and to be accompanied by a letter with a corresponding Motto on the outside, and containing the Name and Address of the Architect.

A premium of Twenty-five Guineas will be given for the Design selected as the best, and which is to remain the property of the Corporation.

The Designs of the unsuccessful competitors will be returned to them.

The Corporation is not to be bound to carry into effect the Design selected.

S. A. NOTCUTT,
TOWN CLERK.

IPSWICH,
October 15th, 1850.

Family'. The prospect of moving from Lower Brook Street to a green field site on high ground opposite the park must have seemed truly inviting.

The choice of site followed from the setting up, in 1848, of an Arboretum Society, which grew out of public meetings and negotiations with the council. W.C. Fonnereau, Esq. was the owner of Christchurch and its park, and other land to the west across Henley Road ripe for residential development. Fonnereau agreed, in return for a rent of ten shillings a week, to preserve the seven-acre cricket ground at the corner of Henley Road and New [later Ivry] street opposite the arboretum itself. The cricket ground, at first intended for more general use, became 'indispensable as an adjunct to the Grammar School', whose buildings were to stand on about one acre at the south-eastern corner. They were to cost no more than £3,000, and should include a school room where 200 boys could be taught, a dining room for 150, and dormitories for 70, as well as suitable accommodation for a housekeeper and the under-masters. The whole character of the scheme was to be 'simple and imposing, the chief object ... a compact and convenient arrangement'.

Fifty-two sets of plans from London and local architects were received by the committee appointed to judge them and much controversy ensued when only the latter seemed to be considered. R.M. Phipson, the diocesan architect who rebuilt the Tower church between 1860 and 1880, planned to re-erect the old Blackfriars dormitory roof over his lower schoolroom. His plans, submitted under a Latin motto meaning 'Be summoned to the books and to the gifts of the Muses', were unplaced in the contest, perhaps because some mischief-maker sent council members copies of the brief with 'Mr Phipson's compliments'. Letters alleging corruption and threatening legal action appeared in *The Builder*. Frederick Barnes and Henry Woolnough were judged the winners but their schemes were passed over as too expensive.[1] The £4,000 scheme of an Irishman

---

1 Barnes' railway stations at Needham Market, Stowmarket and Bury St Edmunds on the Cambridge line demonstrate the quality of his work. Little remains today of Woolnough's work; his Corn Exchange of 1850 was replaced in 1882. The controversy, some of it obscured by the anonymity of correspondents, can be followed in *The Builder* vol. IX (1851) on pages 10–11, 26–27, 40, 63. 109 and 808.

working in Ipswich, Christopher Fleury, apparently unplaced, was suddenly adopted, after modification 'with considerable improvement', and Samuel Simpson of Museum Street was chosen as builder.[2] The style is Tudor, consciously reflecting the colleges at Oxford with which Wolsey was associated. The tower (intended for use as a sanatorium) copies Tom Tower at Christ Church, although that was erected long after Wolsey's time. Could Fleury have seen the Turret House (see page 40) with its pepperpot crowned towers? The main entrance porch is modelled on Wolsey's Gate at the southern end of the Cardinal College site.

There are many ways in which Rigaud's headmastership marked the beginnings of the modern school. It probably helped that he was both mathematician and Classicist, and that from Fenwick he inherited as resident French master the 32 year-old M. Auguste Thibaudin, known to the boys as 'Thib' and renowned for 'his wondrous grey velvet waistcoat'. At the census of March 1851, the Rigauds had four children under nine and 52 boarders aged 12 to 19 living in the Brook Street Master's House. Rigaud chose to assume that the school was founded by Elizabeth's Letters Patent of 1565 and changed its name, apparently without discussion, to Queen Elizabeth's Grammar School. To emphasise the change, boys nominated to free places by members of the council were now called 'Queen's Scholars' and the title has persisted, in modern times, for those winning the awards in open competition. In the beginning, their usual modest ability was recognised by the boarders and fee-paying dayboys, who unkindly made them

---

2 An oil portrait of Samuel Simpson was presented to the school by Henry Bullen.

play at the east end of the Brook Street playground and quizzed them about their fathers' occupations.[3]

From February 1852, *The Elizabethan,* one of the earliest school magazines, appeared in monthly instalments with M. Thibaudin's *Dictionnaire de Tous les Verbes* advertised on the wrappers. One of the surprising features of early issues was that the editors and most contributors were senior boys; breaks in the tradition coincided with moving spirits leaving the school.

The foundation stone for the new building was laid on 4 July 1851 by HRH Prince Albert, who had travelled to Ipswich by train the previous day to address the annual meeting of the British Association for the Advancement of Science. He stayed at Shrubland Hall with the Broke-Middletons, descendants of Broke of the Shannon. The year of the Great Exhibition was a busy one for royalty but as, whilst at Westminster, Rigaud had tutored at the Palace, he knew those who could persuade the Prince to perform the ceremony at the site of the new school. Wallace Morfey published the whole story[4] to celebrate the centenary of the visit and the re-enactment of the ceremony held in Christchurch Park then. Henry Davy's coloured lithograph displays the scene in great detail. One hundred and twenty boys, all smartly dressed in short Eton jackets and white collars, were marched up from Brook Street. The band of the Queen's Bays was ready to play the National Anthem as the Royal Standard was unfurled above the canopy covering the

3 Walter, son of William Goodchild, miller at Stoke entered the school as a QS in 1851. His lively article 'Eighty Years Ago' is in the *Magazine* for March 1934, when he must have been about 93. He left after three years but his sons went from the school, one each to Oxford and Cambridge.

4 *Ipswich School 4th July 1851*, with Henry Davy's coloured lithograph of the scene in black and white on the cover, Ipswich 1951, reprinted in the *Old Ipswichian Magazine* No. 4, for 1956. See front endpaper.

principal participants, the 12cwt stone and the artist's impression of the building which would rise from it. The stone then laid now forms the north-east corner of the tower over the main entrance; the engraved brass plate is illegible, the result of over-zealous cleaning.

Those who stayed until the evening were entertained with a grand display of fireworks. In his speech, Prince Albert expressed his pleasure at 'assisting at the commencement of works having for their object to give this ancient and valuable Institution extended means of usefulness'. To the boys he said: 'Under the Superintendence of such a man as the distinguished scholar who now presides over it, I cannot doubt that it will amply carry out the intentions of its Founders and merit a continuance of that support from the Throne which it has hitherto received'. As one looks at the print one imagines a grand occasion of some length but the Prince arrived from Fleury's Museum of 1848 at three o'clock, leaving in time to visit the Fonnereaus at Christchurch *and* the Ancient House in the Buttermarket (where Mrs Pawsey had 35 minutes' notice of the Royal visit), before the Royal train steamed out of Ipswich station at a few minutes after four.

An unexpected incident marred the visit, with most unfortunate consequences for Ipswich and perhaps its school. During the Prince's journey from the station by open carriage, a shout in broad Suffolk was heard (but probably only by a courtier) from the crowd: 'Goo hoome, yer rotten ole Jarman'. When the Queen was told, she was sufficiently indignant to place a 75-year interdict on Royal visits to the town and the next was in 1926. Ipswich remained in disgrace under three monarchs, so that it was no fit place for a county memorial to Albert when he died in 1861. It was decided to found the Albert Memorial College for the Sons of the Middle Classes at Framlingham, and that shout probably cost Ipswich School better facilities and larger endowments. The fact that no matches were played against Framlingham until 1919 can have nothing to do with the interdict, which was kept a dark secret until long afterwards.[5]

After the excitement of the Royal visit, there was still nearly a year to wait for the buildings to be completed and the council became increasingly alarmed as costs escalated. The builder was pressed to cut corners and, for example, the stone framed and mullioned windows shown on F.B. Russel's painting became wooden frames. It was discovered, in the 1980s, that the large openings needed to house stone had been crudely packed to take slighter wooden frames. The Big School roof gave trouble from the beginning and, despite the addition of metal tie-rods to hold it up, its rapid deterioration was indirectly responsible for the departure of Rigaud's successor Holden. It is not known who, signing himself PASQUIN, drew the double cartoon (see over) contrasting the difficulty of taking down the roof of the Blackfriars dormitory with that of holding up the new one for Big School. There was even talk of doing without the parapets and pinnacles, without which the building would have looked undressed. The pinnacles became unsafe in the 1950s and were taken down then, at a greater cost (pound for pound) than that of the whole building in 1852.[6] The building's enduring charm is its early date; schools built in the 1870s and 1880s may be sturdier but they lack the grace and ornament.

5 Morfey's 'Ipswich Inderdict 1851–1926', is in the *Old Ipswichian Magazine* No. 32, for 1984. He had prised the long-kept secret from Edwin Booty, who served in the Town Clerk's department from 1900 until 1948.

6 In 1991, eleven pinnacles, of moulded bricks around stainless steel rods, were erected over the main entrance and the two flanking, now unused, doorways to restore that section of the building's elevation.

Ancient and Modern Building in Ipswich.
CONTRASTED

This shews the earnest endeavours of the Corporation to Pull down the Old Grammar School room.
Erected 1351

This shews the earnest endeavours of the Corporation to Keep up the New Grammar School room.
Erected 1851

To the Mayor Aldermen and Common Councilmen of the Borough
these sketches are (without permission) respectfully dedicated.

Rigaud's wider connections helped him to recruit some talented boys, and eleven university awards were won. A drawing
by the future President of the Royal Academy, Edward Poynter, is on page 155; his architect father, Ambrose, was a close
personal friend. John Wordsworth, a future bishop of Salisbury, was the son of a Westminster canon, previously headmaster of Harrow. The younger Wordsworth sounds rather a
prig, but there was evidently too little supervision:

> The morals of the School both inside and out were – when I
> now think them over – unwholesome. I did not get as much
> harm from them as I might have done, but I got a good deal.
> I was greatly protected by one or two good friends.

At least he was sufficiently soundly grounded in classics to continue his education at Winchester and Oxford but he mentioned a feud between boarders and day-boys, 'some of whom were of a rough class'. Perhaps he deserved the roasting before the fire in Tom-Brown style which he apparently suffered. From his first term, Rigaud was recruiting strongly enough for there to be too little space in the Brook Street schoolroom. For the last six months before the move in July 1852, some forms had to use the council chamber in the town hall. Business in the magistrates' room was sometimes disturbed by the boisterous young gentlemen overhead but this will only have served to underline the need for the new school. Rigaud, for pastoral and spiritual reasons, wanted to fill the school with boarders and seemed less interested in the day pupils. Even before the new school was ready for occupation, another foundation stone was laid, for a free-standing chapel. On 18 March 1852, the anniversary of Elizabeth's Letters patent, the guest of honour was the Mayor, George Josselyn, whose three sons came to the school. The cost of £640 was raised by a successful public subscription, Rigaud himself leading the way with £200. His speech on the occasion revealed his motives. 'Now, by the kind assistance of many valued friends, I shall obtain the privilege of speaking to you week by week, not only as your master, but as the minister of Christ, in a building specially dedicated to his service.' From the following Michaelmas term, boys would attend service in the Tower church each Sunday morning and the School Chapel in the afternoon.

The new school was opened on 1 July 1852, the mayor presiding at a ceremony during which Rigaud gave his own version of the school's history, giving Queen Elizabeth sole credit for its foundation. He paid tribute to his predecessors Ebden and Fenwick, both present on the occasion and whose busts adorned the new entrance hall. He announced that Pembroke College had agreed to combine Smarte's fellowships and scholarships into one scholarship and two exhibitions. Prizes were presented and Rigaud conducted worship to close the formal proceedings. At the Soirée that evening, the band of the 4th Light Dragoons played and, after fireworks, the future chapel choir, trained by Robert Foster, Tower church organist, sang 'God save the Queen', honouring Elizabeth as well as Victoria. The empty Brook Street properties could now be sold to defray some of the cost of new school.

Rigaud and his deputy Greenfield made the first service in the completed chapel on 5 August an entirely domestic occasion; they still had a fortnight to wait before the bishop licensed it until the consecration. That ceremony was performed on 22 October 1853 by Dr Robert Gray, Bishop of Cape Town, acting for Bishop Samuel Hinds of Norwich.[7] Fleury, again the architect, chose the 'late Perpendicular style', matching the school itself. The ground plan was a double square, 48 by 24 feet, and college-style inward-facing benches were provided for 130 boys, the number of pupils at the time. Rigaud had anticipated this the realisation of his dream by preaching a course of *Sermons on the Lord's Prayer* at St Mary-le-Tower, published before the year's end.

The old-fashioned practice of teaching the whole school in one large room persisted and, with the help of early photographs and diagrams, the layout of forms with their masters in the 1850s can be reconstructed. The headmaster's almost cubical desk, still at the school,

7 NRO DN/CSR 3 pages 52 and 97-100.

commanded the south end of the room and a fine clock hung on the north wall facing him.

This was presented in time for the opening in 1852 by Rigaud's father-in-law Benjamin Lewis Vulliamy, the Royal clockmaker. It was found in the early 1970s without its pendulum, the face tarnished black, in the then open corridors of the Sherwood building. It has hung in the Little School since that building was opened. The Latin inscription 'NIL CARIUS TEMPORE' supplies the motto 'Nothing [is] more precious than time', which an Old Ipswichian recalled seeing in Latin below the clock when he was at school.[8] In early photographs (see page 224) the desks and

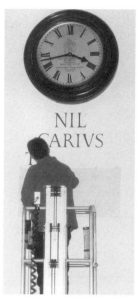

forms appear old and worn; one can almost feel the splinters waiting to penetrate the next sitter's trousers. They were old, having come from Brook Street, and probably from the Black-friars. A boy would have needed something rigid between his exercise paper and the desk if he cared anything for the longevity of his pen nib. All the forms were rearranged for Mathematics classes under Mr Greenfield, because when that subject was in session nothing else was being taught in Big School. Now that the school had left its 'unhealthy hole' in Brook Street, a greater range of subjects and activities became possible.

8 'The School Clock', another article by Morfey, is in the *Old Ipswichian Magazine* No. 24, for 1976. Granville Haskell, OI, made an excellent job of renovating it at his watch and clockmaker's establishment in Tavern Street. The succinct motto was suggested by Dick Burnell, lettered by Lida Kindersley and painted by Mike Scoging.

Arrangement of the forms in the schoolrooms in 1855

South End

Big School

Sixth ⬜ Upper Fifth

The Reverend Headmaster

Third
Mr James Bartlett

Under Fifth
Mr Henry Leech
Upper Fourth

Remove
Mr Montagu Williams

Fourth
Mr William Delta Poore
'Dinah Power'

Little School
The Lower School

Upper Second Under Second First
⬜
Mr Charles Robinson

The Vulliamy Clock
North End

174

The Remove master, Montagu Williams, became a classical master here within a month of leaving school and stayed only a year; he was only 20 years old, and described by a pupil as 'a great dandy'. He became a highly successful criminal barrister, a Queen's Counsel, and his *Vanity Fair* caricature shows the humour in his countenance. His *Times* obituary[9] comments that his first post was 'perhaps, on the whole, the last place in the world to suit a high-spirited adventurous youth of William's stamp, with literary, theatrical and military tastes

and a vague desire to make his way in the world. The [American] Civil War breaking out, he decided to become a soldier, joining the South Lincolnshire Militia, the 96th Foot.' Henry Leech became head of the Laxton School at Oundle.

For *Mathematics classes* the school was completely rearranged. The Revd William Frederick Greenfield sat at the north end of the Big School, with the forms arranged in order going south: Sixth, Fifth, Fourth, Remove and Third.

In addition to those named on the diagram on the previous page, Mr George Wilkinson was a second assistant (with Robinson, known to the boys as 'Cock Robin'), Dr Edward Christian taught French and German, until he became Founder Principal of the Ipswich Working Men's College, and Mr Thomas taught drawing. The partial opening between the Big and Little

9 *The Times* 24 November 1892.

Schools was later completely closed to prevent shrill younger voices disturbing senior classes.

The use of the small library was a sixth form privilege, extended, under some conditions, to members of the newly formed chapel choir. Rigaud, noticing that 'there does not exist in Ipswich a single choir from which we might derive any instruction or assistance', at his own expense engaged Lindley Nunn as choir master, principally for chapel music, and he remained until the end of Holden's time. At the opening of the Michaelmas term 1853, old scholars and friends of the school showed their appreciation of the headmaster's 'untiring efforts in forwarding the erection of our School Chapel' by presenting him with an organ by Russell with seven stops. It cost £140 but lasted only until 1898. In 1854 Rigaud became a Doctor of Divinity.

One unusual feature of the Chapel is an indoor burial. A diamond shaped brass in the centre of the nave marks the resting place of Charles William MacDougall who died, aged ten, on 3 June 1854. A few days previously, he had been struck on the head by a cricket ball. His father, the Bishop of Labuan and Sarawak, had left the boy with the incumbent of Winston, near Debenham, as his guardian, to be educated under Rigaud. In a window to the south of the brass is the boy's other memorial, which includes the kneeling figure of the boy Samuel listening for the voice of God.[10]

10 'Victorian Scenes in Chapel', by Morfey appeared in the *Old Ipswichian Magazine* No. 25, for 1977.

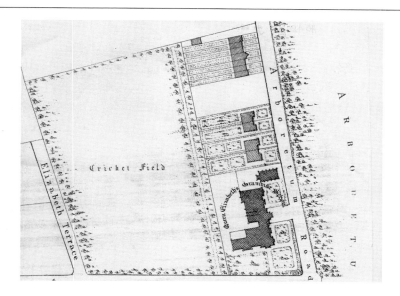

Between the school buildings and tree-lined cricket field was what was called the 'dry playground'. The double avenue of limes on the eastern side of the field was planted about 1856 and a dozen or so of the original trees survive. There was a wall running alongside with a gate linking field and playground. At the north end of the avenue was a coach house with stable (now Drift Cottage) for successive headmasters' means of transport.

Rigaud, despite his many lasting achievements, was by no means happy at the school, which he always had to subsidise from his own pocket. He failed to maintain numbers, leaving his successor Holden only 77 boarders and 28 day-boys. When Holden published his own reasons for leaving nearly thirty years later, he recalled his predecessor's warnings. He had learned from those close to Rigaud that he had repeatedly threatened to resign, taking his boarders to a private school. Resentment at the cost of the new school persisted in the town even as Holden was leaving, which gives some idea of Rigaud's position.

His blackest day must have been 26 April 1856, when he faced public prosecution in the Ipswich Police Court, charged with too severely punishing a dayboy for alleged misbehaviour on his way to school through the Arboretum. Joseph Wingfield Tracy was the 14 year-old son of John Tracy, a Tacket Street dentist and liberal councillor. Rigaud had received complaints from the nurseryman who was lessee of the arboretum, W. D. Jefferies, but should probably have made more enquiries before giving this particular boy, as Thomas Churchyard, prosecuting solicitor, maintained, '20 to 25 blows upon various parts of the body, legs, thighs and back'. The boy's father and three surgeons described the injuries received. Tracy senior called on the headmaster the same evening to complain and was told that 'the boy had behaved in a blackguardly and ungentlemanly way in the Arboretum and, that he had in the winter time, behaved improperly in throwing snowballs'. The boy denied misconduct but had declined to speak in his own defence because he believed that the headmaster would only increase the punishment. Rigaud fell back on Jefferies' evidence, but the father had interviewed him, finding that he had no specific or topical complaint against the boy. Tracy and Churchyard (the gifted Woodbridge artist) were known radicals, unlikely to share political ground with Rigaud, who, in any case, tended to prefer boarders to dayboys. Rigaud spoke briefly in self-justification but no witnesses were called in his defence. In a circuitous statement he said that he 'thought the evidence of Mr Jefferies showed that repeated acts of disorder had been committed in the Arboretum – one that particular day – and, though he could not lay that particular act to Tracy, yet he showed that Tracy had been the most troublesome of all the boys and that upon several occasions'. His punishment record read 'Tracy. Complaint of Mr Jefferies of repeated disorderly conduct. Caned severely – 18[cuts]'. He exhibited a cane on the magistrates' table. They, three Blues and three Yellows, were equally divided in their verdict, so that the presiding Mayor, a liberal, announced that no judgement could be given.

The Grammar School Committee promptly held four meetings and produced a pamphlet reviewing the Tracy case in two pages and, in fourteen more, discussing punishments at the school more generally, dwarfing the impact of the case in question. The nine Yellows, including Tracy senior, outnumbered but did not overrule the four Blues, for the findings were strongly in Rigaud's favour. Much oral and written testimony from staff, parents and old pupils was considered, overwhelming in its support for him and his regime. Only Tracy dissented from the unanimous findings, protesting 'that it is drawn on evidence unsupported by facts'. One can only be impressed by the expressions of support for Rigaud, and denials that he favoured any particular boys, but sceptical about the entirely subjective statement that his system of punishment was 'less severe than that adopted at many other public schools'.[11]

It would not have been surprising if Rigaud had departed immediately but his last eighteen months, during which numbers declined, were fairly tranquil. Before Rigaud left in early February 1858 to become bishop of Antigua, the corporation formally 'waited upon him ... with mixed feelings of regret and congratulation'. In return, he expressed enormous sadness at leaving and dwelt somewhat on having fallen short of the standards he had set himself. He continued: 'It is to kind support and encouragement that I owe much of the power which I have been able to exert – And it is to your kind construction of

11 *Report of the Grammar School Committee presented to a special meeting of the town council and ordered to be printed, May 19, 1856.*

my acts and motives that I owe the expression of feeling which I have received from you.' In his long published farewell sermon, *Growth in Grace and Knowledge*, he rather gloomily concluded 'though I may not rest here, yet remember me when my time comes, and bear us on your hearts in prayer until [then]'. The family took with them to the West Indies a cabinet of ambrotype portraits of themselves, colleagues and some pupils (including a few who had already left). These early photographs remained in Mrs Rigaud's family, the Vulliamys, and eventually came back to the Suffolk Record Office in Ipswich in the 1980s. Few schools will have such a complete pictorial record of those who taught and learned in the late 1850s. By studying them we can almost feel that we have met some of the young men and masters Rigaud had recruited. Some are in gowns (then called 'togas') and a few mortar boards are in evidence. Perhaps the top hat at one boy's elbow is a studio prop. The boys called Delta Poore 'Dinah' Power, recalling him as 'a thin, sallow little man, with a bald head and scrubby whiskers,... a stern look, but humour in his eyes'..., in all 'a good fellow'. As for Rigaud himself, he who had looked so debonair in Maguire's lithograph of 1852, seems scarred by his experiences still; his wife looks no more cheerful. The new bishop had little opportunity to make his mark in Antigua, for he was struck down by Yellow Fever only fifteen months after his consecration. A massive stone memorial marks his grave in the grounds of the cathedral there. The trust fund set up to support the bereaved family later endowed the Rigaud prize.

First page of ambrotypes

First line: Mrs Lucy Rigaud (*née* Vulliamy), 39; Lucy, 15; Louisa, 8; and a younger sibling; The Revd Stephen Jordan Rigaud, 42.

Second line: The Revd Charles Preston Lanchester of Yoxford, Clare College, Assistant master, 26; Charles Browne Goldsonof East Harling, Caius College, 24; Frederick Clarkson Francis, Caius College, 26.

Third line: Thomas Day Turner of Halesworth, 19, later priest; Edward Goldson of East Harling; William Bancroft Espeut of Kingston, Jamaica, 19.

Fourth line: William Delta Poore, later ordained; The Revd William Frederick Greenfield, Second Master; Three younger boys,perhaps brothers.

Second page of ambrotypes

First line: John Jordan, 25 (army officer); Gibbes Walker Jordan and Percival Walsh Jorda, sons of the Revd John Jordan, rector of Enstone, Oxon, and cousins of the headmaster. Gibbes was Captain of Cricket '55 (went to Oxford) and Percival left school '56.

Second line: William Henry Tuck of Woolpit, Emmanuel College, 18; the brothers Dillingham William Seppings (left '55 for Caius College) and William Seppings (left '57), both of Fakenham, Norfolk.

Third line: Thomas Beard of Ovingdean, Sussex, left '60; Henry James Edgell of Nacton, left '55; Walter Stewart of Spanish Town, Jamaica, arrived '56.

Fourth line: Unidentified pupils and perhaps Stephen R. Rigaud, 13.

All ages estimated in 1858.
The Vulliamy cabinet of ambrotypes, in Suffolk Record Office, Ipswich, is JI 18/21.

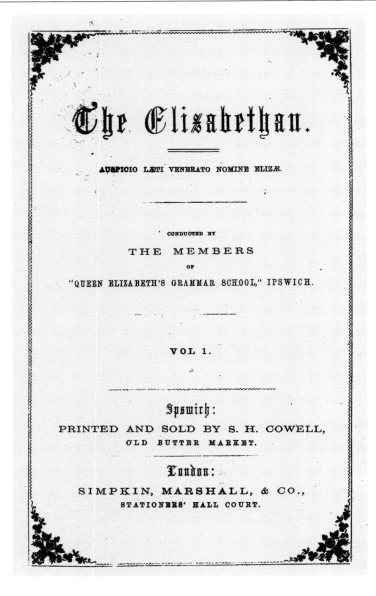

The first number appeared, price fourpence, on 21 February 1852. In a survey to find the earliest magazines in HMC schools, there were no earlier claims.

184

XIII

Hubert Ashton Holden

A scholar unappreciated, 1858–1883

Holden, a classicist, was certainly the greatest scholar in the school's history, and he and his loyal second-in-command, Sanderson, were revered for their teaching and the humane regime they fostered in the school. Holden knew how badly Rigaud had been treated and quickly found himself in the same position. He was too proud to temporise in his relations with the governors, and a great gulf opened up between them. Despite his many fine achievements and improvements (some of which he paid for himself), when he rashly made a gesture of resignation the governors leapt at the chance of ridding themselves of a man they regarded as above himself. He left unthanked and unsung by the governors but almost deified by his loyal colleagues and pupils.

WHEN, AFTER 25 YEARS in post, Holden published his *Plain statement of the circumstances attending my resignation*, he started his account at the beginning. Born in Birmingham, he was educated at King Edward's School[1] there, after which he was successively scholar, fellow,

---

1 It is said that he was put straight into the sixth form aged 12, and soon rose to the top of it.

185

tutor and Classical lecturer at Trinity College, Cambridge. Most recently he had been Vice-Principal of Cheltenham College. He had never previously visited Ipswich and was without local connexion [his spelling of the word] or influence. Admittedly his wife, Laetitia, was the daughter of Robert Lofft Esq of Troston Hall, near Bury St Edmunds, which may have enabled them to cope with the unforeseen costs of the appointment. His brother and cousin were headmasters, respectively, of Uppingham and Durham. He was one of those selected from 23 candidates for interview and the appointing committee found him pre-eminently suitable and took his name only to the full council. Two councillor governors wanted all council members to have a chance to read three candidates' testimonials (one was John Tracy, the parent who accused Rigaud) but their amendment was defeated.[2] Holden was thereupon elected and brought his family to Ipswich in February 1858, having been given no guidance about managing the school, beyond the stipulation that he should educate twenty boys nominated by the town council – the Queen's Scholars – without fee. From now on, these boys should be given a general as well as a classical education, including mathematics. Numbers had fallen from Rigaud's maximum of 200, to about 125 including free place boys, and the full tuition fee for the others was £8 per annum. This income, and the profit from boarders, had to cover the salaries of five or six assistant masters and the wages of a large domestic staff. The nominal endowment of £107 was insufficient to pay the rent on the school buildings and cricket field (£126 per annum), let alone rates and taxes. Holden was required to pay nearly £1,000 for the school plant: desks, forms

---

2 Holden submitted only 28 testimonials (cf. Rigaud's 63), but all but five were addressed to the governors of Repton where he had been an unsuccessful candidate four years before, in 1854.

and stoves, the latter almost immediately proving useless and beyond repair.

Holden recalled that the first letter he received at Ipswich was one offering him the mastership of the newly-founded Wellington College. He soon realised that 'there was a strong party in the town who, having never approved of the new School Buildings, had transferred their hostility to the Grammar School as an institution'. He next discovered 'the low standard of scholarship in the boys and the professional insufficiency in the existing staff'. Although three of Rigaud's most senior masters were still in post when he arrived, in 1859 Greenfield left to become the first head of Alleyn's School, Dulwich, and Delta Poore became archdeacon of St Kitts. Holden found that a strong hand was needed to restore order, for, as he observed, 'boys are quick to discover when they are ruled by men unequal to their duties'. His first action was to publish an order that no boarder should be given credit by tradesmen. By Midsummer 1859 Holden had chosen his own men for all the full-time posts.

The main problem from the beginning was the inadequacy of the facilities, although the entire establishment was less than ten years old. Newly-founded public schools elsewhere had excellent buildings and were well-endowed. Ipswich had 'very inferior accommodation, utterly inadequate class-rooms, no gymnasium, no bath-rooms, not even an infirmary...'.[3] Other schools could offer more financial help to able pupils on arrival and, more important, awards to support them later at university. He had sometimes been blamed for the decline in boarding

---

3 Although the tower had originally been intended as an infirmary, it was clearly then in more pressing permanent occupation.

numbers but, in the circumstances, that can hardly have been surprising.

After pointing out the main difficulties he had encountered on arrival, he began to recount the successes: average pupil numbers just below one hundred over the whole of his time; 133 distinctions won at the universities and elsewhere, including six fellowships, 54 scholarships, forty honours in the class lists, nine university prizes – the list was a long one. To give credit to his predecessors, he published at Midsummer 1859 the eighteen university and college distinctions won since 1848 but, by Easter 1860, sixteen new honours had been won, albeit only ten at the universities. This was indeed a promising beginning. In August 1862, despite the county memorial to the late Prince Consort being the foundation of Framlingham College, the worthies of Ipswich met to establish an Albert Scholarship by investing donations in Albert's memory to provide £50 to support an Ipswich School leaver at university. People were aware of the refoundation of Woodbridge School, with the ample resources of the Seckford Foundation behind it. William Howorth, son of the former master, in seconding the motion, said that Holden was 'one of the most profound and accomplished scholars of the age', under whom the school had already 'attained an emi-

nence which it had never before enjoyed'. Appropriately it was one of Ebden's sons who held the first Albert scholarship.

The main reason for the governors' inactivity on Holden's arrival was their belief that the Schools Inquiry Commission would very soon put such schools as theirs on an entirely new footing. As Holden wrote to a trusted colleague much later: 'I was inveigled into becoming a candidate by an assurance on the part of the Chief Electors, that there would certainly be a fresh scheme for the administration of the School, issued by the Charity Commissioners in the course of a year or two, whereas the local Charity Trustees made no effort to get one until 25 years afterwards'. The nationwide survey took the commissioners from 1864 to 1868 to complete, Mr Douglas Richmond visiting Ipswich in 1866. His report, after visiting 54 grammar schools in Norfolk, Suffolk and Essex, singled out Ipswich (rather than Bury) as the largest classical school in Suffolk. He stated that the endowment was inadequate to cover the rent of the buildings which belonged, not to the school, but to the town. He considered that the school was therefore 'a private adventure', the salaries of head and masters 'entirely derived from profits on the pupils'. The head alone set fees, chose staff and all the pupils except the free scholars, who came mainly from 'gentle, but not wealthy' families. The head would have liked the Queen's scholarships to be competed for but it happened that the present nominees of council members were holding their own and it could 'hardly be said that the existing system of admission was working unsatisfactorily'. As well as the classical, there were civil and military sides, with a broader curriculum, including German as an alternative to Greek. Richmond found that 'discipline was excellent and the conduct of the boys throughout was attentive and high-toned'. The report entirely confirms Holden's analysis of the school's problems and leaves the reader in no doubt that boys were receiving as fine an education as they were capable of in a school well staffed and managed.

The printed draft scheme which followed in 1869 contained one provision which, though universal, did not suit the governors. At all schools in future a head could be dismissed at six months' notice, without cause stated, but this would not apply to existing heads. The governors' objection to giving Holden this security shows that they were already tired of him, despite his eminence and the high standards he had achieved. The commissioners took Holden's side but the argument was not resolved for twelve more years. In November 1881, the newly formed Charity Commission agreed and published the new Scheme with Royal assent. Early that year, the governors, according to Holden, 'importuned, not to say, persecuted' him to abandon his immunity but, in the event, they gave way to avoid further delay. The new governing instrument provided not only for the Grammar School but for two new Middle Schools (one for boys and another for girls, eventually the Northgate Schools), to be governed by a single governing body of councillors. The schools of Christ's Hospital, day and boarding, were both closed.[4] Holden, always doubting the governors' competence to run his school, found it beyond belief that they should take on responsibility for two completely new ones. He pleaded for some non-councillor governors in addition to the newly proposed representatives of Cambridge, Oxford and London universities. In July 1879, Holden told Commissioner

---

4 Christ's Hospital was founded by Letters Patent of Elizabeth, dated 16 May 1572, and should have provided education for poor children as well as supporting their elders, but only after Nicholas Phillips, portman, left Kersey's Farm at Debenham in 1670 was a school founded. By 1881 there was a day school on part of the Blackfriars' site in School Street and a boarding school over Stoke.

Latham in a letter that 'The Trustee most averse to the strengthening of the governing body with a county element is the original of Nupkins in Pickwick'. He was referring to S.A. Notcutt, their clerk, lightly veiled as George Nupkins Esq, the puffed-up principal magistrate in Chapter xxiv of Dickens' most humorous novel.[5]

On 21 December 1869, in 'the cruellest winter weather', fourteen headmasters, invited to Uppingham by Thring, laid the foundations of the Headmasters' Conference. Holden was invited but had to send his apologies. He was there the next year and never missed a meeting thereafter, nor did Browne his successor.

The Doctor's old pupils never tired of recalling the impression he made on them in the Big Schoolroom. The following abridged quotations come mainly from anonymous accounts published in school magazines in later years.

> He used to say that he enforced his ideas 'totius viribus'. He chose as his motto 'Praeceptor animorum pareus', and with a sublime disregard for boys' crude and flippant criticisms, had it inscribed on a scroll above his desk, like a captain nailing his colours to the mast. To the boys of the lower forms he was a somewhat austere figure, an exalted dignitary, to whom approach was most easily made through the unpleasant medium of the Detention Book. But the austerity was largely on the surface, and he kept himself closely acquainted with the work and progress of every boy in the school. To have been under him in the sixth was a privilege indeed, for he was a fine teacher, who endeavoured before all things, to

---

5 In 1835, when Dickens came to cover the parliamentary election for the *Morning Post*, he must have met the first Stephen Abbott Notcutt, solicitor and town clerk, but the clerk to the governors in 1879 was his son and namesake. Holden's letter to Richmond is PRO ED27/4379. The passage in *Pickwick Papers* immortalises the school in imagining boyish misbehaviour in the town in Ebden's time, ending, as Constable Grummer explained, 'consekens of the boys having dispersed to cricket'.

form, by careful and exact study, the discipline and habit of mind which are essential to true education.

Holden's first 'submaster' was Henry Barclay but the Revd Robert Sanderson was the next; he gave twenty-three years to the school and certainly left his mark. The portrait photograph which hung near his memorial bookcase in the Holden Library had, at some stage, been used as a dart board, but was rescued in time to preserve a record of his Herculean presence. Sanderson, a Pauline, maintained that he, Holden, and Mr Gladstone were the only three men in England who really knew their Homer; he certainly knew the first six books of the *Iliad* by heart and could continue from any line he was given. Nevertheless, he was a good foil to the immaculate Holden; he was carelessly dressed but cared for every boy, irrespective of ability, and adored games and the whole gamut of school activities. A former pupil remembered his laughter in Big School as Homeric and the sound of his wrath almost Olympic – he was universally known as 'Guts' Sanderson. He fired at least one of his pupils with his own passion for Romany lore. Norse sagas were another interest and he and two colleagues invented a fictional account of their own doings as residents at 'Swevensby Castle in the Debatable

Land', strange effusions in the school's archives still. Although for many years Sanderson was Holden's assistant, he was not given the opportunity to deputise when, for a month in September 1869, the head was absent through indisposition. Instead the Revd William Collett, head of the school in 1857, but by then a fellow of Oriel, was made acting head.

The 30 year-old Revd Thomas Ashe (whose published poetry won him a place in the *D.N.B.*) took charge of mathematics and the modern side from 1867 and, though a shy and somewhat withdrawn fellow, he would row with the boys down to the Ostrich at Bourne Bridge. The historian W.H. Richardson had arrived in 1871, then 27, to combine teaching with work on a scholarly edition of *Nathaniel Bacon's Annalls of Ipswich*, whose extracts from borough records ended with the king's execution in 1649. Bacon was town clerk, recorder and MP for Ipswich and chairman of the Parliamentary Eastern Association Committee at Cambridge in the Civil War. Richardson, a fine schoolmaster and a bachelor, was naturally fascinated by the school's long history and made collections in the forlorn hope of eventual publication. His nickname was 'sugar', because of the cane he kept to hand on his desk. Holden, however, was careful not to repeat his predecessor's mistake and kept all punishments, including the cane, to the necessary minimum. His 'almost blank punishment books', available to Gray and Potter, have since disappeared. Richardson was shocked by Holden's treatment but left the school in 1880 in order to complete his edition of the *Annalls* which appeared in 1884.

The Elizabethan, silent since 1854, began again in June 1858, with a respectful *envoi* to Rigaud in the first number. After only a year, it was announced with regret that 'in consequence of the disapproval of our Head Master' the second series would be discontinued. The next revival, from 1867-69, owed its impe-

tus to Francis Hindes Groome, son of the archdeacon of Suffolk, who left Oxford after only a term to join the gypsies. With
Sanderson's encouragement, he became a lifelong student of
the Romany life, much later enjoying a turbulent marriage to a
beautiful gipsy girl called Esmeralda. Groome's elder brother
John belonged to Holden's finest year-group: ten boys who left
in 1866 for Cambridge, six with open scholarships and two
more later made foundation scholars of their college.[6] Under
the new title *The Ipswich School Magazine* and in a larger quarto format, the fourth and liveliest series ran from 1874 to 1879.
The first of the new issues greeted the new cricket pavilion,
built at a cost of £136 and ready for the new season, and praised
Ford the professional. Fictional contributions were now more

6 The fact that only one of the ten took a first suggests that, under Holden, each
had reached his ceiling.

entertaining and 'School News' and letters from the universities more informative; people had also begun to ask questions
about the history of the school, requesting lists of heads and
ushers and even asking where they might consult a copy of
Wolsey's *Rudimenta*. It was in 1877 that former pupils were
first called Old Ipswichians rather than Elizabethans. The
head's 15 year-old son Edward made a very fine job of catalogu-
ing the 229 works in the school's valuable and ancient Classical
Library in December 1877, publishing names and brief biogra-
phies of the original donors in the *Magazine*. As soon after as
1889 an anonymous former librarian wrote to the magazine
confessing that he weeded out 'antiquated arithmetics of the
seventeenth century, and the like'.[7] But this does not explain
why only twenty works remain today, for more old and valuable books were lost when most of the remainder were sent off
for pulping at the outbreak of the Second World War. The remnant is kept together in one of the Morfey rooms, set up in the
Tower to house the school archives and museum and opened by
Wallace Morfey in 1988.

In June 1879, at Richardson's suggestion, the arms of Ipswich were replaced at the mast-head of the *Magazine* by the
Royal arms of Henry VIII which the school has used as an
achievement ever since. When the king used dragon and grey-
hound supporters, the former was to dexter (viewer's left), but
they were reversed in error over Wolsey's Gate and remain so
on the school's arms. The College of Arms has never been asked
to authorise their use by the school but a good case could be
made: Henry did refound the school, and the error is a useful
difference, and to that extent specific and less presumptuous.
The last word of the Latinised name 'Schola Regia Gippovicen-

7 *Ipswich School Magazine*, p. 600.

sis', favoured by Rigaud, was changed by Holden to 'Gippesvicensis'.

The lack of a magazine for the remainder of Holden's time only underlines the headmaster's own progressive disenchantment: for example, by 1879 Ipswich had 72 pupils to Woodbridge's 200 and this despite Holden's doing everything he could to broaden the curriculum whilst, of course, preserving the supremacy of the Classics. He held no Speech Day after 1876, perhaps because he objected to sharing a platform with the governors. League tables, surprisingly enough, began in the *Guardian* in September 1879, with an analysis of the list of successful candidates examined by the Oxford and Cambridge Schools Examination Board (still operating as recently as the 1970s, then merged in the Midlands Examining Group, now OCR). Ipswich had 72 pupils, seven successful in that year, obtaining in all eight distinctions. Comparable figures for the East Anglian schools show that Holden prized quality above quantity:

	Pupils		
	Total	Successful	Distinctions
Ipswich	72	7	8
Norwich	130	6	2
Woodbridge	200	3	1
Felsted	200	2	-
Uppingham	325	14	2

Holden encouraged Lindley Nunn to refound the choir as a choral society with former pupils to strengthen the lower parts, affiliating it to Trinity College of Music in London. He employed Dr J.E. Taylor, the inspiring curator of Ipswich Museum from 1872 to 1895, as a part-time teacher of natural science from the late 1870s, the governors eventually providing some basic apparatus. When Arthur Churchman, later Lord Woodbridge, gained first prize in this subject in 1880 with only 18 marks out of 100, Holden unkindly pointed it out but admitted that his nearest rival scored only 3.

When the 1881 scheme was enacted, all the old borough charities had been combined and were now shared out between the three Ipswich schools. The grammar school was at last given the freehold of its site and buildings, the sum of £6,000 in Treasury Stock, and five twelfths of the residuary income of the whole Foundation. Holden was reimbursed for the property he had been forced to purchase, and could be dismissed without cause being given by the governors, on six months' notice. They would in future prescribe the curriculum, after consulting the head. His salary and the fees to be charged were now laid down and ten Queens' Scholarships would be competed for openly.

Ironically, it was the governors' belated efforts to do something to improve the fabric which led to Holden's departure. Unbelievably, a large programme of works began on 21 August 1882, with the new term due to open on 13 September. Holden, who had made himself available for the whole summer holiday to assist the work run smoothly, was frustrated that the governors seemed indifferent; not one of them appearing at the school. He took the decision to postpone term for one week and asked the governors to agree to a few more days but they refused. On learning this on 14 September, he wrote offering his resignation and the chairman of governors immediately visited the school and ordered extra workmen. Nevertheless, the pupils were all crammed into one room from 22 September, the noise and dirt making useful work and proper discipline impossible. On 27 September, Holden wrote again, offering to withdraw his earlier letter if 'the Governors think it best that the school should remain in my hands'. They did not, but requested him to carry on until the end of the current term. He immediately suggested that there would be a 'greater facility for providing a properly qualified successor' by the end of the Easter term and this was agreed. Had he been more politically astute, Holden would never have given the governors the chance they had so long looked for to get him out. It was Richardson who much later tried to make a balanced judgement. Holden was regarded with 'feelings of intolerant dislike and hostility... by some of the magnates of the town... so that they were prepared, in the excess of their ill-will, to damage the school by refraining from doing anything to help its necessities, if by such inaction they could annoy the headmaster, thwart his plans and restrict or obstruct his usefulness... Strange feelings, indeed,... but they arose... from the attitude of reserve and social exclusiveness which Dr Holden firmly and unswervingly maintained towards the town, in the affairs of which he never took part'. It cannot have helped that he never appeared in the streets of Ipswich without cap and gown, something he expected his senior pupils to emulate.

Contrary to the last statement one has only to read the speeches made at the opening of the new Museum, Free Library and Art School in High Street in July 1881 to see how much of a moving spirit Holden had been in this large improvement in the educational facilities of the borough. His own speech on the occasion was lively, even humorous, and his view of education and the new universities broad and all-embracing. A former pupil recalled Holden as 'conspicuously spruce and refined. As he went for an afternoon ride on a well-groomed horse, himself well-groomed and erect in carriage, he looked every inch the scholar and the gentleman'. His scholarly editing of whole lists of classical texts 'may have clashed with school requirements'. [8]

Holden was not without useful employment for his remaining years, editing and examining, but he confided his feelings about going in letters to Richardson. On 8 March 1883 'The time for my leaving is fast drawing near: I have not yet realised its proximity: & I fear the wrench more than I can tell you'. Three months before, no doubt thinking of Rigaud, 'I have no progress about houses, & I am not likely to have an episcopal palace or even a decanal residence'. In good time he took 20 Redcliffe Square in South Kensington, where he spent his remaining years. Holden had made provision for Sanderson before he left, presenting him to the living of Wyverstone north of Stowmarket in his own gift. Sanderson avoided the school in the next head's time (partly because all the masters except one left with Holden), but kept in touch with Holden. In Raynor's time Sanderson made a popular appearance on the 1895 Speech Day platform.

Let us leave Holden on the last occasion he appeared in the Big schoolroom. He called every boy to him, and, in bidding goodbye, spoke privately to each one.

8 W.M. Morfey's essays on aspects of Holden's time add much colour to this account. 'A Sixth of Holden's' is in *OIM* 13 (1965), 'Scholar Gipsy OI' in *OIM* 37 (1989), and in *The Ipswichian*, 'Guts Sanderson' in 1990 and 'Holden Outed' in 1991.

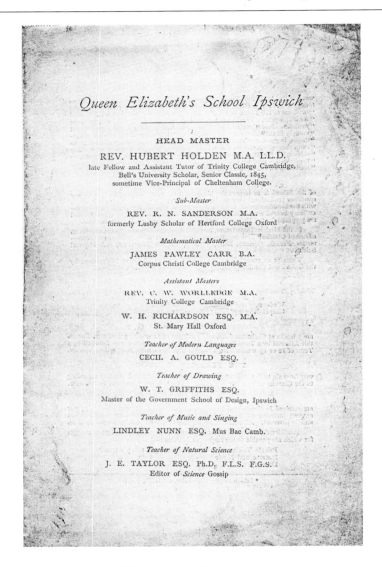

Queen Elizabeth's School Ipswich

HEAD MASTER

REV. HUBERT HOLDEN M.A. LL.D.
late Fellow and Assistant Tutor of Trinity College Cambridge,
Bell's University Scholar, Senior Classic, 1845,
sometime Vice-Principal of Cheltenham College.

Sub-Master

REV. R. N. SANDERSON M.A.
formerly Lusby Scholar of Hertford College Oxford

Mathematical Master

JAMES PAWLEY CARR B.A.
Corpus Christi College Cambridge

Assistant Masters

REV. C. W. WORLLEDGE M.A.
Trinity College Cambridge

W. H. RICHARDSON ESQ. M.A.
St. Mary Hall Oxford

Teacher of Modern Languages

CECIL A. GOULD ESQ.

Teacher of Drawing

W. T. GRIFFITHS ESQ.
Master of the Government School of Design, Ipswich

Teacher of Music and Singing

LINDLEY NUNN ESQ. Mus Bac Camb.

Teacher of Natural Science

J. E. TAYLOR ESQ. Ph.D. F.L.S. F.G.S.
Editor of *Science* Gossip

Staff list in the 1879 prospectus

XIV

Frederick Herbert Browne
Flawed genius, 1883–1894

It was hardly to be expected that Holden would approve of the late applicant, Browne, but the new head had many strengths and the school moved forward impressively, even in academic prowess. Through Mrs Browne's Irish connections, boarding vacancies were advertised in Dublin, and a steady influx of able boys arrived to the school to leaven the East Anglian intake. Like his three predecessors, Browne had to pay for some of the improvements he thought essential, and that never endeared Ipswich heads to those who governed the school. The allegation that he was the father of the child of a School House maid led inexorably to his departure and untimely death.

UNFORTUNATELY, the bitterness caused by Holden's virtual dismissal spilled over into the next headship but it might have been different if one official word had been spoken in praise of his quarter of a century of service. Holden's assistant masters, with the sole exception of Henry Richmond, a gifted young games player and coach who taught mathematics, left just before or with him, as did more than one university governor. None of the governors were present when Holden and Sanderson were feted in Big School by speeches from old boys and parents and presented with lavish tokens of admiration and affection. The field of candidates applying for the headship was neither large nor strong. A senior and highly-respected head had been forced out of office and the word quickly spread, as it would today, that interested applicants should ask some very searching questions before accepting the post. Holden wrote in his *Plain Statement* that he knew of six men, among them two, 'either of whom in happier circumstances I could gladly have welcomed as my successor', who visited but decided against applying.

Of 43 applicants, the Endowed Schools governors considered six, discarded two and interviewed four, eventually offering the post to Charles Gibson, a master at Merchant Taylors' School. A week later he wrote declining the post but those who met urgently to consider the next step were shown an application with testimonials from the Revd Frederick Herbert Browne, second  master and boarding housemaster at Reading School. A boy at Manchester Grammar School and a scholar of Wadham College, Oxford, he took a first in Mathematical Moderations and a second in his finals. Sterling Westhorp OI and R.C. Ransome were despatched to Reading to meet him; a week later he appeared for interview and was appointed forthwith. Holden described him as 'a gentleman who, though not one of the four candidates originally selected, had visited Ipswich in the Christmas vacation and was not daunted by the difficulties which the others were unwilling to face'. He wished him 'every success in the arduous task which he has undertaken with such confidence'. This faint praise will not have helped Browne to win people's esteem but, although his headship ended even more tragically than Rigaud's and Holden's, his achievements were considerable and must have surprised doubters. It clearly hurt Holden to see his successor apparently hand-in-glove with the governors and holding Speech Day again in 1883 after a seven-year lapse. He should have had more pride, however, than to write to a Suffolk paper after the 1884 event criticising his successor's public coverage of achievements by former pupils. Browne gave a statesmanlike reply, having at his first Speech Day described Holden as 'one of the first scholars in England'. Another lapsed afternoon function was immediately restored by Browne: the end of Christmas term Concert, with prize distribution. Haydn's Toy Symphony was the musical highlight of the first, with seventeen boys and only one master in the orchestra. Concerts ran on annually through three head-masterships.

The governors were aware that no time should be lost in winning back the confidence of the school community. As Holden wrote, 'no sooner is my resignation an accomplished fact than we find the Chairman [Westhorp] busying himself to collect subscriptions for a school gymnasium and swimming bath'; the donors are listed in the December magazine. After the two principal benefactors, Browne comes next with £50, while the governors seemed to have agreed upon £20 each.

New classrooms, studies and dormitories were soon built at the northern end of the school around and above the passage which today leads from the antechapel to the quadrangle. Brightwell Binyon, the architect for these additions, chose a site for a gymnasium (see over) which served as such until it was converted into a laboratory in the 1930s. To the south of it, also abutting the Lime avenue, one of the earliest school indoor swimming baths (see over) was built and opened in 1884 by the

principal donor, Sir William Broke-Middleton, Bt of Shrubland, in memory of his ancestor Admiral Sir Philip Vere Broke,
Old Ipswichian, whose Shannon defeated the Chesapeake in
the American War of Independence. Browne soon found, however, that, for such essentials as lattice doors on the dormitory
corridors, he must pay himself, awaiting reimbursement as and

when the governors could afford it. Luckily, like his predecessors, he had capital to draw upon, and the Brownes were very generous to the school.

For three reasons, Browne's head-
ship is very well documented. Firstly,
his wife Frances assiduously pasted
newspaper and magazine cuttings
into albums which, with other
papers, were deposited by their eldest son Maurice (who was only two
when they came to Ipswich) at the
University of Michigan Library at
Ann Arbor in 1948. The archive was
rightly embargoed until the last of
the Brownes' children had died. Secondly, the minute books kept by the newly constituted Ipswich Endowed Schools Governors, from 1 March 1882, are still at the school. Thirdly, the magazine began again in June 1883 and has run continuously ever since, becoming *The Ipswichian* in 1968.

Apparently, only about fifty of Holden's pupils remained in the school but from Reading Browne brought thirty boarders, C.H. Garland came as his second master with other teaching colleagues, including Moore Neligan (Bishop of Auckland from 1903), who worked with his sister Mrs Browne to resurrect the chapel choir.[1] On Trinity Sunday 1883, 25 surpliced choristers sang at 11 a.m. and 6.30 p.m. The long-established tradition of boys attending Tower church services ended as the chapel came into its own again. After Easter there were already 95 boys and the numbers continued to climb steeply until, in 1887,

---

1 Moore Neligan lived in the tower rooms; he would invite the youngest boarders to view fireworks from his windows whenever they were let off in Christchurch Park. Neligan helped with plays as well as music and sport.

there were over two hundred in total, including 75 boarders. Mrs Browne, much admired for her beauty by the boarders, was born in Dublin, where her father, Canon Maurice Neligan DD had arranged for boarding vacancies at Reading to be advertised; now a steady stream of clever well-bred Irish boys came to Ipswich instead. Also from Ireland came the lame 33 year-old Miss Hannah Hunt, formidable (but very kind to the smallest boys in her charge) and a legendary figure to her past pupils long after her retirement in 1912. The smallest fry, in knickerbockers, had the choice of caps and boaters. Older boys still wore gowns (togas) and mortar boards, even in the town, and boaters in summer. A boy coming to school on a penny-farthing tied his gown round his waist. Another, going on a butterfly-collecting excursion thought fit to leave his toga at school but was caught by Browne who deprived him of the privilege of wearing one until the following Speech Day. The Brownes brought colour, even for games, to the school, taking it another great stride towards modernity. The school day became 9.00 to 1.00 and 3.00 to 5.00, with half-holidays for games on Tuesday,

Thursday and Saturday, a routine that persisted (with afternoon school three-quarters of an hour earlier) until the early
1990s. There were two sources of 'tuck' (the edible kind and
imposition paper), a cart which came to the Ivry Street gate and
'old Mother Scrutton's' cottage window- sill in the Drift, acces-
sible only by climbing over the wall at the top of the Lime avenue.[2]

The first cricket match against Norwich School was held
there in 1885. The centenary match on School Field in 1985 was
made the occasion for the publication of *A Century of Cricket*,
giving the history of the fixture and listing the captains of both
sides since the beginning. The distinguished Old Norvicensian
Lord Blake wrote the Foreword. The score over the period was
Ipswich won 43, Norwich 20 and there was one tie, so that there
was some justice in the visitors adding a victory to their tally
that day.[3] In May 1887, the governors agreed to Mrs Browne's
idea of building a south transept as an extension to the chapel
'provided that the expense was not to be borne by them or the
school funds'. Fortunately the Brownes and their friends were
ready to cover the cost and it was opened at a special service in
November, Mrs Browne thanking donors through letters to the
press.

In October 1887, the *Pall Mall Gazette* published a list of
schools winning two or more Oxford and Cambridge Awards;
these tables went on appearing, latterly in the *Times Educational Supplement* until all awards were abolished in 1984. Ipswich,
with seven other schools: Bradford GS, Charterhouse, Christ's
Hospital, Marlborough, Rugby, and Winchester, had six
awards, only bettered by St Paul's, Manchester GS, Eton, Clift-

2 Full but anonymous recollections from 1886 onwards can be read in the
Magazine for December 1933.
3 Copies of the booklet are still available from the School.

on and City of London School. Holden's fears that his successor might not maintain the highest academic standards were certainly unfounded but something quite unpredictable arose at a governors' meeting on 16 September.

Browne's Sixth

The governors had received letters from Alice Jane Neale, the Brownes' parlour-maid until the previous January, stating that she had given birth to an illegitimate child in July and naming the 37 year-old Browne as its father. A week later, they asked Browne for a statement. He denied the charge but the governors were not convinced, whereupon Browne left them with a letter resigning. A fortnight later he returned to complain at his treatment but refused to co-operate in an enquiry. Neale had left for Australia with her baby son, leaving her mistress with a letter declaring that she had lied about Browne. The headmaster withdrew his resignation, encouraged to do so by a memorial from his prefects and monitors and knowing that a deputation of parents would be meeting the governors.

By now, the local papers were full of the scandal and for the third time since Rigaud left all the assistant masters declared that they would leave if the headmaster did. So it was that, on 4 November, five days after the Brownes' extension to the chapel had been opened, the governors allowed Browne to withdraw his resignation and the matter was closed. However, the minutes show that they were not satisfied with the head's explanations, nor with his attitude to their enquiry. In short, they perhaps wisely acceded to the widespread feeling that he should stay in the school's interest. Back in office, the next item on the agenda was Browne's request to be allowed to charge higher fees so that he could increase assistant masters' salaries; it was turned down.

Maurice Browne only had a chance to read the family papers after his mother's death in 1935. In 1948 he deposited them at Ann Arbor, and later questioned Miss Frances Latimer ('Lat'), the remarkable woman who was matron in School House at the end of the Browne's time but who for fifty years continued Frances Browne's closest friend, at the time elderly but of sound memory. He wrote about his parents' time at Ipswich with considerable detachment in his autobiography *Too Late to Lament* of 1955. It was the butler who gave the maid's letters to the governors when Mrs Browne refused to allow her husband to be blackmailed. She was then only 32, quite fearless, and very stubborn. Lat believed that the maid wrote withdrawing her accusation in exchange for the fares to Australia and an allowance as long as the child lived. The butler was later imprisoned for stealing; Lat believed that Mrs Browne had framed him. "When her mind was set on something nothing could stop her. There were five people in her world: her husband and you four children." Lat's final judgement of the headmaster will come later.

The year 1889 was a great one for innovations. The formation of the Volunteer Corps was announced in the March Magazine, and Captain Dunstan, Sergeant Austin and 30 cadets paraded in their forage caps, their Norfolk jackets of dark green serge with light green facings and rifles for photographs that July. Two of those boys went on to serve in the Boer War and four in the Great War. To mark the centenary, David Warnes, then and still head of history, wrote *The Ipswich School Corps 1889-1989.*[4]

The notably colourful fund-raising event held in the Lime avenue on two days in July was called a Fancy Fair. An album of William Vick's professional photographs is a fine record. Money was needed for a new school boiler, the means to warm the swimming bath for use all the year round, and for more classroom accommodation. As Lord Elcho MP was detained by Commons' business, the eminent novelist Rider Haggard, who

4 Still available from the school.

boarded at the school from 1869–72 and told his first stories to his peers after lights out, opened the proceedings in his place.[5]

Rider Haggard by 'Spy'

He was most impressed with improvements to the school since his time but urged those concerned to acquire the field beyond the School Field before houses were built on it. Unfortunately nothing was done. Lady Elcho presided at her pottery stall. At the Old Boys' stall Mrs Rider Haggard was in charge. The Army and Navy stall had Wellington memorabilia. There were stalls called Liberty, Dairy Stall, Flower Stall and a Post Office. Mrs Browne and other masters' wives manned the double-sized Queen Elizabeth's School Stall. There was even a gipsy encampment, but not a real one. The lime trees were remarkably sturdy after only thirty years' growth. Indoors there was Punch and Judy in the headmaster's classroom and Edison's phonograph was demonstrated in the lab. Almost £400 was raised.

The Old Ipswichian Club was founded at a dinner at the Great White Horse on the same Saturday. The Club's hundredth birthday was celebrated in 1989 and the final separate issue of the *Old Ipswichian Magazine* (No. 37) listed the distin-

---

5 The Greek legend in Haggard's novel *She* in the style of Herodotus is believed to have been hastily composed by his headmaster, Dr Holden, during a social occasion.

guished old members who had held the Presidency as well as giving the history of the Club and its sporting off-shoots.

On 11 November 1890, Browne conducted a survey of recent punishments in order to send a printed four-page letter, individually addressed, to each parent with his response to three allegations: that half-holidays and games were interrupted for detentions, too much work was returned for rewriting and that corporal punishment was excessive and frequent. The governors, who received some of these complaints, quite properly left the matter in the headmaster's hands. Browne's day-book contains his instructions and requests to the staff, which were usually initialled as read but sometimes drew opinions and suggestions from masters themselves. The tone is democratic, the common room co-operative with a head who expressed himself courteously and clearly. The punishment survey covers one page-opening, all in the smallest writing. A total of 35 boys had been caned, some at the head's request and one or two in his presence. He wisely delegated the task itself to his assistants. A boy received six strokes at most, usually fewer. Most revealing is the sentence 'I most thoroughly disapprove of it for untruthfulness; an offence which requires the most kindly personal care.'

The following March, a three-page letter to parents tackled 'the wide-spread feeling that the education given at this School is not, in some respects, quite that which is suited to the more general requirements of the town and neighbourhood' by agreeing with it. He had, since his appointment, worked for higher standards in languages and mathematics, also succeeding in the sciences. He had asked his governors to agree to some boys being prepared for the very broad 'Commercial Certificate' but now needed parental views before pursuing the matter. That June, he read a paper on the subject to the Head Masters' Association at Bedford. A year later, recognising that the

Classics were waning, he persuaded the governing body to agree to change the time allocated to subjects in the 42 hours of the week (30 in class and 12 of prep) as follows:

	From	*To*
Latin, Greek or German	24	15 hours
Mathematics	7	10
French	4	5½
English	4	5
Chemistry	2	5½ [with Physics]
Drawing	1	1

His aim in future would be to turn this First Grade Classical School into a First Grade Modern School and hoped that the parents would feel that the school would be doing the best for the majority of boys of average ability, instead of concentrating on the minority of boys of marked ability who would still be specially catered for at the right stage. Browne truly believed that he was doing what was right for Ipswich but it was also a useful response to the growing popularity and success of the town's Middle School.

Governors' minutes, however, tell another story for, at most meetings, letters were read from Browne, sometimes from his wife also, asking for improvements to the servants' dormitory, the sanitation, a proper laundry and also better salaries for assistant staff, particularly bonuses for those who worked hardest – performance-related pay! Usually the Brownes offered to pay for what was needed, on condition that they were reimbursed when they left but this condition became decreasingly acceptable and, worn down by these constant demands, the governors quite often ruled against improvements, even at the head's expense.

In April 1892, Browne was asked to report about numbers and standards. He laid down three criteria for a First Class School: 100 pupils or more, membership of HMC and an adequate representation of its former pupils at Oxford and Cambridge. At the time, Ipswich had 120 day-boys, twenty fewer than in 1887, but the grammar schools at Norwich, Bury, Chelmsford, Colchester, Lincoln and Yarmouth all failed one or more of the three criteria. He would not recruit more boarders until the servants were better housed and the sanitary arrangements improved. He hoped that day-boy numbers would increase following the agreed curriculum change. He ended by asking governors to attend more functions at the school, to allow him to take less salary while paying his masters more (which they at first mistook for another request for money rather than an offer on his part which they accepted) and the telling phrase 'before I relinquish to the Governors the trust placed by them in my hands, to do the little I am able...'. This weary and despondent phrase may have cheered some governors, but it was two years more before matters finally came to a head.

In Browne's view, the governors continued to give greater support to the Middle School, which was now competing with the Grammar School for the ablest boys. There were few applicants for Queen's Scholarships and, in 1893, none could be awarded. Nothing was done about the servants having to share a dormitory between those of the boarders and a final letter from Browne on this subject precipitated his dismissal. On 16 February 1894, their clerk communicated the governors' opinion 'that in the interests of the Grammar School a change in the Headmastership is desirable'. They refused to meet Browne for a discussion and he was given six months' notice, dismissing him 'without assigning any cause' under the first paragraph of

Section 38 of the Scheme. Having no alternative, he resigned, under protest, from the end of the summer term and, like Holden, published the whole correspondence. The governors who, in only their second year of office, cut their teeth on the dismissal of the learned doctor had struck again. The papers were full of the story and the governors came under heavy fire from aggrieved parents and old boys but this furore they ignored. No one, however, could accuse them of anticipating, let alone desiring, the tragic sequel.

The Brownes were invited back to Reading School and its boarding house but they decided instead to find somewhere suitable in the Bournemouth area to open a private school of their own. The resourceful Mrs Browne would have made a success of such a move for the sake of her husband and their children but her husband, had since the February dismissal, lost the ability to sleep, was depressed and in poor health generally. His doctor recommended a change of scene and air and, for a fortnight, he toured in Wales, returning only in time to attend Speech Day on Wednesday 25 July. There, tensions between the governors, on the one hand, and the Brownes, cheered to the echo by parents and boys, on the other, only just remained in check. Presentations and eulogies of the Brownes followed but only after the governors had left, and then term was over. On the following day, Mrs Browne travelled to Dorset, leaving her husband at the school. It later emerged that he had, during the last year, lost most of their capital by gambling. He now disappeared and was found in London, the worse for wear from drink, and was brought back on Sunday. His wife was still away, when, sometime around dawn on Tuesday, he was found dead in his dressing room, with his throat cut, by the maid bringing shaving water. Mrs Browne and her family received much kindness in their distress; she in fact founded St

Bede's preparatory school for boys at Eastbourne to support herself and the family.

Canon Barrington preached the funeral sermon in the Tower church and it was published at the same time as another, which Browne had preached, at Tuddenham two years previously. This followed the suicide of the Revd John Pickford, Browne's schoolfellow and a former colleague at Ipswich, frustrated at his sister's selfish destruction of a much longed-for letter offering him a university appointment. Neither preacher had taken a high moralistic or condemnatory line on what had for so long been regarded as the mortal sin of *felo de se*. It was not until 1898 that Frances Browne applied to the governors for permission to erect a tablet to her late husband's memory in chapel. By no means a foregone conclusion, it took many letters from her and several meetings on their part before they agreed to a brass not exceeding 14 by 9 inches. It is mounted between the windows on the south wall of the extension the Brownes paid for, and is of the specified size precisely.

Years later, Maurice Browne asked 'Lat' what his father was really like. Let her reply stand as his epitaph here:

Splendid, and mad. The most gifted man in the English educational world of his day; and, for all his kinks, brave, just, generous-minded. A great classical scholar, an even greater mathematical scholar and the finest teacher in the conventional sense whom I have known. Look at the scholarships won by his pupils during that decade; no school in England proportionately to its numbers could hold a candle to Ipswich then. Look at men like [Judge and Privy Councillor Lord] Roche and others; they owe what they are, first to God, their parents and themselves, but next to your father.

XV

Philip Edwin Raynor

A modest and generous sportsman, 1894–1906

Raynor arrived having had only modest success as head of two Australian schools. He was 'perhaps too unassuming', yet under him the school rose to new heights in academic and sporting spheres. Believing that his assistants were underpaid, he bankrupted himself to help them; the governors paid his debts and dispensed with his services.

THE NEW HEADMASTER was appointed during Browne's last summer term. There were 113 hopefuls, five of whom had taught in the school in recent years. Six men were interviewed, four were eliminated and two were put to the vote, eight governors choosing the Revd Philip Edwin Raynor MA, against four favouring a physicist who never moved from Clifton College. Raynor, who  had been teaching at Westminster for a short time, was, like his three predecessors, unlikely to know what he was taking on. Whereas Browne seemed always to avoid meeting governors and preferred to deal with them in writing, Raynor, at least in his early days, was welcomed at meetings.

Between Raynor's appointment and arrival, one other matter caused a stir. Complaints from parents and others to the Charity Commission triggered an enquiry into the condition and management of the grammar school and the boys' middle school. Held in the Town Hall on 2 July, the report which appeared in September upheld Browne's complaints but he gave his evidence in person, while the governors only sent their clerk. A posthumous vindication, however, is no consolation.

> 'the accommodation for domestic servants in the School House is unsatisfactory, if the number of boarders received there by the late Master is maintained;' *and* 'I have to urge upon the Governors the necessity of such supervision as will prevent the impression that boys who should otherwise be attending the Grammar School are retained as scholars at the Middle School for Boys, though nominally there in the capacity of student teachers.'

Raynor was born in 1857 at the rectory at Kelvedon Hatch, where his father George was curate. After a year at Tonbridge, at ten years of age he won a scholarship to Winchester, whence in 1875 he took the top award at New College which he justified by taking Firsts in Mods and Greats. Prevented by a football injury from rowing or playing cricket at Oxford, he took up bicycling, a new sport, and rode his penny-farthing against Cambridge. While teaching at Highgate he was ordained, moving on to Marlborough and then Wellington. He married Jessie Cursham, from Nottinghamshire, and their eldest son was born just before they left for the headship of Christ's College, Hobart, Tasmania. Whilst there, the Raynors rode around the island on a tandem and, in three years, the school doubled in size to nearly 80 pupils. During his second five-year headship, at St Peter's College, Adelaide, pupil numbers again doubled to 242, before a recession caused a fall to

170. Raynor and the St Peter's governors fell out over his refusal to adopt economies which, in his view, would only lead to further decline.

When, after a similar period at Ipswich, he applied (unsuccessfully) for the headship of Tonbridge, Raynor claimed that he had raised numbers from 75 to 118, the ten boarders he took on had grown to 40. Browne had claimed that a tenth of his pupils were removed when he resigned and that half of the remainder gave notice to leave with him. Raynor was 37 and his wife 30 when they arrived in Ipswich with their three sons and a daughter. The governors were forced by the recent report to do many of the things they had refused to contemplate in Browne's time. Once more there was an urgent need to restore public confidence in the school. It was helpful to Raynor to have the support of Holden's stalwarts, Sanderson and Richardson, who had kept away from the school in Browne's time but who now re-emerged as stout supporters of school and Club.

An illustrated article about the school, one of a series in the London periodical *St James's Budget* for June 1896, began by praising Browne's energy over eleven years and the school's successes in work and games. It went on to describe Raynor as 'learned and courteous' but then touched on the quality which may have been especially attractive to the governors who appointed him: 'perhaps too unassuming'. The writer further observed that the buildings were the most compact of any of the public schools he had seen. 'Cramped' would have been more accurate.

By Speech Day the next month, Raynor could demonstrate the extent to which he had already pulled the school round. Three more open scholarships had been won in the last year, as well as two more by boys who had had seven years at the school (but who probably left with the Brownes), making a total of 28 in the last ten years. In the *Daily News* league tables, allowing for the size of the school, Ipswich was 10th of 128 schools and, over ten years, 5th. Holden and Browne would have warmed to his next remark: 'Ipswich easily defeats schools with great names, like Winchester, Eton, Rugby, Harrow and Charterhouse, as well as those of more modern repute, such as Marlborough, Repton, Shrewsbury, Rossall and Clifton.' He went on as others had before him: 'It must not be forgotten, moreover, that nearly all of these schools are richly endowed and are able to offer far greater attractions to clever boys in the way of scholarships than we can.'

That September, Sanderson died and, in December, Holden. Appeals for funds to honour both men were launched; they were eventually reunited by memorial brasses in chapel and in the headmaster's former classroom. Holden always regretted the lack of an adequate library and would have been glad that his room between Big School and Chapel was to be refurnished and replenished as the Holden Library. The Sanderson fund, however, had first to help his widow, left in abject poverty. Enough of their furniture was purchased to fill the small clergy house she was allowed in Ipswich until her death in 1903. The furniture was then sold and the triple-fronted bookcase on the west wall of the Holden Library was constructed in Sanderson's memory.

Richard 'Roly' Slator joined the school as a mathematician from Jesus, Cambridge the next term, retiring in 1938 after serving four headmasters, three of them as second master. He did take two years' break at King's School, Bruton, returning with an external London B.Sc. added to his M.A.

In 1898 the boarding numbers justified the opening of a new house in Anglesea Road. During the brief existence of Holden

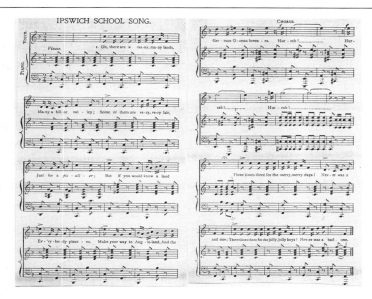

House, Mr John Evans, the music master and composer of the rousing School Song[1] was its housemaster. That year, a new Bishop organ was installed in the chapel, reusing some of the 1857 pipework. Bunnell Burton, organist at the Tower church and a future chairman of governors, gave generously to the fund and played the opening recital. The photograph of the east end of chapel is our only record of that organ and the complete Six Acts of Mercy window.[2] Its main lights were sucked out by a landmine which fell in the arboretum in 1940. In March 1898, the bishop of Norwich confirmed 24 boys at what

1 The Ipswich School Song was printed in the 1899 Magazine, and, despite having led to rebellion in Watson's time, was revived at Speech Day in 1966 and reprinted in the *Old Ipswich Magazine* that year, with an article by W.M. Morfey.

2 C.H.B. Bisshopp was the sixthformer who took the photograph. His father E.F. Bisshopp was the architect of the large houses on the south side of St Edmund's Road and the owner of No. 15. Since 1972, No 11 has been the head's house. The east window, probably by the O'Connors' London workshop, was placed in memory of two Ipswichians, John E.D. Alston BA, aged 23, and John Josselyn, aged 17, who both died in 1863. The causes of their deaths has not yet been discovered.

was probably the first visit of the diocesan to the school, despite the four hundred-year connection.

In the Michaelmas Term of 1900, Raynor appealed for funds to celebrate fifty years at Henley Road by refurnishing what he called the Great Schoolroom. Raynor was unclear where the school began: 'The old desks, which were in use in the original School Building in Silent Street [*sic*], are not only heavy, clumsy and out-of-date, but are now absolutely past repair.' He supposed that they were only fifty years old. It is likely, however, that they were provided when the school moved to the Blackfriars' refectory, about 1612, and they are certainly those shown in engravings of the dormitory schoolroom. 'As there is a considerable amount of sentiment and interest attaching to the old desks and to the names carved upon them, the lids of these will be preserved and placed in some position where they can be seen by visitors, so that an old scholar can still revive the memories of his school days by searching for his engraved name.' The money was raised quite quickly, though a loss of

two shillings and fivepence on a lecture about Generals Gordon
and Kitchener did not help. Rider Haggard, guest of honour at
Speech Day 1904, talked about
going 'to see the furniture he
had damaged when a boy and
the wall where he had kicked
out the bricks'. He had not
shone academically in Hold-
en's time but the desk-lid with
his name carved on it is still
admired in the museum.
Apparently boys gently prised
up the surface of the old desks
and buried slips of paper with
their names and dates in what
then became known as
'graves'. Unfortunately boys
with no taste for history

and archaeology had exhumed and discarded most of these
mementoes long before the desks were replaced. The patent
design chosen by Raynor enabled the room to be converted
from classroom to auditorium in minutes.

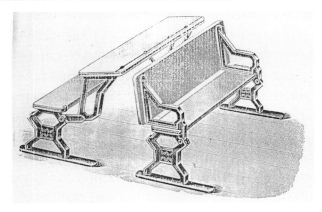

W.H. Richardson's collections include all his invitations to the major events of the school year: The Athletic Sports at the end of March, Speech Day and the Old Boys Cricket Match in July, the Past and Present Football Match and the Christmas Concert in December, replaced by a scientific Conversazione in 1903 to celebrate the new laboratories. Designed by Munro Cautley, they were 'lofty, large and well-ventilated, arranged on the most modern lines, and fitted with the best and latest forms of apparatus'. Before the physics laboratory was built, boys had used one at Christchurch Mansion. Five hundred people came to see the wonders of science exhibited, including a rash demonstration of radium by S.A. Notcutt, clerk to the governors. The good ventilation soon led to the complaint that those resident in 27 Henley Road 'had suffered annoyance from offensive gases issuing from the laboratory' and the headmaster, as always happens, was 'asked to attend to the matter'.

Many societies now met regularly: The Natural History and Scientific founded in 1895, in succession to the Field Naturalist, the Penny Readings, the Literary and Dramatic and, not the same thing, the Literary and Musical Entertainments (a Browne initiative), the proceeds of which were used to swell the Games Fund. Regular lectures were held, mostly dealing with remote parts of the world. In 1900, during the second Anglo-Boer War, the time was ripe for the revival of

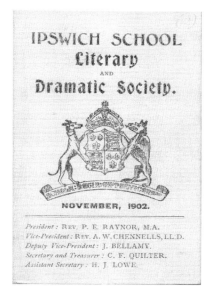

the School Corps, which had foundered after its first two years a decade earlier. The Old Ipswichian Club had 250 members in 1902, enough to support a Paddington 'OI Club for Working Lads in London', run by the Revd James White, at school in Holden's time.

Academic achievements had kept the school ahead of its East Anglian competitors, as shown by a table of awards over 17 years extracted from the *Daily Chronicle* for July 1903:

	pupils	*awards*		*pupils*	*awards*
Ipswich	100	45	The Leys	155	38
Felsted	240	38	Perse	145	35
Norwich	112	16	Bury St Eds	61	12
Ely	35	6	Walthamstow	150	5

Nine blues were won by former pupils in Raynor's time, two of them by his son Kenneth whose younger brothers displayed other talents. Malcolm and Ronald Raynor left the school early and, given their passage to Australia, were advised to take up farming at which they notably succeeded. Unfortunately, however, yet another headmaster, under whom so many good things flourished at the school, was running into difficulties with the governing body.

Around 1900 a national debate about the regulation and funding of secondary education was dividing the politicians. Some wished to assist schools which taught the traditional grammar school subjects; others wanted a more utilitarian curriculum. By September 1902 the school had submitted to four inspections to establish its entitlement to support from public funds. There were the usual criticisms that the curriculum was too narrow yet, of 82 boys, in the upper school, 39 learnt Greek and 43 either German, bookkeeping or commercial arithmetic. French and mathematics were almost universally taken and there was even a shorthand class.

A new Scheme, promising the school a securer financial future, came into effect that September but, by then, Raynor was gone. For some years he had been silently subsidising the salaries of his assistant masters from his own pocket and was now bankrupt. His creditors in the town agreed to settle his debts by accepting ten shillings in the pound. Raynor, given six months' notice to depart in the summer (without cause stated), prepared to take his family to the New College living of Tingewick in Bedfordshire. He requested, and was given, a short testimonial which paid tribute to his achievements. It ended: 'The general spirit of the School has been all that could be desired. Zeal for the welfare of the School and conscientious hard work have characterised Mr Raynor's management of the School.'

Raynor's last Speech Day, in the total absence of governors, became a domestic occasion. After Raynor had distributed the prizes, Roly Slator made presentations from boys, parents and staff. In his reply, Raynor is reported as saying that 'he might, under the circumstances of his retirement, have stirred up strife and made it a public question – but he felt it would be bad for the school and he loved the school too well to do it a hurt, even for the purpose of his own justification. If then, he himself had been able to sink personal matters, he thought they might do so too'. This last was clearly a reference to the absence of his employers. 'He left the platform amid deafening cheers.' The new Scheme provided for Raynor to receive a pension of £200 a year for life, it being open to the governors to help his wife and family if he pre-deceased them.

Ipswich   School.

The Governors and the Head Master
request the pleasure of

W. H. Richardson, Esq's presence

AT A

Conversazione,

TO BE HELD AT THE SCHOOL ON

Wednesday, December 16th, 1903,

IN CONNECTION WITH THE OPENING OF

The New Science Laboratories.

ADMIT ONE.   8.0 TO 11.0 P.M.

PLEASE SHOW THIS TICKET AT THE DOOR.   R.S.V.P.

Should this Ticket not be required, kindly return it to the SECRETARY, SCHOOL HOUSE, IPSWICH.

Ipswich   School.

Speech Day, 1904.

The Head Master requests the pleasure of

W. H. Richardson, Esq presence

On Thursday, July 28th, at 3 p.m.,

WHEN THE PRIZES WILL BE GIVEN AWAY BY

H. Rider Haggard, Esq. (O.J.)

An answer is particularly requested.

PLEASE BRING THIS TICKET WITH YOU.

XVI

Arthur Kenelm Watson

Gentleman headmaster, 1906-1918

If a head's success were to be measured by the admiration and affection of former pupils, Watson would go down as the greatest in the school's history. A layman after several clerics, a countryman, sportsman and a good scholar, his ample means enabled him to take a rather independent line with the governors. He was also somewhat radical in his views, and, as the chairman of governors expected his headmaster to wear a hat in the town, he had to go.

NO SOONER HAD Raynor been dismissed than a group of governors visited Oundle to interview its great headmaster Sanderson. They also quizzed Keeling at Bradford Grammar School, asking whether Raynor had been right about maintaining classical and modern sides in a small school. They also asked what salaries should be paid to assistant masters, what provision of classrooms, laboratories, workshops and equipment was adequate and whether there should be separate accommodation for preparatory school pupils. The advertisement for a successor reflected their discoveries and was 'sent to all the principal public schools for exhibition in the masters' common room', exactly as would be done today. The new head's salary would be £700 per annum, plus £3 for every pupil in excess of 100. 128 applications were received, from which seven were chosen for interview. The Revd E.C. Sherwood of Westminster School withdrew, accepting instead the headship of St Lawrence College, Ramsgate. He applied again in 1919 and came then to build on his predecessor's achievements.

The governors' immediate choice fell on Mr A.K.Watson, who for fifteen years had taught at Rugby, significantly the first lay headmaster since the 1650s. Previous heads had been chaplain also. But, just as the Puritan Commonwealth dispensed with bishops, an anti-clerical mood stirred in the land as the Liberals again prepared for government. The 1881 Scheme had officially severed the school's links with Church and Crown a quarter of a century earlier. The bishops of Norwich would no longer have to approve heads before appointment, and 'religious opinions or attendance or non-attendance at any particular form of religious worship' would not be required of governors, headmasters or their staff. Holy orders would neither qualify nor disqualify heads or assistants. Religious instruction was to be in the principles of the Christian Faith (not specifically Anglican therefore). Now that public funds would be applied in the school, the 1906 Scheme laid down that 'no expenses in any way connected with ... the Chapel ... or with any services therein shall be defrayed out the funds provided by the Council'. Paid for by public subscription in 1852, the chapel and everything to do with it had been given by those who cared for it. In 1907 the governors asked the bishop's registrar whether the chapel had ever been consecrated (it had in 1853), only to be misled that it had been licensed (only)

in 1852 pending consecration. In July 1909, the bishop of Norwich (in absentia) licensed the Revd John A. C. V. de Candole as chaplain two years into his ministry, and his successors have been Anglican priests ever since. Tales of de Candole's otherworldliness are legion. When, in mid-sermon, his surplice caught fire from a candle, one of the choirboys drew this to his attention. "Thank you", he said, quietly extinguishing himself with his hand rather than his sermon: that went on.

Watson's grandfather had been a successful carpet manufacturer in Kidderminster, with a Bond Street showroom. His father shone at Rugby and Balliol and taught at Harrow. His mother was a Digby, niece of the 9th baron Digby, and there were a dean of Durham, an admiral at Trafalgar and several distinguished clerics and lawyers in the family. AKW was at Harrow but followed his father to Balliol and took a First in Mods, a Second in Greats and gained a Cricket blue which was assured to such a schoolboy hero. Having scored 135 for Harrow at Lords, he took the last two Eton second innings wickets in the final over of the match. The new head was a large bear of a man with tight curls of black hair in some disarray. His tweed suits were ill fitting and his trousers creased, but not in the right places. His apparently staring eyes, which seemed to look through you, were, on closer study, twinkling and benevolent.

Under the new Scheme, a governing body solely responsible for Ipswich School held its first meeting on 28 September 1906. The sharper focus this permitted was of immediate benefit to the school. The three separate subcommittees for finance, buildings and 'visiting' then instituted were still functioning in the 1970s.[1] Graduated fees for tuition and boarding (Raynor

1 Members of the third committee in their turn checked that the school was in good repair, and that all was clean and tidy. When much later governors realised their proper role, this became the academic subcommittee.

having discreetly and without permission reduced the latter to boost custom) and the salaries of the assistant staff were agreed in detail. The total number of free and subsidised places available from 1907 was forty and this helped Watson build up numbers from the 80 pupils he inherited, only six of them boarders, to 145 in one year and 177 when he left. Boarding numbers did not rise as healthily, indeed for some years they fell but, by personally subsidising some boarding scholarships, he had thirty boarders by 1914. None of this, however, was the reason that his honeymoon with the governors lasted only two years, the first signs of trouble being his exclusion from automatic attendance at their meetings, but his popularity in the school only grew.

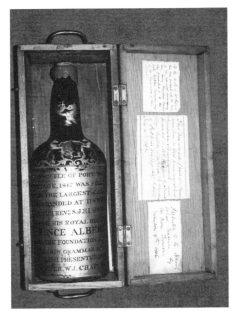

Burton and Watson met sixty OIs after the first Christmas concert and play in the dining hall and warm were the mutual expressions of approval exchanged. S.A. Notcutt, the clerk with a taste for amateur scientific experiments now turned antiquary and 'in a neat and explanatory speech', handed over to Mr Watson a memento of the School for the museum. This consisted of a box containing a magnum port bottle. On the box was the following inscription: 'This box was made from part of a beam taken from the Old Grammar School, Foundation Street, Ipswich, and presented to

Mrs Rigaud by James Day, builder, to place the Magnum of Port Wine, vintage 1847, bottled July 4th, 1851.' The bottle, with its illuminated inscription, is still in the museum and, though it was empty in 1906 and again today, it was refilled in 1980 by J.K.T. Webb, Club president, on the occasion of the election of the first British woman Prime Minister but consumed at the celebrations of the Club Centenary in 1989.

There was one very small matter over which Watson found it hard to have his own way. Which of Watson, Hockey the music master, or even Bunnell Burton took against the School Song of 1899 is unclear. Whether it was the genuinely uplifting and rhythmic tune or the banality of the words ('ripping' rhyming with 'Gipping' for example) which made it unacceptable, Watson banned it from end-of-term concerts. However, old boys returning for the entertainment were unimpressed by the head's substitution of Harrow's 'Play Up' and 'Auld Lang Syne' and followed them with impromptu renderings of their Song. While they were, of course, beyond school discipline, boys seen joining in were beaten for their rebellious behaviour, yet the annual protest persisted for six years.

Funds were available now for improvements to the buildings. In 1907 the new Manual was opened, as well as the changing rooms which joined it to the swimming bath, and the next year Miss Hunt could bring her charges down from their room overlooking the chapel yard to the new Preparatory School beside the Ivry Street gate. It seems unbelievable that the site, so

IPSWICH SCHOOL

Edward Ardizzone Prize

233

close to the headmaster's drive and garden, had been occupied by piggeries. Whose pigs were they?

Adulation is not too strong a word for the way in which Watson's pupils remembered him with respect and affection and one wonders whether, had Sherwood arrived in his place, they would have adopted him as a role model in their lives. As late as the autumn of 1982, there were about thirty of them alive and willing to help Wallace Morfey compile memories of the school in their time. The fact that some of them were nearly ninety probably served only to sharpen their recollections of a remote period of their lives. Vice-Admiral Sir Frank Mason, a brigadier and a colonel, Irvine Gray of the 1950 History and, of course, Morfey himself were reliable witnesses allowing for the element of hero-worship. The modern term for Watson's pleasantly powerful personality, 'a great man physically and morally', would be charismatic. The oddest thing is that no mention of Watson being a married man was encountered in anything written about his time until his obituary published in 1947. He had arrived with Caroline Margaret Warrack, whom he married in 1897, and two daughters. A son, C.P. Watson, and another daughter were born at Ipswich.

At his first Speech Day the chairman of governors Bunnell Burton was eloquent in the new headmaster's praise; the local reporter was farther-sighted, discerning that he was imbued with a thorough democratic reformer's spirit. Burton, who had aspirations to parliament, but *not* on the radical wing, will have read the newspaper account with some misgivings. Watson found some things which needed tightening up. He wanted no excuses from parents about games or chapel attendance. The school was open, and boys should be there, six and sometimes seven days a week. All boys would be taught to swim and take military drill - the Cadet Corps, now commanded by the German master Dr F.G. Bakker, would be virtually compulsory. To show how much he valued games, he invited the Bury headmaster to bring a colleague and play Fives against him and his science master James. The Ipswich pair triumphed totally. He told a boy, who had sworn when he dropped a catch at Cricket, that he was to leave the spectators to do the swearing next time. He was vocal in his support of the soccer elevens and a dignified umpire in top hat and tails at the athletic sports. He could be seen digging up plaintains and other weeds on the pitches and organised the boys into teams to pull the huge roller, made to be horse-drawn.

Watson would never have been happy in a large school, for he enjoyed teaching at least one subject to every boy and to getting to know him outside the classroom as well. At Speech Day in 1909, he read out the examiners' report as usual. The methods of teaching German employed were peculiar. "That's me", he said. The report then pronounced the classical work satisfactory. "It does not satisfy me", he commented. But in some ways he was easy-going and enjoyed working in an untidy study. Arriving at Ipswich station with no money, he borrowed a pound from a parent for the fare to Norfolk, deducting the sum from the next bill. Bunnell Burton was horrified as chairman to see his headmaster in the town without a hat, a thing unheard of in those days, and warned him in vain; he was not pleased to learn that he would sometimes drink whisky and discuss politics with the music master, William 'Mop' Hockey, at his house down Fonnereau Road. The governors refused to increase the salary budget by £65 a year and would not allow Watson to pay it himself. Finding that their head could afford to build himself a house in the Lutyens manner at Upton Green on the Norfolk Broads, they wondered whether he was truly their servant. He liked to break the news to successful entrance scholarship candidates but the chairman regarded that as one of his own Speech Day privileges. Twelve of Morfey's thirty contemporaries were beaten at some time by AKW but regarded the experience almost as an honour. For the eyes of the first headmaster in the school's history to find caning unnecessary,[2] Morfey wrote: 'equally incomprehensible to Watsonians then would have been this era's idea that corporal punishment is degrading and an offence to the dignity of the recipient'. When, in 1905, Edward Fison wished to underwrite a leaving exhibition of £25 for three years, his letter to the chairman ended with a paragraph on the same subject: 'My own reminiscences of the School go back to Dr Rigaud's time and that of his distinguished successor, and they centre very much, especially as regards the earlier part of the period, around the numerous canings I received, which I am sure were well deserved, highly beneficial and by no means as unpleasant as is generally imagined.'

2 It was in about 1980 that Morfey challenged the author about beating. "We would never have appointed you if we had realised that you would not cane." "But you did not ask me. The governors of Sevenoaks made an issue of the matter and that is an important reason why I am here and not there."

Throughout his time, Watson had to depend almost entirely on his chaplain to take services and to choose suitable objects for collections; on 28 April 1912, a massive sum, almost three pounds, went to the survivors of the Titanic tragedy. In Sept 1915, in his first year as bishop of the new diocese of St Edmundsbury  and Ipswich, the Right Revd Henry Hodgson preached in chapel. Poor de Candole was taken seriously ill in February 1917 and his memorial service was held that May. When the head boy told Watson that the boys wanted to send messages of affection to their chaplain, he angrily asked "Who says Mr de Candole is dying?" and that was the end of the matter. The saintly de Candole's patient tutoring of young Edward Ardizzone earned him a line drawing in that artist's autobiography[3] and his painted oak memorial in Chapel in English (to which donors were invited to subscribe a shilling) is in pleasant contrast to half a dozen brass plates with Latin inscriptions. In fact, brass was unobtainable; it had all gone to the war effort.

When war broke out, the younger staff who joined the services were replaced by older men. There was a problem over Dr Bakker, who, no longer commanding the Corps, was seen scan-

---

3 In 1973 Ardizzone gave permission for one of his illustrations from *The Young Ardizzone* (Studio Vista 1970) to be used for Junior Art Prize label. The drawing of de Candole tutoring him from the same source is reproduced here by kind permission of Victor Gollancz.

ning the Orwell with powerful binoculars, and heard singing 'Die Wacht am Rhein' in his house at night. Following a Zeppelin raid (which, presumably, Bakker was suspected of masterminding), the mayor asked the governors to arrange urgently for him to retire to Cambridge well away from the coast, and to consider replacing German with Spanish in the school. Watson stoutly defended Bakker and his mother tongue, incautiously calling the banning of a great language 'the most fatuous of all experiments' on Speech Day. At the southern end of the field, huts were built to serve as hospital wards for the wounded. Ivry Street was blocked by the covered way constructed to join them to the Hospital itself. The huts later did sterling service as classrooms as the school expanded under Sherwood; the last of them only came down to make way for his classrooms in 1934 and the Great School of 1956.

Trivial criticisms now began to appear in governors' minutes but Watson argued strongly that the inspectors considered the staff badly paid. The cleverest boys from elementary schools were not being encouraged to take the free places available at the school. AKW planted vegetables on the land between the school and Henley Road, and did not mind being seen digging there on Sunday afternoons, almost up to the time when Sergeant Austin rang the Chapel bell. On one occasion he was so angered by the latest batch of complaints that he growled at an uncomprehending first form "The governors are a pack of fools". At the 1917 Speech Day both chairman and vice-chairman stayed away.

When Watson told the board that he would retire at the end of the War, they replied that that might not come soon enough. In December 1917, they gave him notice to resign after the next Speech Day and, when he refused to agree, they tried and failed to pass a motion to terminate his appointment immediately. On demanding to know their grounds of complaint, he was told that both teaching and discipline were poor. This he successfully refuted at a special meeting. In his twelve years he had sent thirty men up to the senior universities, half of them with scholarships. Such martinets as Slator, Bakker and their colleagues, and Sergeant-Instructor Austin, were not the men to tolerate indiscipline. Watson wished to stay until July 1919, so that he could continue his practice of writing to every serving OI and master from the school until the war was over and they were safely home. At the outbreak of the Great War there were already 150 OIs in the services but that number soon swelled to 407, of whom 71 were killed or died of their wounds and 74 won honours. As 1918 progressed it became clear that the Armistice was in prospect, and Watson left at Christmas, his successor Sherwood having been appointed the previous July.

That summer, Watson cycled with a party of masters and boys down to Shotley Gate to witness the moving sight of the surrender of the German U-boat fleet. One of them was the school historian Irvine Gray who, when he got up to Cambridge in 1921, visited the 84 year-old H.T. Francis, a Rigaud pupil, formerly a fellow of Caius and still Under-Librarian at the University Library. Francis remembered as a sixth former in 1854, being taken down to Landguard Point to see the British fleet, under Sir Charles Napier, sail for the Baltic during the Crimean War with Russia. Over five hundred years earlier in 1346, Edward III and the Black Prince sailed out of the Orwell Haven to triumph at Crecy. How many Ipswich schoolboys had sufficient notice of that spectacle to see it for themselves?

At his last end of term Concert, as was his habit, Watson sang some rousing solos including 'Hope the Hornblower'. Other favourites of his were 'Forty Years On' and 'Invictus'. The next day he visited each form to say goodbye, telling the third form:

"Well, I'm going, and if any of you boys grow up as big fools as the Governors, then God help you". For a time he taught at Cologne with the Army of Occupation then, for two years, was principal of Durundulum, the Indian establishment run on English public school lines. He then retired to Norfolk and there, and at Harrow, loved to welcome his old pupils. The governors had come to realise that their headmaster's views were a good deal more radical than they had bargained for when they chose him as forward-looking. His pupils counted it their good fortune to have had a head who was so many things: scholar, country gentleman, millionaire (in today's terms), staunch advocate of the best aspects of the public school tradition yet socialist enough to wish for wider educational opportunity and a fairer distribution of wealth. It must be clear that the author owes this account of Watson very largely to Morfey and his schoolfellows.

Below: Bisshopp and Cautley's Drain Plan for the School, 1909

XVII

Edward Charles Sherwood

A professional headmaster, 1919-1933

Charles Sherwood may have suffered by comparison with his charismatic and popular predecessor, but he had the application and the vision to develop the school, appoint good staff and keep them. He also had the diplomatic skills necessary to become the first headmaster since King in 1798 to leave with the governors' unreserved approbation, but that says more about the qualities of the governors over that long period than of their chosen heads.

THE GOVERNORS INTER-VIEWED three clergymen, all headmasters, from the list of 121 applicants to succeed Watson, ensuring that there would be no difficulty (as there had been since de Candole died) in finding a chaplain. The 46 year-old Sherwood had had twelve successful years as head of St Lawrence College, Ramsgate. Educated at Magdalen, Oxford, both school and college, he had rowed for the university and taught for ten years at Westminster. The governors sensibly informed him that he could attend all their meetings and celebrated the drawing of a

line under past difficulties by starting a new volume of their minutes.

The Slators had agreed to open a junior boarding house in their own house, 27 Henley Road, so that boarders could be caught young. Unfortunately, Roly tested the fire escape harness from the upper floor without checking that it was anchored there and broke both his legs. "It's quite safe, boys", he is reputed to have said before the descent. He will not have enjoyed greeting his new headmaster from a wheel chair.

During the fourteen years of the Revd E.C. Sherwood's headmastership, the school took great strides towards its modern size and standing. From 197 boys when he took over, Sherwood brought numbers up to 240 in his first year and to over 300, for the first time, when he retired in 1933. Succeeding a notably extrovert headmaster who had made the school the greater part of his life, it was, however, some time before Sherwood enjoyed general approbation. Watsonians, particularly, felt that a Golden Age was lost but the comparatively reserved Sherwood was strongly supported by his wife Claire, a sister of the poet James Elroy Flecker. Speaking at his first Old Ipswichian dinner, Sherwood said that all his life he had longed to be the headmaster of a school with a past, and a famous past. That was a promising beginning. He avoided the limelight but knew how to use his stature and personality on important occasions. The first magazine editorial predicted accurately that 'Mrs Sherwood will win the respect of all by her kindly feelings, and thoughtfulness for the comforts of the boarders, and the great interest she is taking in the school as a whole'. Charles and Claire Sherwood were genial and generous hosts to the entire school community and came to be much loved.

It may have been in response to a feeling that boys did not look smart enough that Eton jackets and uncomfortable stiff collars were introduced immediately, a not entirely popular move. Grey flannel suits were worn in summer. Gowns were the mark of those who had matriculated. Setting boys by ability replaced the rigid form system and three-weekly reports were used to monitor progress. Sherwood strove for better classrooms to replace the huts but missed the pleasure of working in them by a single year.

Equally importantly, yet unostentatiously, cultural standards were raised, in large measure due to the headmaster and the calibre of the staff he appointed. For decades, a mixed diet of songs and choruses and playlets by unheard-of composers and writers had been the stuff of concerts and end-of-term entertainments. He insisted (against Hockey's advice) that abridged, later full, versions of major plays such as *Macbeth*, *Twelfth Night* and *School for Scandal* should be staged annually. Despite their being long enough to need no musical introduction, these performances were still called concerts for a year or two more. From 1922, the new School Musical Society began performing works by recognisable composers, Gibbons, Morley, Stanford, Parry and Elgar. Sherwood and Stanley Wilson the new music master (who quickly formed an orchestra and a choral society) were clearly men of discernment. Even the programmes printed for school events took on a newly stylish appearance, and when the Cercle Français, founded by A.H. Legh, put on a play in French local businesses advertised in that language. Perhaps to compensate for not being as enthusiastic a sportsman as Watson, Sherwood established day houses: Broke, Holden and Rigaud, which could compete internally with the boarding School House on an equal footing. Interhouse competition was good training, he believed, for matches against other schools. Mid-term exeats, abolished by Raynor 'in common with the headmaster of many other schools' in 1903, were reinstated to general approval. The overused school field had to be reserved for athletics and cricket, and two fields north of Park Road – Avenue field and King's field – were temporarily hired. Some cricket was played at Portman Road in the closed season for football. In 1925, twenty acres of what is now known as Notcutt's were much needed acquisitions. Sherwood, with considerable prescience, believed that it would be prudent to move the whole school to that site. Will such a move ever become a necessity?

The memorial in chapel to those who gave their lives in the Great War was unveiled in July 1922 by the senior Old Ipswichian officer, Lieut-General Sir E.A.H. Alderson KCB, who had commanded the Canadian Corps in the War. For those who think that only today's journalists get things wrong, the *EADT*, reporting the service, had Parry's anthem 'I was glad when they said unto me' as 'I was a *lad*...'. The next year electric light was installed and the growing choir was moved from the chancel nearer to the centre nave.

Sherwood was adept at choosing and recruiting good staff. He visited Hugh Grimwade, revising for finals in his digs at Oxford, and invited him to join the staff on coming down; he had identified in him a fine science master who became Tanqueray's second master when Slator retired. Reginald Jennings also came, by Sherwood's invitation, to teach history, English and the Classics, bringing his many enthusiasms for things cultural and sporting. Jennings founded a school Antiquarian society and organised joint expeditions to churches with the Photographic society recording interesting features. For six years from 1921, he was resident tutor in School house, before moving to Marlborough to teach for nearly forty years more. His judgement was good to the end and, holding both schools in equal affection, he kept in touch until he died in 1987 and wrote about his early experiences with sensitivity.[1] 'Charles Sherwood's quiet watchful Christian wisdom was an example to us all', he recalled. 'It is boys and not buildings which make a school. The sixth, fifth and fourth were in the original building and all the rest were in the huts, relics of the war. A boy went to school to practise courtesy, industry, discipline and intellectual integrity, and to learn to live with other people. The school was a wonderful social mix in those happy days, before the innumerable little snobberies arrived to degrade so much of England today but East Anglia was, and is, a most healthy province. The proportion of boarders to day-boys was about one to four, and there were no tensions between them.' When one knew Jennings, the next quotation is easier to understand and believe: 'The general discipline and manners in the school were wholly admirable. I can only recollect one "incident" and I am ashamed to say that I hit a boy (long since dead, I fear). This is the only time I ever did so wicked a thing but at least I had no more trouble.' When he contributed to Sherwood's obituary in 1947, he emphasised how decisive he could be, yet how seldom he rebuked anyone. When he needed to do so, it lasted seconds only. 'No headmaster's armoury should lack the power of nuclear fission.'

1 'Ipswich School, 1921–27', in *Old Ipswichian Magazine*, No. 23 for 1975.

In 1922, the 15th Ipswich Scout Troop was inaugurated for boys who preferred a less military organisation than the Corps; scouts ran the school tuck shop to augment troop funds. At the end of 1924, Sergeant-Instructor Austin retired having been a popular and respected figure in the school since 1884, setting high examples of fitness and integrity. His punishment drills were an institution, boys alternately running and marching around the quad for half an hour, encouraged by his light cane. Sadly he could not adjust to life without the school and took his own life only a few months later. The 1925 magazine contained a seven-page obituary of Sir Rider Haggard (he was knighted in 1912), who had been throughout his adult life such a friend of the school. That December, an Ipswich School Club was founded for parents, OIs and senior pupils to enjoy social and improving activities on Saturday evenings at the school. It flourished under that name until 1934, when the change of name to The Ipswich School Night Club was thought 'very unfortunate and unsuitable'; it soon became the Ipswich School Arts Society.[2] When Miss Hunt died in 1926, her obituary recalled her abhorrence of seeing boys with hands in their pockets. She would order them to be sewn up and checked that they had been. She used to sit for hours on end on a hard seat in the Lime avenue watching the cricket. Her unmarked memorial is the oak desk-lectern in chapel, more often chosen than the pulpit by preachers.

Expeditions at home and abroad were a new feature of school life. Sherwood took the sixth form to Paris, Versailles and Vimy Ridge at Easter 1925, and urged parents to open a Savings Bank Account to pay for their sons to join him in the Low Countries: Bruges, Ghent, Antwerp, Louvain and the battlefields of Waterloo and Ypres. At the total eclipse on 29 June 1927, sev-

2   It was, however, the Night Club again which staged *Trial by Jury* in 1934.

enty boys paid 18s 6d for a train journey to Leyburn in North Yorkshire to experience '23 seconds of darkness'. Not all were impressed, feeling that they might have seen more at the Picture House for sixpence. Looking ahead to 1999, the account went on 'Undoubtedly aircraft will be chartered, the journey will lack fatigue owing to its short duration; our children's children will rise above all obstruction. The corona will be seen; the clouds will be conquered'. At the end of the 75-year Interdict silently placed on Ipswich in 1851, Prince Henry of Gloucester opened the Gainsborough Exhibition at Christchurch Mansion on 7 October 1927 and visited the school afterwards. That term, Jennings left for Marlborough, and a housemastership three years later, but Stanley Pink arrived, whose schoolboy performance as Henry IV in 1924 while unwell had drawn real tears from some of the audience. He was successively master, chaplain from 1931, and, when archdeacon of Hampstead in the 1960s, a governor.

At the 1929 OI Dinner, Rowley Elliston, in toasting 'The School – Past', made some succinct retrospective judgements worth recording. He recalled that Fenwick was unusual, for it was said of him that he spent far more of his own money on the school than he ever drew from the governors. Elliston's own headmaster, Dr Holden, assembled a remarkable staff and was the best scholar ever associated with the school. Browne was not a good scholar but probably our best ever administrator. In the last thirty years the school had produced presidents of the Royal Academy (Poynter), of the Royal Society (Sherrington), and of the British Medical Association (William Elliston), a High Court Judge (Lord Roche), and a Lieut-General (Alderson) who commanded a Division in the Great War. Nine of his contemporaries at School were knighted. The renowned yachtsman, Sir William Burton, immediately responded that at school he was a dunce, and lazy, but one thing he had – character. He wished that he could tell the masters to come down from their exalted level to that of the dullest boy. "Do that and you never need repeat yourself, for he will understand." This is perhaps the earliest one-line teachers' training course.

The Classicist Norman Stonex was made Broke housemaster and the chemist Tom Glover given Holden to run in 1929. Hard on their heels came T. B. 'Poppa' Job and then James Young to run Rigaud and help Hugh Gleave with the rugby. These men were the backbone of the school staff until the 1960s.

Reading the exchange of compliments between Sherwood and his powerful chairman Burton on public occasions, it is clear that this headmaster was a diplomat determined to avoid the fate of so many of his predecessors. But in 1930, there were only eight OIs up at Oxford and just three at Cambridge. The school was not achieving the highest academic successes in proportion to the greater numbers of pupils. Admittedly, one of the light blue trio was Charles Frank, later professor and FRS, and another, George Notcutt, who made an enormous contribution to the life of the school as boy and master, particularly as second master under two heads. He was particularly good at welcoming OIs and keeping them interested in the school.

In 1932, new oak panelling of the chapel chancel was dedicated, that on the south side in memory of H. C. Lawrence, the friend and colleague Sherwood had brought from Ramsgate to teach Classics. When the next year Sherwood announced his voluntary retirement (a luxury denied to every head since Ingram), there was genuine disappointment and warm appreciation of his work. Both governors and head commented on the pleasantness of their relations. Chairman Bunnell 'I was born to command' Burton must have mellowed since he removed two headmasters from office: Raynor in 1906 and Watson in

1918. The magazine editorial mentioned 'very real and sincere regret' at losing a head who had encouraged so many fresh interests and brought the school all-round success. Sherwood had been invited by the archbishop to prepare candidates for ordination in a Canterbury 'peculiar', the living of Whittlesford in Cambridgeshire. To assist him in founding St Andrew's college there he took with him the chaplain, Stanley Pink. 'I do not believe that a man contemplating Holy Orders should be above blacking his own boots and washing his own crockery', Sherwood told the OIs. The governors' minutes at the time contain a nice slip on the part of their clerk. 'Should the old boy Sir Charles Sherrington OM receive a letter of congratulation from the board on winning a Noble prize?'

A pioneering drama tour to Germany in January 1933, with performances of Shaw's *St Joan* in Trier, Aachen, Bielefeld, Brunswick and Hamburg, should have added lustre to Sherwood's last year, but an equally unprecedented outbreak of pupil politics somewhat marred his pleasure in the event. A promising sixth form scientist, Robert Haward,[3] resigned from the OTC as a pacifist gesture before going on tour with the cast. The whole company so enjoyed the hospitality they received that they could not imagine another war with Germany, particularly so soon after the horrors which they had been told about as children. A debate was held at the first Literary and Dramatic Society after the cast's return on the motion which had already caused a stir at the Oxford Union: 'That this House will under no circumstances fight for King and Country'. Dewandeler,[4] who

---

3 Haward went up to Queens' College, Cambridge, with State and Open Scholarships, to take Firsts in both parts of the Natural Sciences Tripos and a PhD. He later held a chair at Birmingham.

4 His endowed award is remembered at Commemoration of Benefactors in March each year.

wrote up the tour for the magazine, was the proposer and Woolner (Archbishop of Rheims in the play) opposed. Haward pointed out that 'he was an internationalist by nature and by profession', and Langdon, later a governor, opposed particularly the words 'in no circumstances'. Rowan-Robinson, for the proposal, quoted freely and skilfully from Shaw. The motion was carried by 16 votes to 5, much to Sherwood's dismay. Of course, the events of the later 1930s changed the balance of views almost universally, and hundreds of OIs fought in the second War, some giving their lives. Nevertheless, since about thirty German newspapers gave long and glowing accounts of the tour, a quarto booklet of reminiscences by members of the party was published in celebration.

Munro Cautley's Sherwood classrooms on two storeys facing the field across quite a wide parade ground were taken into use in January 1934 without any ceremony. They were described by some of their first occupants as rooms with 'windows that opened and doors that shut'. Compared with the former hut classrooms, this was no doubt true but it made a vast difference when the three entrances were filled in with double doors and the semicircular openings on the first floor were glazed in the 1980s. Then at last the school had a memorial range worthy of headmaster Sherwood, who, as the Performance chapter shows, brought real music and fully staged plays to the school.

XVIII

Truman Tanqueray

Daunted by difficulties, 1933–1950

Tanqueray, wounded in the First World War, had to run the school during the difficult days of the Second. When the governors took the drastic step of turning the school fully independent in 1945, it is not surprising that, by then, he lacked the vision and the energy necessary to take it forward.

TRUMAN TANQUERAY began his headship in the summer term of 1933, chosen from about 140 applicants. The governors decided to advertise the salary at £1,100 per annum, less one hundred pounds to cover the twin benefits of free accommodation and the profit on boarding. The Board of Education felt that this was too generous but the  governors stuck to their guns. After Tonbridge and Magdalene College, Cambridge, Tanqueray taught at Eastbourne for three years, before joining the Queen's Royal West Surrey Regiment at the outbreak of the First War but was soon wounded at Gheluvelt. When recovered, he commanded a company of No 13

Officer Cadet Battalion, for which he was mentioned in despatches. Returning to Eastbourne in 1919, he founded Pennell House and the Rowing Club and retired from commanding the OTC after eleven years with the rank of major.

This was the first time in the school's history that a change of head took place without a major exodus of staff; from then on masters had a loyalty to the school and each other which depended less on who was in charge. A popular, but perhaps unwise reform, was the immediate abandonment of three-weekly orders by which Sherwood kept a check on boys' progress. The new chaplain was J.G.T. Castle, not often allowed to preach if the headmaster was available, perhaps an early sign of Tanqueray's leaning towards ordination. Charles Mollard and J.H.S. Smitherman (later head at Woolverstone Hall) were lively new recruits. The latter was the first to introduce community service; with boy volunteers he organised the Pottery Street Boys' Club, mainly for sporting contests. Boxing was surprisingly popular with both groups, even though the school usually prevailed. When Pottery Street was demolished the families living there were relocated to the Gainsborough estate which gave the club a new name. One sign of the fine *esprit de corps* in the Common Room was that, when *Trial by Jury* was staged in 1934, the headmaster joined all the senior men in the jury with Mollard as foreman.[1] T.G Powell retired after running the prep for 22 years; it was ornithology and his fine bird photographs that had earned him the nickname 'Polly'.

---

1 The jury photograph really belongs in Performance, but is shown on the next page as a common room group: *From the left*: Barton (pupil), Tanqueray, Legh, Gleave, Grimwade, Job, Rose (pupil), Stonex, Castle (chaplain), Young, Glover, Smitherman and Mollard. Mollard and Ken Seacome, who came the next year, each retired after long service at RHS Holbrook, did fine work as the school's first honorary archivists in the 1980s.

In 1935, Sir Percy Everett OI, Baden Powell's right hand man and later Deputy Chief Scout, began to take an interest in the school, joining the governors in time to succeed Burton as chairman when the latter died in 1943. At Everett's OI dinner as president of the club, held at the Mayfair Hotel in London, the three most recent heads were present. Peter Brunt won a State Scholarship and an open Classical scholarship to Oriel,  Oxford. He became Camden Professor of Ancient History, an F.B.A., and was a governor at the 1972 headship appointment. Another OI died, leaving it to his widow to summon expert help to investigate mounds in their field, now internationally renowned as Sutton Hoo Burial Ground. [2]

---

2   The sporting farmer, Lieut. Colonel Frank Pretty (at school 1890–91), died on 28 December 1934 on his 56th birthday. His widow Edith called in Basil Brown from the museum to investigate the mounds visible from their windows which had so long intrigued them. Sutton Hoo, for ever a national treasure, owes something therefore to an Old Ipswichian who chose not to plough his field too deeply.

Magazine editorials contained rumblings of impending war but this did not prevent the staff and boys from staging

J.T.C.

The Mikado. Newsletters from Oxford and Cambridge OIs appeared regularly in the magazine; for the first time one arrived from those studying at London University. From 1938 and throughout the war, the magazine's presentation was enlivened by the cartoon headpieces Ken Seacome drew for every regular feature. By 1954, when they were dropped and 'bled-off' photographs became more numerous, their humour had worn thin.[3]

Martin Squirrell's full-page drawing of the Narvik set a precedent for reproducing pupils' work. His artist father Leonard made the pen-and-ink drawing of the main entrance (ivy-clad once more) which became the frontispiece of the magazine; it was also adopted by the *Old Ipswichian Magazine* from its inception in 1953. When in 1940 *Charley's Aunt* was chosen as festive fare on stage, action shots appeared in the magazine where previously only group photographs of successful elevens and fifteens had been seen.

In 1937, it was decided to replace Holden's pavilion; Cautley waived his fees for designing the handsome timber-framed and

---

3 They were given another airing in the 1999 *Ipswichian* looking fresh and funny again.

cedar-tiled building and loyal OIs raised the cost of £1,100.[4] In 1938, the legendary Roly Slator retired[5] and Hugh Grimwade took his place as Second Master. George Notcutt joined the staff that year. The next year Gleave took over the Prep from Moir who had run it for five years but, a term later, went to the war, during which J. G. Taplin took charge.

Despite the outbreak of hostilities, a finely-equipped new Gymnasium next to the Sherwood building came into use in 1940. Because the tower of the school was thought to be a land-mark for enemy bombers, numbers fell and families evacuated, the boarders dwindling to a handful. For the same reason, and because space was so limited, no other school was sent here for the duration. Tanqueray, who had been a good tennis and fives player, now took up golf and became a great walker. Changing his mortar board for a tin helmet, the head-cum-housemaster

4 The pavilion was extended and refurbished in 2000 and OIs and friends gave over half the cost. Cyril Perkins, shortly to be 90, performed the reopening ceremony.

5 He and his wife spent much of their retirement in Minneapolis with their children. The silver cross in chapel was Mrs Slator's memorial, and the chalice and paten added when he died a widower in 1949. The Slator library came in 1951.

led the firewatching team of masters and senior boys. A Savings Association and a Rabbit Club now became fashionable school activities.

One can picture the finely-furnished drawing room in School House (since 1972 the main common room) and family portraits lined the walls of the dining room opposite. An Anderson shelter was built in the garden, chickens were kept and tomatoes grown in front of the Preparatory School. The family slept in a ground floor room fortified with stout beams. Alice Tanqueray provided meals for the whole establishment from meagre rations,[6] even running a canteen for troops, with help from masters' wives. Lonely soldiers and sailors were welcomed to family meals and, when one Christmas the Poles in Ipswich wished to celebrate their freedom to continue the war effort, they were given the use of the Dining Hall. When School prefects were invited for formal supper after Sunday chapel, the ice was broken by games organised by Alice.

In 1943, Sir Bunnell Burton died after 38 years as chairman of governors and Everett took over in time to prepare for the most crucial decision ever made in the schools' long history. He was in failing health and had to resign before the end of 1945. He was greatly assisted, however, by Richard Brook, who had arrived as bishop of St Edmundsbury and Ipswich in 1941. Having been principal of Liverpool College for nine years after the first war, Brook had an absorbing interest in schools and their management and he joined the governing body as the Oxford University representative just as the school's status changed. When he took his turn as visiting governor he brought a

---

6 Her shopping list, which somehow fell into the prefects' hands, included the item '5lbs of the cheapest possible fish' – for the boarders' Friday supper, of course.

head's-eye view to his tours of the school and always discussed current problems at length with the head.[7]

After VE-day, it took only two months to arrange a general election and Attlee succeeded Churchill as Prime Minister. The new Labour Government made haste to reorganise secondary education nationally on the lines of 1944 Education Act. The school had a difficult choice. It could become just one of the maintained secondary schools in Ipswich but in that case the Prep would have to close. It could apply for the Direct Grant, a new scheme whereby the Ministry would pay agreed fees at independent schools for half the intake, the remainder paying full fees but for them the school would receive £16 per head towards running costs. Almost every parent, and the borough council, supported the school's application but the minister, Ellen Wilkinson, turned it down, refusing to reconsider her decision or to give her reasons. Woodbridge School and Framlingham College, the only providers of secondary education in their areas, were accepted as Direct Grant schools. In Ipswich, however, the minister preferred the Northgate Schools to expand to provide free grammar places for the abler children of the town. Full independence was the only realistic option for the school, and, with the support of four-fifths of the parents, this is what the governors decided before the year was out.[8] In the longer run, it was fortunate that Miss Wilkinson ruled as she did. Many Direct Grant schools, whose fee increases were liable to be pegged by government, found themselves unable to provide new facilities or to maintain their buildings properly.

---

7 Andrew Cockrill (1948-1956) has gathered pupils' account of the war years for a booklet which he plans to publish.

8 A.L. Clouting was the only governor who abstained from the final decision. A Labour councillor who gave long and loyal service to the governing body, he was renowned for travelling to meetings by bicycle.

When the scheme was abolished in 1976, D.G. schools had some catching up to do relative to their fully independent neighbours. For over thirty years, Ipswich was the only fully-independent day-and- boarding school in the county. Although Ipswich education authority ceased taking up places in the school, an arrangement with East Suffolk continued, whereby able boys from an area north of the town and others from the Shotley peninsula could win free places. There were casualties from the doubling of the current fees and the parents of 65 boys from 58 families applied for assistance. More than 50 boys were helped to complete their course but some of the others had to move schools. Two important intentions expressed at the last meeting of 1945 took an incredible 27 years to be implemented: the taking over by the governing body of financial responsibility for boarding and catering and the provision of a new residence for the headmaster.[9]

After the war, reparations were needed inside and out at the school – trenches to be filled in and shelters dismantled on school field – and on 'Top' field there were arguments with the War Office over the cost (nearly £3,000) of removing wartime concrete obstructions. A substantial command post and four gun emplacements had been built on the northern part of the field and rugger posts were put up at random to make it difficult for aircraft to land on the field. Rugby practices sometimes involved the soldiers who manned the guns, their kit left on the touchline in case duty called. But now masters returned from active service and others moved to new posts elsewhere. The long-serving Stanley Wilson moved to Dulwich College and Osborne succeeded him, refounding choirs which had been

---

9 The long run of vellum-covered minute books ended abruptly, the new volumes being bound in half red morocco with green cloth sides. The clerk's copper plate script had given way to typewriting in 1934.

silent for the duration. Bill Potter, author of the post-1800 part of the 1950 history, was an able but temporary addition to the Physics department. An appeal for funds to support the school's new status and the formation of the Friends of Ipswich School brought in the magnificent sum of £21,000 by July 1946.

One of the school's most pressing needs was a better Great School but that was still a decade away. Martin Squirrell's drawing of assembly in the old Big School is a precious record, showing the senior boys occupying the raked 'chicken perches' at the back. He also drew one of James Young's lessons from memory (above) and his peer group showering after games (see page 264). Speech Days now needed a larger venue and the Public Hall in Westgate Street served in 1946 and 1947 but burnt down before the 1948 ceremony. The minister and deacons of Burlington Baptist Church in London Road came to the rescue, generously allowing the school to hold the first of ten Speech Days there. It was the clerk to the governors, rather than the headmaster, who had to work through lists of possible guest speakers before one accepted. Lunch for the guests in 1946 was held at the Great White Horse, rather than in School House, but Mrs Tanqueray earned the governors' gratitude for providing it the next year. In 1949, the Head Boy's Latin greeting to the guest was repeated in English for the benefit of all but those who taught Classics.

In 1947, Watson and Sherwood died, and tributes to both men appeared in the magazine. The Gables, formerly the Notcutt family home, was purchased that year to accommodate the Prep, freeing the 1908 building for the sixth form. Mollard and Seacome moved to Holbrook and Bill Dodd, who made Ipswich history an important part of the course, and the linguist Noel Sullivan took their places.

IN HONOUR OF

AUBERTIN. R.
BAILEY. R. A.
BENNEY. F. A.
BENTLEY. M.
BICKFRRDIKE. H. F.
BODIE. C. A. W.
BOOTH. P. D. S.
BOWMAN. R. J.
BREWSTER. C. R.
CASSON. S.
CATCHPOLE. D. E.
COBBOLD. J. M.
CROUCH. E. C.
EDGE. H. N.
ELDRIDGE. D.
FENN. G.
FREANE. A. A.
FRENCH. J. H. R.
FRIEND. J. F. A.
FROUD. R. F.
GOLDSMITH. A. L.
GREENFIELD. R. L.
HARVEY. W. M.
HICKINBOTHAM. H. G.
HUNT. H. N.
HUNT. J. W.
JARVIS. P. G. V.
KENNARD. J. H.
LAMBERT. E. C.
LIVINGSTONE. J. D. W.
WORRALL. C. C.

LOW. J. N. A.
McNAMARA. S. R.
MALONE. L. F.
MILLS. H. P.
MOFFAT. D. R.
PALMER. D. C.
PELLS. P. H.
PLATTEN. D. J.
PLATTEN. H. W.
ROWBOTHAM. W. D.
SAWARD. J. F.
SHAW. W.
SLATER. H. J. M.
SPRUYTENBURG. R. F.
STAMMERS. H. J.
STONE. G. C. W.
SWAIN. A. P.
SYMPSON. J. P.
THORPE. D. S.
THOWLESS. W.
TREHEARNE. R. H. M.
TUFFEN. D. P.
VAN DEN HEI. DEN. J. P. M.
WALTON. M. P.
WARD. R. E.
WARD. W. A.
WARD. W. P.
WEST. D. E.
WHITMORE. J. N.
WILSON. P. W. C.
WOOTTON. R. B.

EDWARDS. R.

THE WORLD WAR
1939 – 1945

There were five Ipswichians up at Oxford and ten at Cambridge, some of them mature men finishing their studies after seeing action. Brigadier Hossack OI unveiled a plain Second War memorial facing its First War equivalent in the Browne chapel transept. 63 Ipswichians had given their lives in this conflict out of some 675 combatants from the school, 143 of them casualties. Lieutenant J.N.A. Low RN was posthumously awarded the George Cross and Lt M.W. Griffiths received the George Medal.

Although the war had ended, many years of austerity stretched ahead. Grand plans to celebrate the centenary of the school's move to Henley Road in 1852 were discussed, perhaps a visit by the Duke of Edinburgh; later it was decided that this might imply that the school was only a century old. Irvine Gray pointed out that the school had no right to the arms it had used since the 1870s but could not persuade the governors to pay some £300 to set matters in order. A metal Chubb safe to store the school's archives would cost £100, so instead they were put in a wooden chest in the Town Hall strong room. Luckily, the governors did afford the fertilisers Fisons recommended for use on Top field. Their clerk was not sorry to be relieved of his duties when the School's first bursar was appointed in late 1949. W.R. 'Bill' Shirley, an amiable and efficient Etonian, who kept a practised eye on school field cricket matches, began his duties just as Tanqueray was retiring. Four years after independence, a new school scheme was needed but the most the Ministry of Education would do was to agree the revised composition of the governing body. When the idea of two governors each from Oxford, Cambridge and London universities was mooted, the response from all but Cambridge was that it would be hard to recruit a second. Three governors are still appointed by Cambridge, reflecting the school's strongest university links throughout its history.

The modest and gentle Tanqueray was a popular headmaster, who led chiefly by example, but two world wars had taken their toll of him and he lacked the drive at the end of the second to take the School from its partial dependence on the local authority to full independence. Bishop Brook, who by then knew the head and the school well, recognised this and suggested ordination, to which Tanqueray readily agreed. He was made deacon in September 1949 and served as a part-time assistant curate at the Tower church. As priest the following year, the bishop made him curate-in-charge of Hintlesham and instituted him to the rectory of Hintlesham with Chattisham a year later. Retiring to Sussex, he died four years later, aged 71, in 1960. At Charterhouse in July 1972, at the celebration of the centenary of that school's move from the City to Godalming, the author had hoped to meet Alice Tanqueray (then living at Peaslake), but in a crowd of several thousand failed to do so. By 1978, Alice was too frail to leave an account of their Ipswich time herself; instead their daughter Judith wrote interestingly about school and family life. Alice Tanqueray read the draft and commented "just say: he never interfered". One colleague wrote of 'his mild and humane rule... the School was in low water financially and much of his time was clouded with the sorrows and anxieties of war, yet for all that the School was a happy place. He stood for something which we all valued...'. The photograph Alice Tanqueray took of her husband with

their five children outside School House at the outbreak of war seems to illustrate this well. David stands behind Anne, whose twin Judith is on the far right. Their father holds Philippa, with Clare on his left.

The small blue note-book titled 'T.T. to P.H.F.M.: A few notes to tell you what have been my practices', intended to ensure a smooth handover to his successor, cer-

T.T.
to
P.H.F·M .

A few notes to tell you what have been some of my practices.

tainly confirms that Tanqueray worked by delegation. He was, however, totally supportive to his loyal lieutenants but felt the need to fill no more than twelve small sides of paper with notes in his neat round hand. The clergy of the parishes of boys to be confirmed were invited to attend the service robed. 'N.B. Some clergy are inclined to be jealous of the school claiming the boys, even sometimes when they do not know them, even by name.' In the Triangular Sports, 'Perse and Hampton Grammar School are due to come here in 1951 – Glover organises all this: some difficulty arises over lunching so many'. At the School Sports, 'Glover arranges & will ask you to find some Lady to present Cups from Pavilion. The Head of School returns thanks to her.' On Speech Day 'After Hymn (in deference to our Baptist hosts who request that every meeting in the chapel shall contain a hymn or prayer), the Head of School welcomes the Distinguished Guest in Latin (Young is responsible for the text).' 'Parents are advised of this special opportunity of seeing masters. Job is responsible for distribution of tea; Grimwade arranges final clear-up during last period; Notcutt for putting out seats and chairs; Osborne for organ and hymn.' 'Prize poems and a Choral display have latterly been dropped. Proceedings in [the Baptist] chapel should not much exceed an hour.' There are clear indications about who will foot the various bills. On 'OI Day, whole day cricket match, buffet tea (OI Club pays).' 'Grimwade organises Exams.' 'Prep Speech Day – arranged by Gleave.' A copy of the folded sheet prospectus printed in blue, with minimal information, is pasted in after the notes peter out. 'A new one is necessary but the expense of production has continually postponed it. It may be better to forgo photographs in the new edition, as they are the chief cost.' But there were none in the specimen and this was a school five years into independence, surviving on the meanest and dreariest sheet, omitting even the names of the staff. A new headmaster with clear vision and strong drive was now urgently needed and the man chosen arrived ready to grasp the challenge; in short, he saved the school.

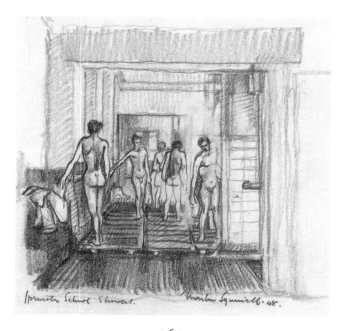

XIX

Patrick Hassell Frederick Mermagen
Embracing independence, 1950–1972

Arriving five years after the school's change to independence, Mermagen had the energy and drive necessary to make up for lost time, to raise standards and to innovate. His experiences as a boy at Sherborne and a master at Radley informed his aims for the school, although it would always be a flourishing day-school with a minority of boarders. It is no exaggeration to state that the school today owes its survival to PHFM.

BISHOP BROOK, who had been a governor since the decision was made to embrace independence in 1945, became vice-chairman early in 1949, and was therefore a most influential member of the subcommittee charged with finding a new headmaster for September 1950. The advertisement for an Oxford or Cambridge graduate under forty-five drew seventy applications. Tanqueray and the clerk, Frank Tempest, selected 25 names for the subcommittee to consider. Three laymen from Rugby, Loretto and Radley and two clerics from Sedbergh and Rossall were given individual tours of the school, and Mrs Tanqueray showed them School House before their interviews. The full board met only Peel from Rossall and Mermagen from Radley but the former withdrew and was still running his boarding-house ten years later. Since Mermagen was the favourite with most of the selectors, he was appointed without further ado. A good deal of work was done on the house and school between the appointment in March and the arrival of the new head who, as an indication of the governors'

sense of urgency for change, was made welcome at all governors' meetings in the interim.

Patrick Mermagen was 38 and the son of a headmaster. After Sherborne he won an open scholarship in mathematics at Pembroke College, Cambridge. He taught at Loretto for six years, then moved to Radley in 1939, only a year before joining the Royal Berkshire Regiment, serving in India and at the Staff College, Camberley. Back at Radley in 1946 as senior mathematics master,  he helped his pupils to conspicuous academic success and with skill and enthusiasm coached rugby (especially the three-quarters) and cricket (calling out 'Get your feet there!' in the nets) and, in 1948, took command of the Cadet Force. A talented cricketer, who had played for Somerset, he made an instant impression at Ipswich by scoring 68 for the Mistics against the OIs in the August 1950 Cricket week. There were three sons and a daughter in the Mermagen family. Sadly, Mrs Mermagen died in 1953 and it was twelve years before the head married again. He and Inge Schütt (of Hamburg) had a son and daughter, both of whom spent some years in the school. The new headmaster found 529 boys in the school but only 28 in the lower sixth and 18 in the upper. He had 40 boarders in School House and there were 33 in Junior House under the outwardly intimidating but fundamentally warm-hearted Tom and Rena Glover.

Change in the new era came at a cracking pace. To remedy the complete absence of Biology, the conversion of the old gym to a laboratory was urgent but new building in post-war Britain needed a licence and that meant a year's delay. Perhaps linked to this lack of freedom of action to provide new facilities, there were rules against a school making a 'profit' on the fees. It has always been essential to budget for a surplus as the only equitable way of maintaining and developing independent schools. 23 Holly Road was purchased as a chaplain's house for the Revd Ronald Jones, just appointed. The OIs were grateful to be invited by the Mermagens to hold their annual dinners in the dining hall, still very much the head's own territory. As part of the Ipswich pageant in the Festival of Britain the school agreed to re-enact the 1851 foundation stone-laying, but in Christchurch Park. Boys uncomfortable in Eton jackets with stiff collars were delighted to give three cheers for the master playing Prince Albert at the end of the ceremony. Peter Marsden, regular producer of school plays since 1948, directed this scene.

Noel Sullivan had given careers advice since shortly after his arrival but the school now joined the Public Schools Appointments Board. Help was readily available from the many well-established engineering firms in the town. Allan and Percy Leggett, who ran their late father Arthur Leggett's

firm 'E. R. and F. Turner', now became ever more generous school benefactors. Allan, who became a governor in 1974, remembered that Sherwood had discouraged their father from sending them to the school ('we do not prepare boys for engineering'); there was a similar response from Tanqueray when Allan came to enter his elder son. In the light of these incredible gaucheries, the Leggett benefactions seem all the more remarkable. The governors agreed that £125 could be spent on a new prospectus, money well-spent through Geoffrey Smith, a director of W.S. Cowell Ltd, colour printers, a new governor in 1951 and a persuasive chairman of the appeal committee. The resulting brochure was the first of many stylish pieces of printing which Cowells designed for the school. There was talk of a register of Ipswichians through the ages, something which Morfey compiled and the headmaster's secretary published in-house much later.[1] With OI Club assistance, a room to the west of the Holden Library was furnished to become the Slator Library. In a strange attempt to provide heraldry for the non-armigerous, the ends of three double-sided bookcases were embellished with the arms of the schools and colleges of the

---

1 *An Alphabetical List of Ipswichians...* listing known arrivals up to 1857 (1976); revised and enlarged 1988.

three headmasters Watson, Sherwood and Tanqueray to commemorate their service to the school.[2] The headmaster made a
case for the appointment of a full-time director of music and
John Ince arrived from Felsted. His chief interest lay in the
chapel music and in rescuing and rebuilding organs. Sixteen
scarlet cassocks, the gift of Mr and Mrs Allan Leggett, added
colour and to the appeal of singing in the chapel choir.[3] In the
Summer term boys could wear blazers with the school arms on
the pocket and seniors were encouraged to wear boaters with
regulation ribbons.

The first service of Commemoration of Benefactors, an
annual event at the Tower church ever since, was held on 7 July
1951 to mark the centenary of the Henley Road buildings. Bishop Brook was the preacher and the collection was for the redec-
oration of the chapel, by then long overdue. On Speech Day the
Rt Hon Richard Stokes MP, Lord Privy Seal, was the guest and
Wallace Morfey arranged an exhibition to illustrate the
school's history. It was suggested that a plaque be placed on
Felaw's House in Foundation Street; if it was, it did not save the
1483 school from demolition in 1963. That February, Sir Percy
Everett died and a memorial window with scouting badges and
knots was put in north of the altar.

2 It was easy enough to persuade former pupils of Watson to help but harder to
raise a similar sum for Sherwood. The Caen stone fireplace, with carved school
arms, was the gift of a stone mason parent, G.R. Saunders. Unfortunately, the Slator
Library always afforded the most direct route from the main entrance to chapel, so
that it was used as a passage at certain times. The permanent change to a passage
came when the new library was opened in 1980 and the bookcases were transferred
there (against the wishes of Birkin Haward the architect, who wanted only modern
furniture). The physics room adjoining the Slator extension was enlarged retaining
a showcase facing the fireplace which is always full of interesting exhibits.
3 Strictly the colour should only be worn by the choirs of the Chapels Royal but,
since 1981, when the Sovereign again became Visitor, it may certainly be deemed
appropriate.

Sir Charles Sherrington OM died in March; as the discoverer of the physiology of the brain, for which he had received a Nobel Prize in 1932, he was certainly the most eminent Ipswichian since Thomas Wolsey.

Another governor who understood schools joined the board in December 1950 and soon made his mark. He was the Hon. George Lyttelton, a retired Eton master living at Grundisburgh. Like the Bishop, he gave the new headmaster strong support and was ready to judge public speaking contests, to propose votes of thanks or stand in should a speech day speaker be prevented; he was guest of honour himself in 1952[4] and persuaded his elder brother, Viscount Cobham, to be the guest in 1955. That literary masterpiece in six volumes, published long after his death, *The Lyttelton Hart-Davis Correspondence*, contains several of his uncharitable comments about Ipswichians and Woodbridgians, which, had he been alive at the editing stage, he would surely have eliminated. It was the custom for scripts of the headmaster's Speech Day reports to be issued to prefects and senior masters on the day, with one and two asterisks indicating applause and more applause and 'groan' where that response was required. After the second Commemoration service, the bishop of Peterborough opened the Sherrington laboratories, one for chemistry

---

4 Lyttelton, an early defender of the purity of the English language, could surely have cited better examples than 'barber' better than 'appearance engineer', and 'working a lift' better than 'operating an elevator'. He was a governor for 12 years, and died in 1962.

on the site of the old fives courts and one for biology in the former gym.

Growing numbers causing overcrowding in chapel made an extension to the west desirable but, in July 1952, the roof of the old great school was discovered to be rotten, putting it completely out of action. A new building, preferably of twice the size, was urgently needed and various sites were considered. The first idea, fortunately soon dismissed, was to widen the hall on its western side and give it a new roof. When Martin Slater and his partner Birkin Haward took over from Cautley as school architects, they suggested building a hall over the swimming pool, and Haward produced deceptively attractive impressions of what could be done. Thoughts then turned to the Holly Road/Ivry Street corner and Martin Squirrell drew a hall presenting a long side to the field where the 1958 Great School and 1966 Fison classrooms stand. There is no doubt that the final solution, agreed in 1955, was the best but it is regrettable that the bas relief frieze of youthful figures which Haward envisaged was replaced by yet another representation of the school arms. Other images are more appropriate to a post-armigerous age.

In 1952, the historian Bill Dodd left for Tanganyika, to be succeeded by Peter Hill, a man of great wisdom, integrity and many talents. Dr Brook took over the chairmanship of governors from Charles Grimwade, who had succeeded Everett in 1946 but was now in poor health. Societies with names like the Jeremy Collier (philosophy and theology), Barclay Head (archaeology), the Bee-Keepers (meteorology) and the Athenaeum grew up and flourished, and there were even two clubs for puppets and marionettes. The first junior plays were staged in 1953. The training corps, now a cadet force – the CCF – did well but the major sports rugby and cricket were central to school life for all right-thinking members of the school. Walter 'Bunny' Howe retired, having been caretaker (and latterly laboratory assistant) since 1905. The eccentric Ramsey Wherrett, who now taught art full-time in 33 Henley Road, had a painting in the Royal Academy Summer Exhibition in 1953. He was prepared to listen to boys who found it harder than others to fit in, at a time before chaplains had developed their pastoral roles. That autumn term, the magazine lost its OI section to a new annual *Old Ipswichian Magazine*, impeccably edited for its first fourteen years by Wallace Morfey. Continuing appeals, with objects varied enough to interest the whole spectrum of friends of the school, drew numerous OIs to school and club functions – 82 dined at the 1953 Ipswich dinner.

In September 1953, the academic year began with 623 pupils, including 197 in the Prep, and there were ninety boarders. The school was moving towards three streams and Westwood House in Constitution Hill, its lodge and grounds of six acres, was acquired for £4,500. At first it was planned to use it for middle-school boarders aged 11 to 14 but it was soon needed for 13 to 18 year-olds on a par with School House and Peter and Constance Marsden were its founders. For some reason, the Lower VI became the Remove. That November the school had its first full inspection since 1931 but the report by ten HMIs concentrated more on statistics than on anything they had witnessed in classrooms. The sixth form had grown from 25 to 57 since the last inspection (still too small) and the proportion of boys living in the borough in the school had shrunk from three-quarters to one-half. In three years, the numbers taking A level had increased from 10 to 18 a year, at O level from 28 to 34. The school's record in open and state scholarships was respectable rather than distinguished. About one teacher to 18 pupils 'was not extravagant by public school standards' and 'The teaching strength was perhaps a bit thin in English and also in science and mathematics. Many of the staff were limited in experience to this school. Some recent appointments were quite promising, one or two not so'. The final meeting of the inspectors with the governors 'closed with mutual expressions of goodwill, cordiality and gratitude'.

Kay Foster, the Prep musician (who later married John Raffe OI), was presenting the weekly 'Time and Tune' on the BBC Schools Programme. With her coaching, Prep boys sang in the first Aldeburgh recording of Britten's cantata *St Nicholas*.

In 1954, Bishop Brook retired from the diocese to live in Grasmere, handing over the chairmanship to Colonel Geoffrey Mason, whose elder brother Vice-Admiral Sir Frank, club president that year, was Engineer-in-Chief of the Fleet; both were OIs. Wallace Morfey became vice-chairman of governors and the new bishop, Dr Harrold Morris, became a governor, as have all his successors. Bishop Brook's scrawled letters to the headmaster had to be transcribed for him before they could be read.[5] He visited the school whenever he came back to Suffolk, and continued to give the headmaster strong support into the 1960s.

The entertainer Gillie Potter opened the 1954 school fete.[6] The old big school was now demolished, leaving ugly scars on the walls opposite the swimming bath. The honours boards which had lined its walls were thrown out and only one com-

5 The bishop apparently maintained that all great men: Shakespeare, Napoleon, Brook, etc wrote illegibly, forgetting that Michelangelo, many English monarchs and Palmerston had conspicuously fine hands. He also invited representative Ipswich and Woodbridge pupils to intimidatingly formal dinners at his palace in Park Road, afterwards beating them at Monopoly by insisting on remaining banker and exploiting that advantage.

6 Gillie Potter, a popular radio comedian of the 1930s and 1940s, was the creator of the fictional village of Hogsnorton, which inspired one of the movements of Percy Whitlock's 1937 *Wessex Suite*.

plete board and a few fragments were recovered in the 1980s. Fortunately the surviving complete board is the earliest, running from 1848 to 1870. It was found in appalling condition in a former chicken house at Westwood and was splendidly restored and mounted in the Dining Hall. With no Great School, plays had to be staged in the Garratt Memorial Hall in Bolton Lane or in the High Street Gallery next to the Museum using a temporary stage provided by George Pipe, a future chairman of governors. The enormous sum of £2,000 was subscribed towards the new hall at a single OI dinner. The physicist Charles Frank, a Sherwood pupil, became the latest Ipswichian FRS. With Rowley Elliston's death, the school lost a good friend and OI governor: a barrister, he had been Recorder of Great Yarmouth from 1913–51.

In 1956, the school had the first of its three Royal visits of the century, when the Duke of Edinburgh laid the foundation stone of the new Great School. He arrived by car from HMS Ganges where, coincidentally, the author was inspected amongst the junior officers. The Guard of Honour of the CCF (Major P.J. Hill commanding) was on parade in front of the main building.[7] Jeremy Barr, head of school, welcomed the duke in English rather than Latin by reading from a long illuminated scroll. After the ceremony the duke asked the headmaster for a whole holiday, 'preferably in term time', to mark the occasion. After displays of cricket, athletics and scouting, the duke visited the prefects in their room in Donachers. He admired the walls, papered with boys' lines and asked about the brass strip on the floor, where those in need of discipline 'toed the line'. He later observed that a boy was re-assembling a dinghy which he had been ordered to take to pieces for the occasion. 'What was the matter – didn't it float?', he asked. Cyril Perkins, head groundsman, was presented with the cricketers, as was the newest recruit to the common room, Ian Prior. He taught English and soon took over cricket and became a distinguished captain of the Suffolk county side.

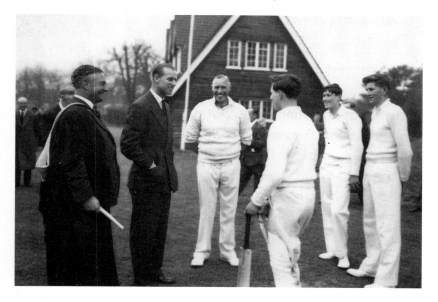

7 Before the visit, Allan Leggett thoughtfully presented new oak doors for the main entrance of the school. Apparently the existing white-painted doors looked as though they were more likely to fall apart than open.

While the Great School was under construction, new Physics labs on two floors filling the space left by the old hall were also being built, provided by a grant of £13,000 from the Industrial Fund for the Advancement of Science. Rather than try to match any of the three shades of red brick already in the quad and to avoid waiting for steel girders, Martin Slater unwisely chose a purple engineering brick which will neither fade nor blend. The school's hospitable Burlington Baptist friends allowed the tenth and final Speech Day to be held in their church on the 4 July 1958. Sir Hugh Beaver, Chairman of the Industrial Fund, opened all the new buildings that day. Martin Slater presented the school with stage curtains which, in textile collage, showed the buildings of the school from Felaw's House, the Cardinal College and the Blackfriars to those of 1851. They were very striking but more appropriate for some productions than others. Maisie Jenkins, wife of Cdr Owen Jenkins (Bursar 1967–82) and sometime relief day matron, worked hard to keep them going well into the 1980s. The house badges, carved in stone and mounted on the north wall of the great school, read from the left: School House, Broke, Holden, Rigaud, Sherrington and Felaw, with the Tudor rose of Westwood added last as it became a senior boarding house under 'Spud' Marsden.

276

On 27 November 1959, Bishop Brook wrote to the head-master from Grasmere:

> 'I have read the OI Magazine with immense pleasure. It is a first rate production. And how happy you must be in what it tells us of the School. How different a place from what it was when you came – new labs: new Great School: now the chapel extension. Numbers going up – 143 boarders: a large VI Form: good certificate results: a wonderfully good XV: flourishing societies, one of them even discussing the ethics of Artificial Insemination by Donor. When I was 16, I had only just abandoned the 'stork' view of the population problem. I thought the three letters from the Universities were excellent – they show you are 'turning out' educated people who know something of the writing of English – one of your old boys, I saw, had obtained a degree for an essay on the Quantum theory – so that not only English and general culture flourish, but even advanced mathematics.
> Well – I do congratulate you. May you continue to go forward. After all, nothing succeeds like success! You seem to have a good body of governors now. I remember the timid days when Grimwade was your chairman. I like to think that I helped to bridge the gap to the progressive policy which now prevails.'

The headmaster's reply praised the interest, ability and energy Morfey brought to editing the *OI Magazine*. He regretted that more scholarships were not being won and that some masters did not support chapel, soon to be extended – 'overcrowding will no longer be an excuse'. He continued: 'I often recall with gratitude the stand you made against the timid attitude of some of the governors ten years ago, and the steps you went to to ensure that you handed over to a regime which would be prepared to move with the times and to have vision and the courage to move forward towards establishing the School as an Independent Public School in the fullest sense of those words.' In his view, 'the school would not have Westwood, the new labs or even the Great School' without Richard Brook's lead years ago. The bishop had indeed played a decisive role in putting the school on its feet but so unobtrusively as to have passed notice until now.

In 1960, Ramsey Wherrett died while riding to school on his Vespa, and John Le Mare moved up from the Prep to take charge of senior school art. In his long career he coached all the major games, commanded the CCF, with his wife Rosemary ran the junior boarding house, succeeded George Notcutt as Head of the Lower School, and well into his retirement became the first non-OI to become President of the Club. A new chaplain, Bill Hussey, arrived that year just after the opening of the chapel extension and the Henry Willis organ brought from Sudbury and adapted to the new gallery. School summer fetes had raised a great deal of the cost. For seven years more one still had to leave the main building to reach the chapel. The first OI Ball was held and tickets sold rapidly. In 1961, 31 Henley Road was purchased from Allen Payne OI to complete the run of school buildings from Ivry Street to the Prep.[8]

In September 1962, Highwood House, with Ian and Marion Prior in charge, opened as the third senior boarding house opposite Westwood in Constitution Hill. Each house (even Junior House) had its own dining hall and meals were prepared, therefore, in four different kitchens around the school. If cook was absent, it fell to the lot of housemasters' wives to fill the gap. Boarder numbers were 169, divided between School 55, Westwood 50, Sherrington (in Highwood) 16 and Junior 48. There were 75 sons of OIs in the school in September 1963. The maximum boarder strength, 179, was reached six terms later.

---

8 Payne, who kept all his school reports and termly lists from Watson's time, presented them to the school archives.

In 1963, Richard Burnell joined the staff, soon to take charge of Classics and to defend them locally and nationally by his energy, originality and first class teaching; Cambridge continued to send him Dip.Ed. course Classicists long after the stream of other subject specialists ceased. He served on the Schools Council's consultative body for his subjects and devised the inter-school Ludi Scaenici competitions which brought costumed plays in Latin to the stage. Another arrival then was the mathematician and all-round sportsman Andrew Gregory, of whom more later. In 1964, Hugh Grimwade died just months before his pleasurably anticipated retirement. His 41 years' service had only confirmed Sherwood's wisdom in head-hunting him before his finals. A patient and effective teacher of Physics, he also served two headmasters as their deputy with high integrity and distinction. Latterly, his hearing deteriorated, but he still kept in touch with old boys and planned to do so in retirement. Cor Visser is shown finishing the masterly portrait he drew from photographs; it nevertheless does the subject full justice. In Grimwade's place the headmaster asked

Hugh Gleave to be second master as well as head of the Prep, to avoid, perhaps, promoting certain senior masters who might have been considered. This was not ideal, for Gleave had already been at the school since 1924 and, while he was an excellent and kindly head for the youngest boys, firm but totally fair, he was somewhat in awe of the older variety.[9] He retired with full honours in 1969, only to take charge of the 70s Appeal, which raised £120,000 by the time of the Royal Visit in 1973. He was succeeded by one of the greatest second masters, George Notcutt.

In 1965, James Young and 'Poppa' Job retired, each having given unstinting loyalty and total commitment to the school for over 35 years. At about this time, a few Chinese boys entered the school from Hong Kong. When the grandson of the shipping magnate, C.Y. Tung, shone through the school and at Cambridge Ipswich found that it had an unexpected cachet in the Far East. Never mind Eton, Ipswich, ahead of similar schools, was the favoured school for the sons of successful Hong Kong Chinese. Westwood, Highwood and, occasionally, Junior House had some delightful and talented boys well into the early 1980s.[10]

To celebrate the Quatercentenary of Elizabeth I's Charter a special service was held at the Tower Church on 18 March 1966 and loyal greetings were sent to HM The Queen who returned thanks and congratulations. To show the school to better effect and in time for the celebration, the entire Henley Road frontage from the main building to the Prep was opened up in a landscaping scheme which won a Civic Trust Award that year. The Fison building joined the Sherwood gymnasium to the Great

9 He is recalled telling the school awaiting the headmaster's arrival for assembly: 'If this sort of thing happens again, – or *many* more times...'
10 There was a revival of the Hong Kong link in the mid-90s which persists.

School, adding a foyer at ground level and six light classrooms above to the teaching accommodation. First impressions in the *OI Magazine* were remarkably penetrating: 'although from Ivry Street it fits tightly into the missing side of an open quadrangle and fits in with strength and felicity, from School Field it has a decidedly brutal appearance. Perhaps in the centuries ahead it will come to be accepted as symbolic, not so much of the Quatercentenary, as of the year of Vietnam, the race riots in Chicago and the murder of the three policemen.' For pupils, however, the new rooms were a great improvement over the draughty huts behind the pavilion which went out of use when deemed by the planners too close to Warrington Road.[11]

Two years later the antechapel was completed and at long last the 1852 chapel was properly joined to the 1851 school, with large built-in cupboards to house choir robes. The entrance doors bear full-length portraits of Thomas Wolsey and Thomas Cromwell in engraved glass, Wolsey for what he tried to do for the school and Cromwell for taking decisive action three years later to save it from extinction. The mayoralty of Wallace Morfey in 1970–71 was a triumph of stylish municipality entirely worthy of a more gracious age. The Mayor's Service was held, for the first and probably the last time, in the school chapel. As master of the Sproughton Foot Beagles he sometimes took parties of boys to follow the hunt.

Three more buildings were erected before the end of Patrick Mermagen's time: the Sixth Form Centre, the Leggett Technical Studies department and a fine first floor chemistry laboratory at the north end of the quad. The budget set did not allow Birkin Haward to do better with either the Fison Building or

11 A line was drawn some 138 feet from the road, to the west of which the school could never operate. Accordingly, all the land to the east of the line was quickly purchased and used.

281

the field corner additions. Certainly, the quality of the Sixth Form Centre, so prominent at the corner of the field, has long given cause for regret, in 2002 it was properly refurbished. The preservation of 'Donachers' within the Leggett Centre was a great mistake; on the clear site a considerably more useful building could have been constructed. It was the ultimate folly to leave woodworking in the first floor Manual around several corners from the new accommodation for work with metal, plastics and electronics, a fault which had urgently to be rectified by an addition built in 1973. The Duke of Edinburgh planned to visit during the summer of 1972 but a clash of dates with a State visit caused a year's postponement. It was unfortunate, therefore, that Patrick Mermagen was not then in post to welcome him and to show him the Great School, built on the foundation stone laid in 1957, and the new facilities for Engineering which Sir Frank Mason and the Leggetts had done so much to make possible.

One event of the final term made the front pages of the local papers. Before the whole-school photograph was taken, the headmaster was determined that all boys should appear with short hair. A few of the worst offenders were called to the study and sheared on the spot by a novice barber, the head himself. Some parents were outraged, others happy to have their sons (or other people's sons) disciplined. The National Council for Civil Liberties offered to take the matter up if they received complaints from parents or pupils. The punch-line of the Holly cartoon in the *Evening Star* was apocryphal: A freshly shorn boy came out of the study saying '...the worst part was when he said, "That'll be 25p, please".' After reading the news in the *Daily Telegraph*, one OI, lost in admiration, sent a donation to the current appeal.

The next month the Mermagens were given a standing ova-
tion at their last Speech Day, a deservedly splendid send-off to
their new home, the Old Rectory at Otley. Lord Belstead, good
friend and sometime governor of the school, was guest of honour and delighted the audience by announcing 'I've had my
hair cut'. In his twenty-two years[12] the headmaster had set
high standards, achieved growth from a two- to a four-form
entry and continued the building programme, whilst sport and
many other activities flourished. Twenty-seven years into
independence, the school stood on firm foundations from
which it would never look back. A fine team in the common
room awaited the new headmaster under whom entry standards at eleven, thirteen and sixteen were destined to rise.

The Rt Hon. Lord Belstead, Guy Pearsons (vice-chairman),
the Headmaster and Richard Cooper, Head of School.

12 George Notcutt worked out that successive heads from Browne to Mermagen
had served for 11, 12, 13, 14, 17, and 22 years respectively, challenging the
mathematicians to continue the series.

*Seven School Year-Books published between 1975 and
1994 provide a permanent record of staff and pupils over
two decades. This photograph appeared on the front cover
of the first.*

XX

John Marcus Blatchly
Encouraging breadth, 1972–1993

From 1972 onwards academic standards rose alongside a general broadening in other spheres. Minor sports came to share parity of esteem with major, and a wide range of activities was introduced. The cultural life of the school developed strongly. Able members of staff were ready and willing to embrace change. The Eighties Appeal enabled enthusiastic and far-sighted governors to provide the library range and other building continued during the whole period.

OF 111 CANDIDATES for the headmastership, eight men were interviewed at Fison's head office in Princes Street (another Birkin Haward building) on the morning of Leap Day 1972. In their turn they had a tour of the school with PHFM, and were shown the threadbare property in St Edmund's Road which would become home for one of them. As the bursar had lived upstairs, house and garden had been partitioned. In the main rooms downstairs there were piles of cricket and CCF equipment and some signs that class music had been taught there; the study by the front door was the Appeal Office. Continuing the longstanding East Anglian Puritan tradition, no hospitality was provided and each candidate was sent off into the town to find his own lunch and told to reappear at two o'clock, when the chairman, George Pipe, named three who should stay, while the rest left. At the school the full governing body was assembled to quiz the survivors, and things livened up. Bishop Leslie Brown, Professor Peter Brunt, and Geoffrey Smith (both

OIs) asked memorably searching questions, and the choice fell on the 39 year-old Dr John Blatchly educated at Sutton Grammar School, Surrey and Christ's College. He had taught chemistry and run science at three schools: King's, Bruton, Eastbourne College and Charterhouse, and was the first chemist to be awarded a Cambridge Ph.D. under new regulations allowing the submission of published research. The work had been carried out in school laboratories with the active and acknowledged participation of senior pupils. At Charterhouse, Blatchly had been much involved with music, run the licensed Sixth Form Club, was joint Librarian with the head of history and Secretary of the Addison and Steele Essay Society. At Ipswich he would teach as much chemistry as time allowed and made no secret of his sporting shortcomings, and was therefore, as PHFM put it when announcing the appointment to the school, "completely unlike me". The only objective evidence which can be offered to support the governors' choice is that only three of the last eight candidates became HMC heads, two in 1978 and one in 1983. When offered the post, John Blatchly asked whether his wife Pam might be consulted, and was invited to ring her up. Perhaps because the Bursar was not at the meeting (instead entertaining the three men waiting in the almost book-free Grimwade Science Library) there is, astonishingly, no record whatever in governors' minutes of the day's proceedings.

The new head began with several advantages not of his own making. The house, No 11 St Edmunds Road, overlooking School Field, was soon put in order and proved ideal as a family house, for entertaining and for society meetings and chamber music rehearsals. The traditional head's quarters since 1851, at the southern end of the school, were quickly converted, the reception rooms for the common room and the bedrooms for history teaching, later for classics. Music took over much space formerly used by School House boarders. As the former common room had been overcrowded, members of staff were visibly cheered by the improvement. Catering was no longer the head's responsibility, and the taking of lunch became voluntary, new serving counters accelerating the flow. The move to central feeding for the boarders took longer to achieve because of bursarial pessimism about employing staff early and late. Mathematics A level had always enjoyed more periods than other subjects, an anomaly which was corrected in time for the new academic year. All these changes were welcomed, for the men at the top of the common room were particularly forward-looking. George Notcutt, halfway through his six-year second mastership, was totally open-minded about change, not something which could be taken for granted in one who entered the school as a boy in 1919 and returned as a master in 1938. He would say, "If we have tried something three or four times, it's time for something different", music to a new head's ears. At the end of his first term, Blatchly was misguided enough to read out form orders for forms one to five, a degrading progress from the bottom boy in the bottom form which was never repeated. As soon as possible, first and second formers were relieved of their sooty grey shirts and black ties (a vague notion persisted that the school was still in mourning for Charles I), and boys looked and felt better in blue shirts and a dark blue tie with the school arms in light blue, formerly known, optimistically surely, as the 'holiday tie'. Fourth and fifth formers were no longer required to wear caps, and a year later only the lower school retained them. The open lawns in front of the school could, now that there was no private garden, be continued to Ivry Street. The old common room became an imaginatively decorated Grimwade Science Library, and its former home housed the flood of school archives arriving in response to an appeal to parents and OIs for school memorabilia of all sorts: books, photographs and pictures. To perpetuate the name of the former boarding School House, a day house of that name was instituted under Howard Jones, and all the day houses were given quarters in 31 and 33 Henley Road. The Scouts, whose hut had been struck by lightning, were given the topmost former dormitory in the main building. The old 'Manual' now became an audio-visual centre with secondhand cinema seating from the Stowmarket Regal. The shell of a new biology lab was built to the north of the existing one, and David Reid, head of that subject, supervised volunteers in wiring and furnishing it as an activity. Sixth form General Studies conferences were instituted on the Cranleigh model, jointly with Ipswich High School but held mostly on our side of the park.

Two minor Charterhouse traditions were imported: the 'Book' on a stand on the Common Room mantelpiece became the repository of important announcements, useful for future school historians, and 'calling over', the headmaster's retrospective of the term given at final assembly. If many things changed, others were retained: Saturday school with games after lunch, not only matches (games also on Tuesday and some on Thursday, Activities and CCF coexisting with top team practices); Sunday chapel services for members of boarding and dayboy houses in rotation, their parents always welcome, and said Eucharist on Sundays and Wednesdays.

The sun shone brightly on 14 June 1973 when HRH The Duke of Edinburgh piloted a Wessex helicopter to land on School Field on his second visit to the school in 17 years. The concert band played while the crowds waited, then, after presentations, brief speeches were made, a welcome by the headmaster, and a reply by Prince Philip, who emphasised his belief

in the importance of technology in education. Sir Frank Mason had worked under him in educational initiatives to promote this, and HRH knew of and paid tribute to the Leggett brothers' provision of the new Centre from their father's Foundation. Richard Passmore, head of school, presented the key, and HRH said that he would next 'declare the Leggett Centre, – not open, which it has been, I have heard, for some time - but more open than usual'. During his tour of the centre, and of activities around the perimeter of the field, the Duke chatted informally with all those he met. In the Great School, the Choral Society sang a Welcome Calypso, and Britten's *Golden Vanity*, and I D Prior's XI beat the School 1st XI by three wickets. The three-hour visit included lunch with the school prefects who sat with the Royal guest in the dining hall extension, while others enjoyed a buffet meal in the main room. The author confesses that, in his inexperience and a fit of false economy, everyone was offered the same NV wine with the meal. The shock to the royal palate of something so remote from Grand Cru provoked the only critical remark: 'Do the governors brew this stuff on the premises?' Altogether it was a happy and memorable day for the whole community of the school. A week later, Sir Robert Birley, former headmaster of Charterhouse and Eton, was the guest of honour at Speech Day. The Great School was used sideways on with half the audience sitting under a canopy on the Fison lawn to the east; the proceedings could be easily seen and the sound was relayed.

The pass rate at A level became 90 per cent in July 1974, and has continued its asymptotic progress towards 100 ever since. When George Notcutt retired in 1975, he generously gave his testimonial fund towards the building of a squash

court, and before his final assembly slipped the head a scrap of card with his own draft farewell: 'This year we see the departure of Mr Notcutt – [pause] – time the old ****** left!' He needed many successors. Peter Hill became senior master, Andrew Gregory (aged 34, with ten years at the school) second master and John Le Mare lower school master. John Nicholson had already taken over games and physical education and Bob Clayton, in a bright purple Loughborough tracksuit, took on his teaching. That year the very first girl, Nicola Barnard, daughter of a governor and a future chairman, left to read biology at Bristol. The next year, five girls arrived in the lower sixth and the school had taken the first steps on the 25-year road to full co-education. Two early projects in the Leggett Centre were the

electronic cricket scoreboard
(number units driven by
cycle chains proved too
unreliable and light units
were substituted) and a
Zuckermann Italian sin-
gle manual harpsichord
made from a £200 kit.
The scoreboard was not

completed until it was opened by PHFM in 1979, but the harpsichord took only two years and it still travels with the chamber musicians all over Suffolk.

In 1976 the gentle and gentlemanly Noel Sullivan retired and
Michael Lee arrived from Trinity School, Croydon to drive
modern languages. Dominic Bell and David Chapman reached
the final of the Observer Mace Debating Trophy that year, and
fought it out with Eton, Marlborough and Calday Grange under
the benevolent gaze of Viscount Hailsham. The last and larg-
est-ever eleven year-old entry of East Suffolk pupils selected
from the Shotley peninsula that September brought record
total entry numbers and fortunately there was no difficulty in
filling four streams in subsequent years. In 1977, the addition
of a scenery store to the west of the Great School stage restored
the understage green room to its proper use and made several
stage productions each term possible. E.J.W. Fiske OI generously gave two hundred comfortable chairs for the Great
School, but Speech Day had to be held in the more capacious
and newly-refurbished Corn Exchange. To make all welcome at
Speech Day, the event had to move to the cavernous Regent
Theatre. In 1978 the first Gaudy of a continuing series was
held, all those who left the school before 1930 being invited,
and over forty OIs came to see what had changed and to

encounter afresh six of those who had taught them: Gleave, Glover, Jennings, Stonex, Taplin, Young, and of course, George Notcutt, who very sadly died the next year after only three years of well-earned retirement, a severe loss to OI Club and school.[1]

Plans were now afoot for an Eighties Appeal to provide several things: the Library range on two stories and on stilts, with six classrooms and a large studio for art. Extra studies were needed at Westwood and Highwood, a second squash court alongside GSN's first and, as soon as possible, an extra playing field to replace the Moat Field which the school had occupied 'temporarily' since 1961. Its inevitable development for housing took place in 1988. When the 450th anniversary of Wolsey's death was celebrated in Ipswich in 1980 the school's contribution was a memorable son et lumière production in front of the flood-lit Henley Road building, the script written by Dick Tucker, head of English. Attempts to have the traffic diverted for the length of performances were unsuccessful, but the Chief Constable, a guest on the first night, experienced the problem for himself, and the second night audience sat alongside a blissfully car-free Henley Road. Rockets let off on School Field signalled the end of the performance. Dan Briden, an inspired head of physics and a patient, gentle and courteous colleague, had retired the year before, but came back to run the sound. Professor Geoffrey Elton gave a memorably controversial view of Wolsey on Speech Day.

When Peter and Margaret Hill retired to Hasketon, Ian Prior became senior master, and it was with the Priors that the Blatchlys flew to Hong Kong to meet several generations of

---

1 Colourful reminiscences overheard by pupils that day were collected for publication in the *OI Magazine* for 1978.

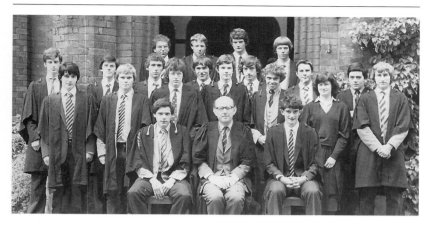

Chinese parents and tell them about the current Appeal. A
great deal of stamina was demanded by eight days of overwhelming non-stop hospitality and sight-seeing. Before the
welcoming dinner on a floating restaurant began all the appeal
donations were promised, and it was only necessary for Ian
Prior and John Blatchly to make brief speeches of thanks and
business was over for the week.

The architect's model of the library was admired, but there
were two questions. It showed only two storeys on stilts: how

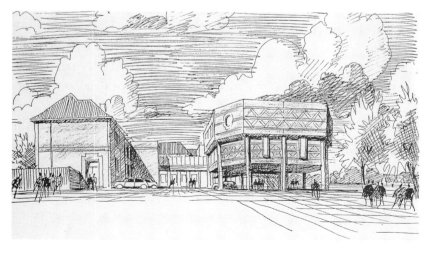

many in total? And, when it was explained that that was all: will boys play games on the roof? Not if we can stop them! School trips to Moscow, the earliest led by Ken Read and Gillian Holt as the main Russian speaker, began in the late 70s, long before the Cold War ended. They became biannual, but are now held every year. When Michael Lee moved to Oundle to run languages there, David Warnes came to be Peter Hill's successor as head of history, not a straight exchange, but a fair one.

The new buildings themselves took over eighteen months to complete and the southern end of the field was caked mud for the whole of that time, but the transformation from a wide and drafty tarmac area in front of the Sherwood classrooms to an interestingly-shaped and partly covered area where boys could play and the enhanced view from the north was worth waiting for. The site foreman, Mr Featherstone, cheerful on the greyest days, became quite devoted to the school and its pupils. The opening ceremony by Sir Hugh Casson, PRA at a special open day on 19 May 1982 was of already occupied and working spaces. This was Birkin Haward's last major commission, and one of

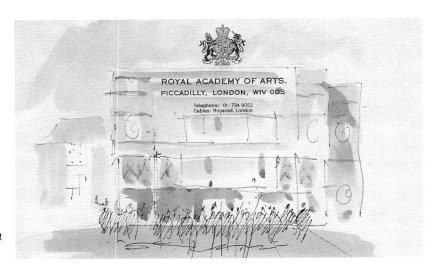

PRA's thank you letter

294

his finest. He was delighted that his fellow art-student John Piper would design four circular windows to fit the top-floor openings in the short sides of the octagonal library building. Made by Patrick Reyntiens and David Wasley, they constantly attract artistic attention and much favourable comment. In honour of Sir Hugh, one of whose predecessors as PRA had been Sir Edward Poynter Bart, OI, an exhibitions of drawings and paintings by OI artists was arranged (see Chapter XXIII). Tribute was paid that day to Commander Owen Jenkins, OBE, DSC, retiring that term after 15 years as bursar, who took great pride in the material improvements which he had helped to bring about.

The ten-acre former Tower Ramparts School field adjoining Notcutt's was at the time used by Suffolk College, but the lack of a pavilion made it useless to them. The governors bought Mann Egerton's field and pavilion in Humber Doucy Lane, and effected an exchange. The Eighties Appeal total eventually reached £140,000, and all its objectives were achieved before the end of 1981, despite the need for a planning appeal over the Highwood studies.[2] Formal assent was obtained from HM The Queen to become the school's Visitor, the Lord Chancellor to act for the Sovereign when necessary.

The Holden Library, now empty of books, and equipped with a piano and white board for music classes, was a forlorn sight. Peter Labdon, county librarian, came to see the old and new libraries, and was shown Holden first. He immediately suggested that the ancient town library of Ipswich, then lacking a home, would fit nicely on the shelves. In November 1983, one

---

2 The school's counsel at the enquiry in the town hall was Thayne Forbes QC, now a High Court judge. The then MP for Ipswich opined that, if this compact building on two floors were constructed, it would 'have a serious impact on the residential amenities of north-west Ipswich'.

thousand books published between 1460 and 1760 arrived in two loads of the mobile library van, and boys carried them into the now empty room.[3] Between 1612 and 1835 successive headmasters had been responsible for the library, so that, in a sense, the books were coming home. The headmaster moved his study there when the reshelving (by Ted Herrington and Barry Askew) was complete, and the new bursar took over his old one. Now it is the Second Master's room and the Bursar works upstairs.

The arctic Sherwood classrooms now received a new heating system and the open corridors were fitted with door and windows. The school, although now in a new Mid-Suffolk constituency, invited the three Ipswich candidates to share a platform for a debate in the Great School. Commenting on independent schools, Ken Weetch, the Labour victor, declared in the local press 'in a free society there will always be private demand, and I am opposed to total abolition.' His optimism has worked. There was a mass exodus from the school to Twickenham to watch Mark Bailey OI skipper the Cambridge side in the Varsity match; he later joined the governing body.

The author is ashamed to find that was not until 1984 that boys first acquired Christian names on Speech Day; it was probably the contrast with girl prizewinners, who were always given them, that led to the change. But at a comparable school it was another 12 years before boys and girls sprouted their Johns and Janes. Awards at Oxford and Cambridge were last made to school pupils in 1984. Instead they were given to undergraduates after their first year's exams. The total number won by Ips-

---

3 It took the headmaster until 1989 to write and Boydell to publish *The Town Library of Ipswich, provided for the use of the Town preachers in 1599: A History and Catalogue.* Mrs A E L Birkby of Bury St Edmunds wrote the catalogue cards on weekly visits to the school over two years.

wich School candidates from 1972 to 1984 was 40.[4]   In 1985 a
new rear entrance to the main building, giving shelter to those
queuing for lunch in bad weather, greatly civilised that area,
and the former Junior House, no longer needed for boarders
was renamed Mermagen House, and all five day houses were
now accommodated there. This left 33 Henley Road free for the
Prep, with a glazed and roofed corridor joining it to No 35. No 31
became the Paolozzi Art School and was opened and named in
June 1987 by Eduardo, whose links with Ipswich were long-
standing. This was just six years after the new studio had been
opened, but it still seems that artists like to move on. The new
Alton Water, an artificial lake between Stutton and Tattingstone, gave all watersports a fresh but all too brief boost. The
centenary of Haggard's *King Solomon's Mines* was celebrated
with a presentation in the library, an exhibition of our Haggard
memorabilia and a generous OI gave a complete set of early editions of the novels. Keith Jones, now Dean of Exeter, preached
brilliantly on the parable of the Prodigal Son at Commemoration and his sermon was printed in full in the *Ipswichian*. In
1986 there were four retirements: John Booth OI from the Prep,
and John Le Mare received a presentation from the chairman
after his 17th Annual General Inspection in command of the

*CCF
Dinner
in the
mid-80s*

4   A quick count on the honours boards at Chigwell showed only nine in the same
period.

CCF. His and Rosemary's contributions to the life of the school were legion. David Clements, Classicist, housemaster of Westwood and a fine games coach, and Ken Read, a long serving linguist, completed the quartet. Kenneth Baker, Secretary of State for Education and Science and bibliophile, visited the town library as a brief interlude in a busy official visit to the town's schools, and Dean Eric Heaton of Christ Church, Wolsey's other foundation, was the guest on Speech Day. He was presented with the first bound copy of the symposium of papers written and read to the Athenaeum by its members and guests (all masters) between 1984 and 1986. In alternate years, David Warnes invited about a dozen lower sixth formers to meet at his house, each in their turn reading a paper. This particularly gifted year group chose topics spanning many centuries and cultures, and their civilised leaving prank that summer was to hold a sedate Edwardian-style breakfast party in front of the pavilion with deck chairs, silver teapot and muffin dishes beside a parked veteran car.

Douglas Yelland, who took over the Prep from Hugh Gleave in 1969, retired in 1987, at the same time as his wife and colleague Pat. With a heart of gold and a tremendous sense of humour, Douglas had been an avuncular and devoted cubmaster who was tireless backstage (with some cameo roles on stage) in Prep plays. As Prep head, he sometimes underestimated how easily small boys could be in awe of authority. Nicholas Allen, succeeding to the Prep headship, had initial difficulties in persuading staff and some parents to accept that a broader curriculum was desirable, but with massive support from the head and senior governors he won through. It should have been more help to him that he had spent one year teaching in the senior school before taking over. As a member of the larger common room he had become involved with CCF and drama and saw at first hand what preparation entrants at eleven needed.

The pavilion of Notcutt's was finished in time for the opening at the OI Rugby match in December 1987, the clock turret the gift of George Pipe, chairman until 1979, and the replica Lord's weathervane the gift of his successor, Geoffrey Barnard. After all their efforts on its behalf they owed the school nothing; our debt of gratitude will never be repaid. Six new brass chandeliers were installed as the main chapel lighting, and chaplain Walter Wilson engraved five of them with the names of great men in the school's recent history: Sir Frank Mason, Wallace Morfey, Patrick Mermagen, George Notcutt and Hugh Gleave. Geoffrey Mason and Stanley Pink have rear-lit stained glass roundels set into the north wall in their memory. The chaplain, creative as engraver and worker in stained glass, leading the demolition activity group, made an interesting discovery when removing the pine panelling of the Holden studies, before that boarding School House studies. Ephemera with which boys had decorated walls a century ago had been covered all that time. A fascinating insight into the tastes and preoccupation of past generations of schoolboy was revealed and could be preserved in the Morfey Rooms in the tower opened by Wallace (with Irvine Gray) in March 1988 to give archives and museum objects permanent homes. Russian joined French and German as middle school languages. Highwood was sold for conversion to flats and a

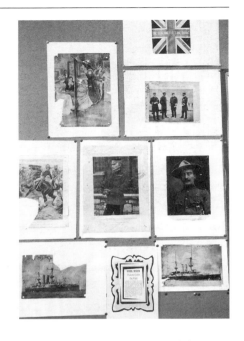

new day house perpetuates the name Sherrington. This enabled a second hall next to the Great School to be afforded and built. Eric Green, a real treasure as head caretaker, retired after fourteen years.

In 1989, Geoffrey Barnard OI, senior partner of Birketts, solicitors, retired after 17 years as a governor, chairman for the last eleven. His undergraduate years at Christ's were divided by his war service, but after that, he gave a lifetime of service to Club and School. The success of the 50s, 70s and 80s appeals owed much to his lead and commitment. In the special Club Centenary edition of the *OI Magazine*, which ceased as a separate publication that year, the headmaster wrote 'His has been the greatest service a gifted *alumnus* of a school can give: to guide it through a crucial decade or so with the priorities clearly perceived and ordered'. The vice-chairman, David Coe, another OI, took over and it was, of course, business as usual.

Both chairman are shown with Michael Williams, OI President and Tony Greengrass, OI Chairman before the London Dinner at the East India Club. After 23 years at the school as head of English and Drama, Richard (Dick) Tucker retired. A very gifted teacher, he it was who convinced the governors of the need for a larger library, where he chaired the Suffolk Book League (the first regional offshoot of the national body) which he had had a large hand in founding. Peter Beales retired too after 17 years; after he and Maureen had ran a happy Junior House, he was the first warden of Mermagen House, but Peter was happiest out of doors with adventure training, CCF, cross-country and all the games. To inspect the CCF in its centenary year, Major Bob Clayton welcomed General Sir John Akehurst, Deputy Supreme Allied Commander in Europe. Sir John's verdict was: 'There is no doubt that you have an exceptionally fine CCF'. The school became involved with Schools Partnership Worldwide that year and, with all the other independent and maintained schools in the borough, with Education 2000. Leadership courses were first run at the end of the lower sixth form year, and the Great School was in builders' hands for a grand transformation to be revealed when it and the new Little School were opened.

Sixth
Form
girls
1991

HRH The Princess Royal was the guest when the twin halls were ready. She was visiting Ipswich as President of the Save The Children Fund, and could spend an hour in the school afterwards. The tall narrow Welsh slate plaque which she unveiled was designed and made by David and Lida Kindersley of Cambridge, the lettering Rustic Roman. There was singing, trad jazz from Trak 7, excerpts from *Doctor Faustus* and the presentation of a cheque for £3,000 to the SCF, raised at the first Ipswich School concert at Snape Maltings. The new Great School had become an excellent auditorium, insulated from light, heat and sound, all of which had made the original hall unsuitable for certain of its most important functions. Examinations in the summer term were often held in sweltering temperatures, and the noise of passing traffic intruded then and during concerts and plays. The Ipswich Chamber Music Society now held its four concerts a year there, the membership rapidly growing to capacity; Nicholas Ridley, a governor, gave half the cost of a new Grotrian Steinweg grand piano. Birkin Haward felt that his conception for the building had been destroyed, and Wallace Morfey told the headmaster that it was no longer bright and uplifting to the spirits, but 'like a place boarded-up'.

The gains have, however, certainly outweighed the losses, and the Little School, with its mini-Snape Maltings' roof, is excellently light in contrast. Rigaud's Vulliamy clock which hangs in the Little School emits a single soft chime once an hour, ruining nothing. Two stacks of one hundred bleacher seats can be moved from one hall to the other through the tall doors; they fill half the larger space and most of the smaller. Dorothy, Lady Foot, left the school a quarter share in (her husband) Sir Dingle Foot's library. His brother Michael Foot came to open the special Foot section in the library and spoke to the Book League about his then recent biography of Byron.

Ian and Marion Prior retired the next year to divide their time between Ipswich and their house in the Languedoc. School and county Rugby and Cricket, housemastering and English teaching had filled Ian's life here since 1956, and for eleven years he had been a wise and devoted senior master. He handed over to David Warnes. A third Eton fives court was built and opened in 1992 with exhibition matches by the stars of school, common room and OIs. At the end of that year there were more retirements of pillars of the common room, John Nicholson, Bruce Andrews – head of mathematics and lower school master, scoutmaster and a fine musician, Ted Herrington and his faithful assistant Barry Askew, both from the Leggett Centre.

A terrible muddy swathe of devastation ran parallel to the Lime Avenue to carry materials for the sports hall, multigym and cricket gallery, built with help from the Foundation for Sport and the Arts. Externally the new hall by Poole and Pattle looks more like a classical temple than an aircraft hanger (as so many sports hall do) and Walter Wilson made a 'kite flying' window for the field end and Michael Scoging a 'sports' window for the other in stained glass. The *Ipswichian Occasional*

began publication in January 1992 to give parents and friends up-to-date news of events and achievements every week during term time. That June it carried news of the new headmaster's appointment.

At Speech Day in June 1993, David Jewell, master of Hailey-bury, and Lord Belstead, HM Lord Lieutenant and a former governor, were joint guests of honour. David Coe, in the chair, took the opportunity to tell the headmaster in public (instead, he said, of being told by *him* what was to happen), that the governing body had commissioned new laboratories to carry his name and that they would be ready for use before the end of the new headmaster's first year. Pam and John Blatchly were overwhelmed by the kindness and generosity they enjoyed in their last term; the OIs presented him with the original John Piper cartoon for the Autumn window in the library and governors and staff presented thoughtful gifts to enrich their retirement. For the first seven years of his retirement JMB led teams to inspect HMC schools all over the country, one a term, and became a governor of three HMC schools in England and one in Paris.

What follows is a summary by others of this headship: John Blatchly's energetic and creative approach to headship ensured that much was built on the secure foundations laid by Patrick Mermagen, and the school became notably more outward-looking. Regular meetings between parents and staff established valuable contacts. Staff and pupils valued both his warm encouragement of excellence and his critical eye for the slipshod, and were motivated to give of their best in an ever-broadening range of activities. His enthusiasm and encouragement extended not only to the spheres in which he had some talent, but to many others where he claimed none. Himself gifted with a mischievous, some might have said sharp, sense of humour, he enjoyed the same qualities when displayed by pupils, and may have been judged too forgiving of the waywardly able. He was fortunate to do his headmastering at a time when there were few changes in the curriculum, and when the culture of performance measurement and accountability which now blights English education was no more than a menacing cloud on the horizon. This meant that the teaching staff had the time and energy to respond to his frequent and invariably creative challenges and suggestions. When curricular changes did occur, as in the case of the transition from O levels to GCSEs in 1985, he did not deviate from his policy of running the school with as few and as brief meetings as possible, trusting the heads of department to get on with the task in hand. He himself was able to be active outside the school to an extent that the pressures of the job no longer permit. He was president of the Suffolk Institute of Archaeology and History, a trustee of both the Suffolk and the Ipswich Historic Churches Trusts, chairman of the Suffolk Records Society, and president of the Ipswich Archaeological Trust. Many of these bodies held meetings in the school, particularly in the new library.

Just as his predecessor claimed, with considerable justification, that much of his best work for the school was done on the
cricket field and golf course, so Blatchly believed that, by getting to know a wide range of people across the county, children
and grandchildren would come to the school as a result. As
Treasurer of the Headmasters' Conference and editor of its
journal, *Conference & Common Room*, he was a well-known
and well-respected figure in the independent school world.
This, together with the increasingly strong academic results
achieved by pupils, regained for the school the national reputation which it had enjoyed under Holden.

*Outgoing and incoming heads and wives on the day of Ian
Galbraith's appointment.*

XXI

Ian Geoffrey Galbraith

Guiding major change, 1993–

Most school histories give little more than the name of the current head but, as IGG has already served almost ten years in his post, extending co-education from the sixth form to the whole age range from three to nineteen, and in September 2002 there were more than one thousand pupils, it is wholly appropriate to give a brief account of the school's achievements in his time.

OF THE EIGHT CANDIDATES on the long-list, four became HMC heads within the following year or two, clear indication that the field was a strong one. The governors' unanimous choice, Ian Galbraith, won a scholarship from Dulwich to St John's College, Cambridge where he read geography and took Firsts in both parts of the Tripos. He taught at Dulwich, with a brief interlude at Kingston Grammar School, and became, successively, head of geography, head of the humanities subjects and head of the sixth form – almost an independent command – under David Emms and Tony Verity. Not long after he and his wife Kathryn, who had taught history at James Allen's Girls' School, arrived in Ipswich, their children Mary and Sam were born. Ian Galbraith has published works on physical geography, led expeditions in Iceland and Greenland and is an accomplished keyboard player and conductor, so that under him the Chamber Group (as the Chamber Orchestra) continues to flourish and perform in local churches.

An energetic visionary, the new head was quick to see the way forward for the School. Negotiations for the purchase of part of the Anglesea Road Hospital site began in 1992, and David Coe was determined to grasp this unique opportunity to acquire land separated from the school only by the width of Ivry Street. While Ipswich High School for Girls was at the other side of Christchurch Park, parents with mixed families had, within half a mile, selective schools for all their children, but after the Girls' School moved to Woolverstone Hall, co-educational opportunities at Woodbridge and Framlingham beckoned. Changing social patterns and growing parental demand both for nursery and primary provision and for co-education helped to shape the early decisions of the headship. These led to the opening of the Nursery and Pre-preparatory Department, and to the introduction of full co-education, a process which was completed in the academic year 2001-02 when the first girl entrants at eleven reached Year 11 and sat their GCSEs. The pressure to admit girls at all levels simultaneously was wisely resisted, for this would almost certainly have meant very small numbers of girls in some years, for whom it would have been impossible to provide the full range of sporting and extra-curricular activities. The Governors decided to clear the hospital site and build from scratch, and the light, south-facing single storey school designed by Poole and Pattle proved an ideal home for the youngest Ipswichians, whose ages range from three to seven. It now made good sense to give forms the nationally accepted year numbers: 1 at age five to 13 at age seventeen.

An energetic marketing campaign reversed the decline in boarding numbers which had characterised the late 1980s and early 1990s, and the remodelling of Westwood made it possible to admit girl boarders for the first time. That Westwood is now

full and numbers in the senior school have risen to an unprecedented 710 in the past three years suggests that the decisions
of the mid 1990s have placed the school in a very strong position from which to face the future.

The move to co-education has involved a change in the composition of the staff, with the appointment of more women
teachers, including the school's first Director of Studies. At the
time of writing, Felaw, Rigaud and Sherrington houses have
housemistresses, and three departments, General Studies,
Religious Education and ICT, are headed by women.

To the post of Head of Lower School, pioneered by George
Notcutt and developed by John Le Mare, Bruce Andrews and
David Walsh, Galbraith added a Head of Sixth Form (Robert
Karling and later Edmund Cavendish) and a Head of Middle
School (Jonathan Cox and later Adrian Brown). The grouping
of tutors into houses, the creation of tutorial time in the school
day and the introduction of Personal, Social and Health Educa-
tion all assisted the development of pastoral care. Other curric-
ular changes have included the emergence of a flourishing
Business Studies department and the introduction of Design
Technology at A level, taught in a splendidly equipped suite of
rooms housed on three floors in the former gymnasium.

Sport, Music and Drama have continued to flourish and the
range of extra-curricular activities available has broadened to
include the Junior Sports Leader Award and Young Enterprise,
a scheme which gives pupils experience of founding and running commercial enterprises. The whole of year 8 now enjoys a
week of outdoor activities and field studies in Cumbria during
the Michaelmas Term, accompanied by their form tutors and
other teachers and guided by professional instructors. Living
together there gives day pupils a taste of boarding life, and the

shared excitements and challenges of the week cement friendships within forms.

In 2002, numbers required the provision of an additional laboratory and classroom which were built on the east side of the 1994 Blatchly laboratories, rising sheerly at the edge of the biology pond. The decorative but inessential polygonal spiral staircase was the only loss. At the same time the long-overdue refurbishment of the sixth form centre and the art department next door put two other buildings into first-class order. HMC schools are now inspected every six years and Ipswich has come through two of these with flying colours, in 1996 and 2002. David Coe, who had served as Vice-Chairman under Geoffrey Barnard, and became his able successor in 1989, retired from the chair and as a governor. He entered the school as a boy 57 years previously, and has long given fine service to Club and School. His Vice-Chairman, Dan Goyder CBE, retired in 2000 having also served for 13 years. The new chairman is Karl Daniels OI.

XXII

Sport at the School

An alphabetical survey by Andrew Gregory

It was Thomas Wolsey, when founding his Ipswich college in 1528, who first ordered recreation: 'Pleasure is to mingle with study, that the boy may think learning rather an amusement than a toil.' The 1571 ordinances were more specific:

> It shall be lawful for the School-Master to appoint times of recreation once in the week and that upon Thursday in the afternoon; unless, at the earnest request of some Honourable or Worshipful Body some other day or time shall be thought more convenient to the School-Master for the time being.

but from the 1880s to the 1990s there were three games afternoons: Tuesday, Thursday and Saturday, though CCF and Activities shared Thursday.

ARCHERY gained popularity briefly as an alternative to mainstream games with the extension of choice under John Blatchly. 'Random aim', when the master in charge was distracted, distributed arrows into gardens adjoining Notcutt's field – luckily no casualties were recorded.

ATHLETICS began to be practised once the school had a field, and by 1860 there was an annual Sports day in March with 23 events for all ages, as well as Wrestling and Fencing. However, for a few years from 1887 the Sports were held in October, the school doctor believing it would be 'beneficial to the health of those competing'. The Open Hurdle Race cup

was first competed for in June 1878 when *G. S. Sherrington* cleared twelve flights in 18½ seconds.

W. H. Dunnett cleared 22 feet 3 inches in the long jump in 1905 which still stands as a school record. Even allowing for the possibility that he jumped down hill or down wind, this was a massive leap which he just failed to repeat in the Public Schools Championships of 1905 and 1906. He also won the high jump and the hurdles. Did he compete at Cambridge whilst reading theology?

The 1929 athletics team, photographed at the now demolished west entrance to the chapel, was trained by Roly Slator and captained by *George Notcutt. Geoffrey Rees-Jones*, much later head of King William's, stands next but one to Slator. In 1931 *Jack Catchpole* held three county men's athletic titles whilst in the sixth form.

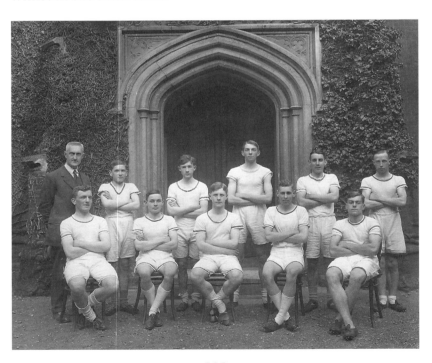

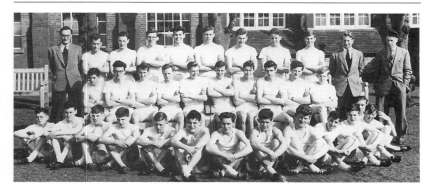

The 31-strong team of 1957 was trained by Noel Sullivan, Peter Hill and John Nicholson. In 1961, *Colin Simpson*, an England Schools' rugby cap (*see below*), had the strength and technique to throw the senior shot 16.60m and the discus 42.54m, distances which have never been seriously approached since. He also ran the 440 yards in 52.0 seconds, a time only improved upon 20 years later in the slightly shorter 400m. *Tim Burrows* ran that event in 1999 in 50.3 seconds, moving the record on to a new level.

In 1966, Sports day was permanently moved to the summer term to avoid what was described as 'the spiteful tail-end of the English winter'. In 1967, in ideal weather, no fewer than three athletes improved upon the senior half-mile record and the time set by *William Mayon-White* that day stood until *Oliver Barrett*, an English Schools' medallist at 800m, beat it in 2002.

From 1977 to 1981, *Ian Knox-Macaulay* set school records in various age-groups at 100m, 200m, 400m, high jump, long jump and triple jump, three of which still stand. His best event proved to be the triple jump and his outstanding U15 record of 12.86m remains better than the more senior records. His talent took him to the English Schools' Championships, where a slightly below-par performance resulted in sixth place. Sadly back problems curtailed his future involvement in the event.

313

In the mid-1990s, *Gordon Irvine* became the Scottish number one at the steeplechase, an event in which there have been few competitors recently.

In 2001, after only one season as an athlete, and in his first year as a senior, *Tom Sharland* achieved second place in the English Schools' Championships at 3,000m, and, in doing so, sliced well over 50 seconds from the school record. He also achieved our first under four minutes 1500 metres and ran the 5,000 metres in just over 14 minutes.

For some years there were allegedly state of the art field events' facilities behind the school field pavilion, but the pole vault area next to the Warrington Road garden fence would have inhibited even a world champion.

Contentious timekeeping and judging incidents, requests for competitors with fictitious names to report to the starter and miscalculated house totals have all added spice to Sports days. Since 1978, Mike Bannan's organisation – computer-free but always running to time – has done much to keep the sport alive. 2002 began to see the emergence of high quality performances from more girl athletes.

BADMINTON, always popular with those averse to afternoons on a wind-swept Notcutt's field, was for long banished to such venues as the YMCA, but from 1993 it has flourished in the sports hall.

BOXING flourished for many years on the 'make a man of him' curriculum. There were eleven bouts in the 1952 matches against Felsted and Gresham's. Gradually, interest subsided down the age groups, but the sport finally vanished into oblivion with the retirement from the Prep School of that great fan of pugilism, *John Booth*, in the 1980s.

CRICKET: From the Brook Street school, boys had to be marched up to the Race Course to play Cricket, but at Henley Road from 1852 the field adjoining, previously intended for town use, gave Cricket a new popularity as the principal school sport. Matches with Bury School began in 1853 and by 1869 the tally was 8 to Ipswich and 7 to Bury. In June 1852, the magazine reported 'six fellows left who played in our matches last year'. Demands for a paid bowler-cum-coach from Lord's were gratified the next year with the arrival of Wigzell. Matches were played between Old and Present Members of the School and against the 4th Light Dragoons (whose band played at the great events connected with the new school and chapel) and Boxford Club.

H E Malden noted 'In the 1860s a Surrey man was Professional but he left Ipswich abruptly without paying his landlady.' 'The best player we ever had as a professional was tried at Lord's later on but had the misfortune to kill a Nottingham man (Summers) by hitting him on the temple with a bumping ball and I believe left off playing'. 'Some of the School Eleven seem to go out to a Cricket Match much as though it were a picnic, simply for the good dinner and pipe or cigar, whereas it is impossible to play as well after a heavy dinner with cucumber, lobster, sherry, beer and what not, as before it. And if anyone must have a cigar or a pipe, he had much better keep it till the evening, when he will enjoy it just as much, and will not injure his play'.

Matches continued against various opponents and the School Magazine became dominated by score cards, reports and averages for both 1st and 2nd Elevens. Matches often resulted in first innings victories and a 'complete defeat' only occurred if a two innings game was completed. Before the turn of the century school players were selected for the Suffolk

County side, and *Kenneth Raynor*, son of the Headmaster, was twelfth man in the Varsity match for Cambridge and gained Blues for soccer and hockey. In 1999, *Chris Swallow* rightly put County before School in line with the principle that people should play at their highest level. The pavilion erected in late 1874 did sterling service until Munro Cautley's stylish and larger one replaced it in 1938, a present from the Old Ipswichians who have enjoyed Cricket weeks on school field in August ever since 1906.

Norwich and Woodbridge Schools have been the longest standing 1st Eleven opponents, Framlingham College joining them in 1919. W.H. Turner was the esteemed professional from 1924–33, but one man overshadowed all others in his contribution to Ipswich School cricket, G.C. (Cyril) Perkins, appointed professional and head groundsman in 1946 after playing for Northamptonshire. There he was short-listed to tour but never played in a winning team in the County championship. Cyril served at the school for 30 years and was Suffolk's most successful bowler. He graciously opened the renovated Holly Road Pavilion in 2000 enjoying his lunch in comfort on the site of his 'ball cupboard' of yesteryear. Ian Prior, who captained Suffolk, was master in charge for much of Cyril's time and helped school cricket develop an esteem that survived them both.

Before and after this period many Old Ipswichians represented Suffolk in the Minor County Championship with five on the field in one match. Indeed three school captains went on to lead Suffolk – *Phil Caley, Mark Bailey* and *Simon Clements,* who also captained Oxford, as well as being important members of the Old Ipswichian team which was fearsome on the field and terrifying off it in the 1980s.

Patrick Mermagen insisted on cricket being played by every-one on three afternoons a week in the Summer Term, senior House matches lasting two days. This made the game unpopu-lar with the rank and file. House cricket gradually faded away, first to thirty overs per side, but the end came in 1987 when Felaw scored 324 for 3 to Broke's 20 for 7 declared.

Ian Hammond, who arrived in 1952 and retired in 1994, became a legend after Cyril Perkins retired, giving advice to anyone about anything – he even offered batting tips to the former Paki-stan captain Majid Khan, visiting with the Pakistani U25 side. When he died in 2002 Mark Bailey gave the address in chapel; later Ian's ashes were interred near the pavilion. The photograph recalls him in the 1970s.

Ian Prior's successor Phil Rees used winter facilities to hone boys' skills in the dark months, and cricket flourished. *Nadeem Shahid* was joined in the England U19 side of 1987 by *Nick Gregory*, and *Shahid* and *Gul Khan* became first class cricketers. The U17 side twice reached the semi-finals and once were finalists in the national Barclay's Bank competition.

An expanding fixture list was extended by a regular end of term Festival usually involving Brighton College, King's Mac-clesfield and, of late, Edinburgh Academy. Tours to Barbados, South Africa and Australia took place. The five cricketers here looking suitably overawed at meeting Sir Garfield Sobers and

Wes Hall in Barbados are *Nick* and *Tim Gregory, James Ledden, Nadeem Shahid* and *Edward Porter*. In recent years, the ever-jesting Ray East, left arm bowler in the early glory years of Essex, has been the driving force behind his former Essex team professionals Andrew Golding and Adrian Brown. The 1995 1st Eleven won 11 matches and lost only to an Old Ipswichian side. In 2001 *Richard Mann* played for England U19s.

CROQUET flourished particularly when *Paul Hetherington* (1977-83) was the driving force on the Christchurch Park Arboretum Lawns.

CROSS COUNTRY began as paper chasing in Holden's time, and the hares claimed to have run 32 miles on one occasion in the 1870s, one *C.E. Hammond* being one of the only boys to finish the course. When a horse shied at paper left in the road at Hintlesham, throwing its woman passenger from the trap to her death, the school's activities were criticised at the inquest. Magazine accounts of the early years of the last century make amusing reading. In February 1905, the twelve-mile course

took the runners as far as Culpho and Playford, but near Tuddenham the bags burst and the paper barely lasted out. By taking a shorter route the hounds gained on the hares, but the first was eight minutes behind them. His fellow hounds could not be placed, 'as some availed themselves of the trams at Lattice Barn'. The Steeplechase was first run at Bramford, but the Finn Valley course was used for about seventy-five years until safety concerns dictated the use of Christchurch Park instead. Watching runners, like lemmings, negotiating the Finn here are Cyril Perkins and Albert Finch. *Sally Eastall* represented Great Britain in the Marathon at the Barcelona Olympics whilst in 2002 *Tom Sharland*, still a sixth former, came second in the UK Cross Country Championships. School leagues have been organised and school teams have competed regularly in national relay events.

CYCLING has been an intermittent interest – indeed it was a common mode of transport for pupils and teachers until the 1960s. The future Headmaster P.E. Raynor bicycled, on a Penny-farthing of course, for Oxford in the 1879 varsity match. In 1988 *Nick Cairns* and *Nigel Scott* cycled the 958 miles from Land's End to John O'Groats in 12 days for charity.

EQUITATION has seldom featured in reports being essentially a private pursuit for a few. *Sophie Deliss* achieved national success during and after her time at school, and was joined by *William Bancroft* and *Thomas Sisterton* in the Inter-Schools Show Jumping at Hickstead in 1993.

FENCING From 1860, the finals were held on Sports day. '*Alastair Cullen* beat his father in 1978' says *The Ipswichian* when fencers still tackled national championship events. In

2002 efforts are being made to reinstate the sport for boys and girls but good coaches are hard to find.

Two RUGBY FIVES courts were built in the main quadrangle in Rigaud's time, to which a third was added in Holden's, but they gave shelter to bare-fist fights as often as to the game. From 1868 the single and doubles Fives finals were played on Sports day. On his arrival in 1906, A.K.Watson provided two ETON FIVES courts behind the pavilion and he and his science master James challenged the staff of Bury School to a match in which the Ipswich pair triumphed. By 1942 the game had died and the Rugby Fives courts with their thirty-inch high back walls were used as coal sheds until they were demolished in the developments of the 1950s. When Martin Shortland-Jones joined the staff, the Eton game was revived in newly covered courts; he married James Young's daughter. The game has remained popular since and a third court was built in 1992. Its survival was ensured when Barry Hoskins learned to love the courts in the early seventies, and *Mike Fenn* and *Peter Boughton*, bursar, gave him every support to expand the fixture list and to encourage female participation. *Simon Woolfries* and *Gareth Hoskins* (captain) won half blues at Cambridge and *Nick Broyden* gained his at Oxford. Staff stars have been the mathematician Karen Runnacles (later Hoskins) who part-nered *Peter Boughton* to win the National Mixed Champion-ships four times between 1989 and 1995, Karen dominated with eleven successive victories in the National Ladies Cham-pionships (with three different partners) 1988–98. The best boys' performance in the National Schools Championships was in 1993 at Shrewsbury when U16s *Charles Robinson* and *James Thompson* reached the semi-finals before losing to the Eton first pair.

FOOTBALL (Soccer) replaced the unique Ipswich School game in 1874 with a full programme of matches against clubs, schools and regiments for the next 50 years. In the final of the Suffolk Cup in 1887, the school played the local Ipswich Association Football Club which became Ipswich Town the following year. The two sides' last meetings had

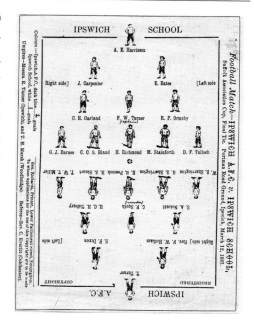

gone the school's way, 5–0 and 2–1, and there was a record attendance for the final, which the local paper described as a red-letter day for Suffolk football. The school, with four masters in the side, were the favourites, but the Association team was strong; at right back, the Revd F. Hotham, making his last appearance at 43, had 'never been seen to such advantage'. 'The School played in brilliant style for some two-thirds of the game... but with the worst of luck, including an oversight by

the referee', they lost 1–2. The pictorial match card shows that there were two Sherringtons and a Notcutt playing against the school. Team photographs from Henry Richmond's album show almost all the players in both sides, but Richmond, who played for both teams when he could, appears in both. It was in 1894 that Raynor introduced marked touch lines and goal nets and ended the inclusion of staff in school sides.

In 1924, headmaster Sherwood declared that soccer lacked the prestige necessary for a successful school, an opinion that would have amused the heads of Eton, Charterhouse, Malvern and Shrewsbury.

In recent decades a team called Gram-marians, compris-ing pupils, teachers and old  boys, competed 'secretly', initially in the Ipswich Sunday League, before in more enlightened times this popular sport was re-established and this group photo (dating from the early 80s) was taken. In 2000 a well-organised and trained team played regular first team fixtures against old rivals and new opponents, and a regular Old Ipswichian football day now takes place in early April.

FOOT BEAGLING: Joint meetings were held with the Sproughton pack led by *Wallace Morfey*, but died out when he retired as Master.

GOLF: The game gradually made its way into the school's curriculum encouraged particularly by Patrick Mermagen.

Richard Evans in 1971 gained a prestigious junior title which indicated a potential to play professionally, whilst *Louise Wright* was awarded a scholarship to Florida State University where she failed by one stroke to qualify for the USLPGA circuit. Several OIs have become professionals at well known clubs: *Peter Rolph* at Royal County Down, *Ian Pearce* at Swinley Forest and *Colin Simpson* at Royal Worlington and others.

GYMNASTICS was a much loved Victorian pastime and indeed it continued in traditional form in the Sherwood Gym until in the late 1990s it was converted to a palatial suite of rooms on three floors for Design Technology and Economics.

Sergeant Austin, who served as instructor for over forty years from 1884, lived for the annual pilgrimage to Aldershot for the Public Schools Championships. In 1894 *Parker major* and *McGhee major* finished seventh and were photographed with their mentor.

Large scale Gym displays on School Field, ending with massed marching to the OTC band, were popular in

Sherwood's day. Mr Bolland stands in front of the lines for the photograph while 'popular music from a gramophone was amplified through a loudspeaker' in June 1929.

George Notcutt, John Nicholson and Bob Clayton maintained the traditional movements and vaults into the 1980s until it was deemed that Physical Education demanded more breadth and less rigour.

HOCKEY was introduced in the Lent term of 1889, 'a great success, though not unattended by some danger'. The day-boys beat the boarders by 16 goals to 2. 'We wish that some other Clubs in the town would start the game so that we might have the opportunity to test our strength.' In 1902 the game was re-introduced in place of football in the Lent term in time to pre-pare *Kenneth Raynor*, son of the headmaster, to win his Blue at Oxford. It was dropped in 1908, and although it made an unh-eralded return a little later, it struggled to compete and was finally dropped in 1942 – a casualty of the lack of sticks and pitches in wartime. In 1950 James Young opposed its reintro-duction because 'our rugger is not good enough to allow time for hockey', but it was still permitted to share the second half of the Lent Term with Athletics. In the late 1960s, thanks to the determined lobbying of Peter Petrie, it became the major Lent sport and by 1979 four-fifths of fixtures at all levels were won, a reward for much effort by Derek Chapman, the long-serving coach. Whereas the red ash pitch at Westwood was not all-weather at all, the three astroturf pitches of Ipswich Ladies, Ipswich Sports Club and Ipswich School were reliable. Then the dedicated efforts of David Fletcher, Steve Godfrey and *David Walsh* brought a surge in interest and a raising of standards to sport in general. In 2001 Ipswich School reached the RAF Cup U18 finals with one club and two other school sides. *James Southgate* – Player of the Tournament in an international competition in Barcelona – and *Oliver Didham* represented England at U18 level.The following year the Under 16 side emulated the achievements of the senior side and *George Pinner* and *Ed Driver* were capped by England and *Tom Parry* by Wales. Girls' Hockey was begun in 1986 by Karen Runnacles who spurred on teams by her competitive nature but standards surged in 2001 at junior level thanks to the enthusiasm and expertise of Kirsten Spencer and Deb Godfrey.

ICE SKATING was certainly practised in cold weather on flooded meadows at Flatford in the 1950s, probably earlier, with *George Notcutt* as organiser.

The IPSWICH SCHOOL GAME was played until replaced by football in 1874. As with similar contests staged in other schools and many villages it was a mixture of handling and kicking played between various nominated sides. It owed its popularity to the fact that it

provided large numbers of people with physical activity. Because every 'club' had its own rules, games were parochial. This is undoubtedly why new games with agreed laws emerged to make inter-school competition possible. The museum has a heavy pumpkin-shaped ball thought to have been used in the game in the 1870s.

NETBALL with indoor and outdoor courts of high quality has become a major girls' game recently.

ORIENTEERING since the 1970s has found some devotees with both *David* and *Joanne West* competing in World Championships, with David taking silver in Israel in 1999.

ROCK-CLIMBING is a modern pursuit practised on indoor and outdoor climbing facilities at home and abroad.

ROUNDERS is certainly the noisiest game ever played at the school.

RUGBY: This sport was coached from the beginning of the Lent Term of 1924, as reported in the *Ipswich School Magazine*: 'Another epidemic of more alarming possibilities has arisen – Rugger; on all sides people are recovering from attacks of it and it is almost as fashionable as an appendicitis.' On 25 October 1924 our XVs took the field for the first time in matches against Woodbridge School. The editorial commented: 'By far the most important point about this term has been, of course, the fact that it was the school's first experience of Rugger. Statistics must be sought elsewhere but we take the opportunity here of congratulating the school on the spirit in which it has played the game in the face of defeats and of hard knocks. The small boys now will be able, when their time comes, to look back on the school's first plunge with pride and with satisfaction'.

The change to the oval ball game was the result of a decision made by Sherwood, headmaster from 1919, a rowing man himself, but keen on games. The change from soccer to rugby met stiff opposition, some from his own staff. It was necessary to bring in an expert to provide coaching for the new game and in January 1924, shortly after the school played its last soccer match against the OI Club (a 5–1 victory to the school), R.H.F. Gleave masterminded the introduction of rugby. R.A.U. Jennings prepared the younger teams the term before Gleave arrived, and remembers a minute boy who wept the first time he missed a tackle. He showed distinct promise which nine years later the Welsh selectors recognised. His name was *Geoffrey Rees-Jones* who gained a Blue at Oxford and several Welsh caps before becoming headmaster of King William's College, Isle of Man.

In an interview given given long after he retired, Hugh Gleave explained that Sherwood's motives for making the change were partly a matter of status. Great public schools played rugby and if Ipswich were to rejoin their ranks, Ipswich must become a rugby school. According to Gleave this meant that Sherwood presented his colleagues at Woodbridge and Framlingham with a *fait accompli*, announcing that from September 1924 Ipswich School would be fielding rugby teams and if other schools wished to continue to enjoy winter fixtures with us, they must do likewise.

After the Second War ended almost any sporting event would draw a crowd and the whole school was expected to watch the XV on a Saturday afternoon, anticipating and usually seeing an Ipswich win. The fixture list grew slowly, and a

IPSWICH SCHOOL
I st XV   1971
RECORD: P 10   W 10   D 0   L 0   Pts. for 284   Pts. against 34

Back row: J.C.NICHOLSON ESQ., N.MORDEY, D.R.ADAMS, W.A.LATTA, P.K.GEELMUYDEN, L.BOND,
               (Master i/c Rugby)   I.B.ADAMS, N.C.FARTHING, W.I.BUCHANAN.
Middle row: N.D.BOURNE, A.R.G.KIDWELL, N.J.S.ABRAM (capt.), F.S.SPENCE, M.J.BERRIMAN.
Front row: M.N.LUSHER,   D.H.KNIGHTS.

mixture of schools and clubs was played until the late 1950s. The unbeaten side of 1959 played eight matches, while the 1987 XV met 22 schools in fifteen a side matches and beat 19 of them. *Colin Simpson* was capped by England and *Tony Hallett* became an important figure in the restructuring of English Rugby Football in the 1990s. In the 1950s and 1960s the ascendancy of the game at the school did not suit all pupils. The 1st XVs of 1958, 1959, 1963 and 1971 (in the group photograph) were undefeated. Peter Williams was a strong influence during his time as coach before handing over to John Nicholson.

In 1963 Wallace Morfey presented a silver trophy for place kicking. The supporters from the school arms guard the posts with a royal crown between them. The motto 'Finis Coronat Opus' – the end crowns the work – is most appropriate.

The winds of change, however, were beginning to blow, as *Mark Bailey,* capped by England in the 1980s and now headmaster of Leeds Grammar School remembers:

> On arriving at Ipswich School in September 1972, I was only interested in two things: wearing long trousers and playing rugby football. When both ambitions were fulfilled within two days of arrival, there was nothing else left but to decipher the timetable, concentrate on serious study and attend *George Notcutt's* incomparable Human Biology classes.
>
> The Blatchly era began late in 1972, but the shadow of an earlier regime still lingered. On a certain freezing and damp afternoon in December, it was traditional for the whole school to stand around the perimeter of the 1st XV pitch on Top field (as it was then imaginatively known). Once in place, we were required to perform the ritual of supporting the annual School versus Old Boys game. Even to a committed follower of rugby, the necessity and wisdom of this exercise seemed dubious. All I remember was that one Old Boy, who possessed the physical characteristics of a giraffe, charged down a kick at goal. The numbing cold seeped into our toes and then crept inexorably up our pink and fragile bodies. Our shoes became indistinguishable from the mud which everywhere consumed us and our expensive and newly-purchased flannel suits turned deep brown below the knees. I don't recall the score but I do recall the hiding when I got home. John Blatchly must have had a similar experience because compulsory attendance at this match was (thankfully) abandoned thereafter.
>
> I was convinced by this experience – and remain so – that rugby is a game for participants, not spectators.

Our teams competed robustly and with no little style. Derek Wyatt, now MP for a Kent constituency, was capped for England while teaching history at Ipswich in the 1970s and encouraged us endlessly to be innovative and resourceful. John Nicholson was an extraordinary man: here was a coach whose primary concern was to equip us with the attitude and technique for us to fulfil our individual and collective potential. Winning matches as an end in itself was never mentioned. Those who were coached by John and didn't acquire some traces of his dignity, decency and salutary disrespect for winning were lost causes anyway.

Another Nicholson era player *Bryan Caley* played for England Colts in 1982 whilst *David Stone*, now a governor, played for England Schools against Japan in 1987.

Neil Cameron, who ran Rugby for some thirteen years, deemed a tour to Canada to be a fitting way to celebrate 70 years of Rugby at Ipswich, and anyway, when *Keith Wilkinson*, who happened to be the manager of the Canada Rugby World Cup Squad, issued the invitation, it would have been churlish to refuse. Since 1995 regular matches have been played in Barcelona and Holland, and Canada is to be revisited in 2002 with Richard Welbourne leading his umpteenth tour.

In 2001, *Charlotte Thurston* was a member of the England Development Squad showing that girls' rugby could continue to develop under Bryan Caley's guidance.

Seven-a-side Rugby

When in 1965 Ipswich lost in the Rosslyn Park final to Coleraine Academy, the result was given on the BBC Nine O'clock News. In the 1960s and 70s the Suffolk U19 competition was often won by the 'Jacobeans' which title was chosen by the school to avoid the sensitive Sunday play issue. National success came in the Oxford Sevens in 1988. In recent years the Old Ipswichian seven-a-side day just before Christmas has become a popular sporting and social event.

SHOOTING, encouraged by the CCF at the Notcutt's field Range has had bouts of popularity. When for many winters it was practised by boarders in the drained swimming bath it was at enormous risk to all concerned. A Cambridge correspondent to the *Magazine* commented that *George Notcutt's* college room was 'virtually an armoury'. From time to time Clay Pigeon shooting has had its aficionados amongst the country lovers.

SKI-ING at various continental venues became a regular feature of the end of the Christmas Holidays from about 1950, at first under *George Notcutt* and then Derek Chapman. The Wherstead dry-ski slope of the late 1970s was useful for beginners. The alcohol-free slopes of North America are now wisely favoured by Simon Duncombe, and the journey time by jumbo to Canada in 2002 is quicker than by steam train to the Alps in 1950.

SQUASH In Watson's time one of the obsolete Rugby fives courts was modified for squash. Even so, Tanqueray turned down a benefactor's offer of squash courts on the grounds that it was not a game for gentlemen. He should have met Peter Hill who arrived to teach History in 1951 with half blues in squash and athletics. For many years the game had to be played at the Airport, until *George Notcutt* generously gave his retirement testimonial fund towards the building of the courts at the rear of the Holly Road Pavilion. Teams then began to compete in the local leagues.

SWIMMING at the public bathing place on the Orwell or in the Gipping at Sproughton was a hazardous and potentially unhealthy pastime. From 1884 the school was one of the first to have an indoor bath, much later called the swimming pool. From then on competitions at House and Year level have been held annually. The pool was upgraded some hundred years after it was built, since when it has become an important facility, also enabling many local children to learn to swim during the school holidays. Water-polo was introduced in 1958 but died naturally.

TABLE-TENNIS, particularly popular with far-eastern boarders, has led to successful spells in local leagues. Ian 'Ping-Pong' Bullock coached many junior teams to county victories.

TENNIS has sneaked into the physical and social life with various degrees of success for over 100 years. In 1878 a letter in the Elizabethan explored the need to 'get up' a Lawn Tennis Club. By 1902 the all-round sportsman *Charles Palmer* had gained a Cambridge Blue.

There is a possibly apocryphal tale from the 1960s of two *Johns – Collett and Lee –* being beaten for truancy on the Monday and extolled in Headmaster's Assembly two days later for winning the Suffolk Doubles whilst illegally absent.

In 1987 the U19 Tennis team reached the final of the Glanvil Cup at Queen's Club succumbing to Repton, St Paul's and Millfield. The French master Gilles Gergaud was the charming coach at the time. However for the last thirty years Headmasters Blatchly and Galbraith have encouraged the game by tolerating the use of the court next to their house. In more recent times girls have been more successful at County level than their male counterparts.

VOLLEYBALL has been a popular diversion these past 30 years, not merely because Dr Blatchly is remembered as a willing but hopeless participant in a pick up game one summer's afternoon on school field.

WATERSPORTS
Rowing On 6 September 1852 the customary half-holiday was granted for the Ipswich Regatta. The school did not take part, but this sparked the idea of learning to row on the Orwell, a dangerous river for novices. A Head of the Water or Captain of the Boats was appointed. The liberty of going on the water was confined to fifth and sixth formers. From about 1865, mixed Scratch Fours of old Ipswich and Bury school men used to compete in those races at Cambridge. *H.W. Schreiber* while up at Trinity Hall was President of C. U. Boat Club in 1855, in the crew which won the Grand Challenge that year, but he did not row in a Boat Race. The Games Committee refused to reinstate Rowing as a school sport at the turn of the century but nevertheless *A.C.L. Hunt* won a Cambridge Blue in 1906. In 1985 *Neil Cawthorn* addressed potential rowers but the pulling didn't last long even on the newly flooded Alton Water.

Canoeing has had spurts of interest. Mathematics master Ivan Hamilton was granted a weekend's leave of absence to attempt a crossing of the Irish Sea, but the weather did not permit it.

Sailing was so popular in the 1950s that participants used to cycle to Waldringfield, and from time to time under an enthusiastic teacher it has been a team sport with inter-school matches. Some pairs have reached international competition level.

Sub-aqua training in the school pool and field courses at St Abb's Head have been popular recently.

Windsurfing has had its aficionados in recent years with *Toby Monk* remembered for posting mock Maths papers from Spain to be marked while competing nationally just before A levels.

The GAMES COMMITTEE has met for over one hundred years. Carefully selected pupils and staff have spent hours designing badges and blazers, debating the merits of various sports and searching for consistency in refereeing. The allocation of points in various competitions towards the Ganzoni Trophy awarded to the House with the greatest total, provides readers of the minutes with much innocent amusement. It was in 1936 that headmaster Tanqueray wanted to abolish the Trophy because of the 'constant bickering'. By 2001 'rational discussion' amongst the Heads of House – staff not pupils – had replaced the earlier methods.

Several *Old Ipswichians* have appeared in the sporting pages of newspapers: *Dick Partridge* took part in the Paris-Dakar Rally from 1988 onwards, and *Bob Spalding* was World Power Boat Champion in the 1960s. *Richard Evans*, once Racing Correspondent of *The Times* is now of the *Telegraph; Michael Williams* was Golf Correspondent of the *Telegraph*, and *Martin White* has gained plaudits for his coverage of Hockey in East Anglia since the early 1990s.

Not quite sports, but:
CHESS has always been an activity for many and interschool matches have existed for years. In 1994, the school won the 'Times Schools' Chess Cup. According to Roger Holt, the *Pert*

334

twins, later at Oakham School, have been the most capable performers with *Nicholas* becoming an International master. *Alison Holt* held the Suffolk Ladies' title in the mid-1990s.

DEBATING, at first the preserve of the Literary and Dramatic Society, ruffled patriotic feathers at the end of Sherwood's time. Tony Ninham's enthusiasm lay behind *Timothy Briden* and *Simon Pudge* reaching the final of the Observer Mace competition in 1969 when they were runners-up to Ampleforth but it was Dick Burnell who coached *David Chapman* and *Dominic Bell* to follow in their footsteps in 1976. The art was revived in the 1990s with the encouragement of OIs, and under Kimberley Wilson debates have raged at all levels under her driving enthusiasm.

SCHOOLS CHALLENGE QUIZ for Under 13 and Under 18 teams has attracted pupils since 1987 undoubtedly encouraged by the general obsession with such competions. The juniors have twice been national finalists whilst the seniors have been regional champions. Many have graduated to join teaching staff in various pub leagues.

BIRDWATCHING, pioneered by T.G. 'Polly' Powell, Prep head from 1912–34, has only grown in popularity in recent decades, entirely thanks to Messrs Gregory and *Walsh*. Regular trips in East Anglia have pursued the calls of the bittern and the nightjar. Others to Majorca, Spain, France and Morocco have been held in holidays. The school's bird library has been moved to Landguard Bird Observatory, where it can be used by ringers and researchers, its ownership still acknowledged. In 1993 Ian Andrews, then house tutor there, published a list of the flowering plants of Westwood which included some 160 species excluding trees, grasses and ferns.

DANCE has recently become a popular pursuit for all ages starting with 'Modern and Jazz' in the Pre-prep.

Gymnastics display at Erwarton Hall Fête in June 1965.
Left: Nicholas Hall *behind* William Notcutt
Right: Brian Peyton *behind* Andrew Lamerton
Centre: Paul Read *on shoulders of* Nigel Leech

XXIII
Performance

Although at times music and drama may have languished unappreciated in the school there have been others throughout its history when the performing arts have flourished conspicuously. This survey over nearly seven centuries contains some surprises: a former choirmaster burnt at the stake as a Calvinist, entertainments in honour of the first Elizabeth, and Shaw's St Joan performed in five German cities just days before Hitler became chancellor.

Pageants involving both drama and music were an important part of life in Ipswich from medieval times; worship in those days was accompanied by colourful ceremonial, solemn enough in church but lively and sometimes entertaining when processions took to the streets. From its foundation in about 1325 the Guild of Corpus Christi celebrated its principal feast on several days during the week following Trinity Sunday, with pageants in procession and communal feasts. The chaplain who celebrated mass for the Guild was responsible for collecting contributions towards the costs of the celebrations from the craft companies, for storing, maintaining and renewing the pageant costumes and properties from year to year and for entertainment, but another all-the-year-round duty was the teaching the sons of the members. Children in costume will have joined their elders in singing, dancing and acting, some presenting static tableaux on carts. In another popular and public annual religious observance between the Feast of St Nicholas (6 December) and Holy Innocents (28 December), the boy chosen to be the Boy Bishop Nicholas with his peers in attendance took part in the traditional processions and ceremonies, the youthful 'bishop' even preaching a sermon. In Colchester, the boy bishop tradition, involving grammar school boys, was established as early as 1422. The first record of the practice in Ipswich was during Richard Argentine's mastership in the Marian 1550s and he will surely have chosen promising pupils for the leading roles.

The importance of music varied greatly throughout the school's history, but the first regulations of 1477 show that the youngest pupils, the Apeseyes, learned to read and sing before, as Donatists, they began to study Latin grammar. William Godyng was collated by the bishop of Norwich to the charge of the song school, the junior school, as early as 1445. Still in his charge, pupils became Psalterians, learning the words, and surely the plainsong, of the Psalms of David. Richard Felaw determined, in bequeathing the school his house in Edmund Pountney Lane that the 'said master shall keep with the said children the Mass of Our Lady by note [*i.e.* sung] at the North altar within the said [Black]friars at six o'clock on the morrow daily'. The Blackfriars' church faced Felaw's House, so that the boarders had only to tumble out of bed and cross the road. Were day scholars expected at school so early? It is likely that they were. Music was almost certainly more important in the late medieval and Tudor school than during the Puritan period which followed.

During the brief but glorious period of existence of Thomas Wolsey's Cardinal College of St Mary, there is no doubting the importance of music, for the establishment included eight singing men – lay clerks, and eight 'children' – treble choristers. An inventory of the vestments and plate of the chapel taken for Thomas Cromwell at the dissolution of the college lists two copes, fourteen tunicles and sixteen pairs of parers [footwear] to be worn by the choristers at services. The greatest festival of the college year was the annual procession on the Feast of the Nativity of the Virgin – 8 September. The music performed would have been as important a part of the celebration as the feasting.

Wolsey naturally recruited the best men available to direct the choir and sing in it; the first choirmaster, one Lenthall, had been his contemporary at Magdalen, Oxford some thirty years earlier. Dean Capon described Lenthall to Wolsey in the autumn of 1528 as being 'very sober and discreet, and bringeth up your Choristers very well: assuring your grace that there shall be no better children in [any] place in England than we shall have here, and that in short tyme'. Lenthall was less good with the singing men who would 'not serve here with theyr good wills' as a protest against low wages and poor food. The Dean unwisely commented: 'without Mr Lentall we cowde in a maner do nothing in our quere', and this led to his promotion to the senior foundation at Oxford. Capon dared to chide Wolsey for poaching him in a letter of 20 December 1528: 'he was the key of our choir and set everything in order'. On 12 April 1529, Capon wrote to Wolsey 'Mr Testwood, one of the choris-

ters [he meant lay clerks] trains the children admirably'. A year later Robert Testwood was paid off with the rest of the choir following Wolsey's disgrace, but Cromwell found him new employment at St George's Chapel, Windsor, but with the condition that he was to combine singing with spying for his patron. How, in 1543, he suffered burning at the stake as a Calvinist associate of John Marbeck, the composer and organist at Windsor, can be read in another of Morfey's articles.[1]

We do not know how much music went on in the re-founded grammar school, but, throughout the Tudor period, groups of touring players performed regularly in the town. The King's and Queen's Players (in the time of Philip and Mary) were paid one mark (13s 4d) for their plays. James Lockwood, court jester to Henry VIII and to Edward, Mary and Elizabeth his successors, came to the town in 1556 for a quarter as much. Bear baiting was a common spectacle on the town's streets, so that schoolboys experienced live entertainment of many kinds. Their own chance to perform came on New Year's Eve 1565, [24 March], when the borough chamberlains paid ten shillings 'for a play, to Mr Scott's lads'. This was to celebrate the sealing by Queen Elizabeth, six days earlier, of Letters Patent formally refounding the school. Six years later (the lawyers took their time), ordinances regulating the school were drawn up and promulgated on 26 July 1571. They included an order for boys to give speeches in the Moot Hall on the Cornhill:

> The Master and Usher shall yearly cause the best learned Scholars of the said Town, to the number of six at least, to make every one a several [different] Theme, or certain verses in Latin, and deliver them to the Bailiffs of Ipswich for

1 'Robert Testwood, Choir Master, Spy and Martyr' is in *OI Magazine* 15 for 1967. The woodcut is from Foxe's *Acts and Monuments*.

the time being, yearly, on New Year's Day, to the intent that
they may see how they profit in learning.

It was only during the 1960s that the authorities discontinued
Latin orations by head boys on Speech Days in an admission
that only those who composed them could understand them.

On 17 November 1582, the master John Smith was granted
forty shillings 'for his paines and charges in presenting certaine publique pageants in joy of the Queen's Coronation'. This
was of course an anniversary celebration, and held on the accession rather than the coronation day. In successive years he was
rewarded for 'frameing [writing] an oration on the Quenes
dayes' – for a boy to declaim – and for 'speech on the Guild
days'. By then the Corpus Christi Guild had reverted to being a
secular guild merchant, a cross between a chamber of com-
merce and a friendly society, with mainly social and charitable
objects. In 1595 James Leman, usher, received the payment
rather than the elderly master, John Berkely, and in 1599,
George Downing, then a private schoolmaster in the town, but
later, briefly, the master, was chosen; whether he used his own
boys or borrowed the grammar school pupils to perform we do
not know. These Elizabethan performances were, therefore,
sometimes formal declamation and at others, plays and pageants.

The religious and political tensions of the seventeenth century left their mark on the school and probably put an end to
stage performance for most of that time. The Puritan minister
Samuel Ward, arriving as town preacher four days before the
discovery of the Gunpowder Plot, soon took on the governance
of the school and found fault with the incumbent master James
Leman, a former pupil and usher, but not a Puritan. There is no
further mention of entertainment, but Ward, loyal to king and

341

bishop provided they made no moves towards Rome, will have encouraged the annual Tower church service celebrating England's deliverance from Spain in 1588 and 1605. Each year from 1615 until, amazingly, 1771, the senior boy would declaim a dramatic Latin prose Gunpowder Plot sermon. One boy, Robert Purplett, son of the town clerk, went on to preach similar sermons before the university in Great St Mary's while an undergraduate at St Catherine's, Cambridge, thus earning himself a capon in 1695 and the whitewashing of his rooms two years later. The son and namesake of Jeremy Collier, briefly master in the 1660s, was prepared at the school for Caius in 1666. If his best-selling *Short View of the Immorality and Profaneness of the English Stage* is any indication, if he did tread the boards at school, he did not retain any liking for the experience.[2]

Robert Hingeston who became usher in 1737 and master in 1743, came of a family with a long musical tradition. His father Peter was borough organist for 55 years and had studied under his uncle John Hingeston, state musician to Oliver Cromwell and court musician to Charles II. In the 1750s Robert Hingeston and his neighbour Thomas Gainsborough belonged to a club meeting weekly for music with the then borough organist Joseph Gibbs and other local musicians. Unfortunately we know little of their proceedings and nothing of the possible effect of this music-making on the school.

Even though the celebrated actor David Garrick gave his first public performance at the Tankard Theatre in Tacket Street in 1741, no more is heard of school performances, musical or dramatic, until Rigaud moved the school to its present buildings in

---

2 David Self (who reviewed at least one piece of school drama in the 1970s for the *Times Educational Supplement*), in 1999 published an account of Collier's campaign to cleanse the stage with the even more enticing title *The Single Source of all Filth*.

Henley Road in 1852. As soon as the chapel was opened the same year, establishing a choir to lead the services became Rigaud's first priority. A one-manual organ by Russell costing £140 was presented to the head by the Head Boy at the opening of the Christmas term 1853. It had been subscribed for in his honour by present and past masters, scholars and friends of the school. Its specification was 'from FFF to F in alt' with 'three composition pedals and one and two-thirds octave German foot pedals, and seven full stops'. Afternoon chapel services were popular in Rigaud's time, but the choir, which always sang an anthem, wore no surplices, despite a veiled appeal in *The Elizabethan* for 22 May 1852:

> Now to the goodly choral fund
> Subscribe, subscribe, for I
> Expect that with the surplus, they
> Surplices will buy.

Lindley Nunn in his *Musical Recollections*, which cover 1826 to 1899, mentions in passing that he was appointed chapel choir master in about 1854 by Rigaud and left with Holden in 1883. He has not one word to add to this, being rather prouder of the fact that he succeeded Robert Foster as organist at St Mary-le-Tower, and took a Cambridge Mus. Bac. with a cantata of his own composition, dedicated to Lady Flower. For the Amateur Concert given by the choir in June 1859, the entire text

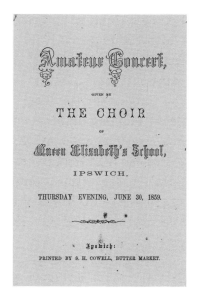

Amateur Concert,

GIVEN BY

THE CHOIR

OF

Queen Elizabeth's School,

IPSWICH.

THURSDAY EVENING, JUNE 30, 1859.

Ipswich:

PRINTED BY S. H. COWELL, BUTTER MARKET.

of items ran to sixteen pages, but Nunn omitted mention of his name as conductor. The lack of surplices was quickly made good by the generosity of Holden's successor's wife; Mrs Browne presented a set first worn on Trinity Sunday 1883. In 1898 a larger chapel organ by Bishop was provided and the brass dedication plates of the first two instruments are now fixed to the vestry screen.

Prose and verse orations in Latin, Greek and English were a far cry from drama, and Rigaud and Holden, who both brought much that was new to the curriculum, would have been far-sighted indeed to encourage fully staged plays. At the 1868 Speech Day, however, single scenes from *The Merchant of Venice*, *Twelfth Night*, Molière and Goldsmith were read. Browne continued with scenes by major dramatists on Speech Days, but also instituted regular Musical and Literary Entertainments with readings, songs and duets, some by boys and others by staff and their wives. Collections were taken to cover costs. In Raynor's time the annual School Concert was held at the end of the Christmas term. The first part was musical, miscellaneous items of an ephemeral nature, but the second consisted of a short farce, usually by some author not worth naming. In December 1903 the souvenir programme printed by the school press included no play, but the music, in four sections, lasted from eight to at least ten thirty. Bunnell Burton OI 'arranged' the music whatever that means. The caste (*sic*) in 1906 included a master and the proceedings closed with the National Anthem and Auld Lang Syne, because the newly arrived A. K. Watson, having heard it, would not allow the School Song to be performed. With his rich bass voice he liked nothing better than to sing himself in school concerts. 'Invictus', 'Hope the Hornblower' and 'Forty Years On' were his party pieces and he would also lead the communal singing at house suppers. He

344

enjoyed a glass of whiskey at the Fonnereau Road home of his part-time music master, 'Mop' Hockey. Had the chairman of governors, Bunnell Burton, known, this would have been another nail in the coffin of this gifted and effective head. But the symposium of gathered memories of Watson's time from thirty of his pupils has nothing more to say about music in their schooldays.

Sherwood, following Watson in 1919, insisted (against Hockey's advice) that major plays, at first abridged but later complete, should be the sole entertainment at the end of the Christmas term. Despite the complete lack of music, the event was still called a concert until 1925. Plays set for School Certificate were chosen, the first *Macbeth*. In 1920, rehearsals had commenced for *The Rivals*, when Hockey's resignation brought them to a standstill, and no entertainment was given that year. *Twelfth Night* and *School for Scandal* were the successes of 1921 and 1922. Coming in Hockey's place, Stanley Wilson quickly formed a School Musical Society with an orchestra and a choral society. Sherwood and Wilson now introduced works by recognisable composers: Gibbons, Morley, Stanford, Parry and Elgar. *The Merry Wives of Windsor* and Molière's *Le Bourgeois Gentilhomme* were put on in successive terms in 1925/6 and the whole cultural climate of the school was thus transformed. Producers (called stage

Souvenir Programme
(Printed at the Conversazione.)

MUSICAL PROGRAMME
WEDNESDAY, DECEMBER 16th, 1903.

8·0.

GLEES ... ... { ... *The Poppy* ... ... Trousselle.
{ ... *The Hop-Pickers* ... ... Philp.
IPSWICH SCHOOL CHORAL SOCIETY.

SONG ..."Two Songs" { *Since my Love now loves* } ...G. W. Cox.
{ *me not* }
{ *In the merry month of May* }
Mr. ERNEST PRETTY.

SONG ... ... *Song of the Toreador* ... ... Bizet.
Mr. W. HOCKEY.

8·45.

SONG ... ... *The Old Grey Fox* ... ...M. V. White.
Mr. G. KING-SMITH (o.I.)

QUARTETTE ... ... *Sleep, gentle Lady* ... ... Bishop.
Messrs. SMITH, EVERARD, KING and WATSON.

SONG ... ... *Onaway, Awake, Beloved* ... Cowen.
Mr. OVERTON MOYLE.

9·45.

SONG ... ... *Sound Argument* ... ... Lane Wilson.
Mr. W. HOCKEY.

QUARTETTE ... ... *Old King Cole* ... ... Macfarren.
Messrs. SMITH, EVERARD, KING and WATSON.

SONG ... ... *I had a Flower* ... ... Laurence Kellie.
Mrs. ERNEST PRETTY.

10·15.

SONG ... ... *The Tinker's Song* ... ... Lane Wilson.
Mr. G. KING-SMITH (o.I.)

SONG ... ... *The Jolly Sailor* ... ... W. H. Squire.
Mr. OVERTON MOYLE.

GLEE ... ... *The Winter Song* ... ... Dorn.
IPSWICH SCHOOL CHORAL SOCIETY.

SONG ... ... *Ipswich School Song* ... ... J. Evans.
OMNES.

God Save the King.

Music arranged by Mr. BUNNELL H. BURTON, (O.I.)
School Choral Society, Mr. M. WRETTS-SMITH.

Printed at Ipswich School by H. B. Buck, C. P. Badsham, T. C. Mellonie, C. C. Ling, M. M. Stuart and C. J. Tempson.

managers) were hardly mentioned, let alone thanked, in accounts of plays before 1928 when Stanley Pink OI returned as a master and with A. W. Steward staged performances of *Hamlet* that really impressed audiences. They produced four more plays jointly, taking their last, *St Joan*, on tour in Germany in February 1933, only three weeks before Hitler became Chancellor. The group photo taken in the main square at Brauschweig by the locally-based manufacturers of Rolleiflex Cameras shows several boys wearing their school caps. That summer, Pink left to help Sherwood with his ordination candidates at Whittlesford and Steward became head of Chipping Norton School. James Young enlisted the help of an OI called Winterbottom to put on *Julius Caesar* the following December. It is to Sherwood that the credit is due for bringing the first real music and fully staged plays to the school.

Tanqueray inherited Stanley Wilson as music master, who in March 1934 staged *Trial by Jury* preceded by an orchestral concert which included the first movement of the Schumann piano concerto. The sixteen-strong orchestra included eight boys

346

The
Tempest
1934

(John Alexander, later a professor of engineering and governor was a first violin), but the chief thing remarkable was a whole jury of common room members and the head, the leading parts taken by boys. That December *The Tempest* cast was well-dressed in imaginatively simple sets, but the group photograph shows how cramped the stage was, less of a problem for *Andro-cles and the Lion* in 1936. In *The Mikado* the year before, OIs took the male leads and masters strengthened the chorus of Japanese nobles. Comparatively few boys were offered musical and dramatic opportunities, and another war was looming. *Macbeth* and *The Comedy of Errors* in 1937 and 1938 were well received, but there was then a two-year gap before *Charley's Aunt* was staged by Stanley Wilson in the spring term of 1941. Thereafter the only year without a play was 1955. A low point for chapel music came when Bunnell Burton, chairman of gov-

Androcles
1936

347

ernors, presented a Hammond organ in 1939 to replace the one he had largely funded in 1898. The governors were told that it produced 'its sound by electrical sound currents', and Burton, an organist himself, must have been persuaded that this was the instrument of the future. Wilson suspended the choral society and the chapel choir during the war, departing for Dulwich when it was over. The next man, Osborne, refounded both, but it was thanks to the next music master, John Ince, assisted by Robert Gower (when a pupil) and Cecil Borrett the carpenter that the electrone was replaced. They rebuilt the present Walker organ which came from a chapel in Sudbury, ideal for the size of the building and a useful practice instrument. The other organ they built in the new Great School deteriorated under the severe contrasts of temperature and humidity which resulted from a thin roof over a mainly glass building. Tanqueray briefed his successor about drama, showing how cut and dried things were in those days, but omitted all mention of music:

> I have advocated a 'classical' play, with a bias to Shakespeare. Marsden produces, assisted by Dodd (scenery). Performances are on the last three nights of [the Christmas] term. Seating and giving out of tickets arranged by Young and Sullivan, or Saunders. It has become customary to invite Governors on last night and for H.M. to entertain them and Staff afterwards. This social meeting has been appreciated by all. Generally each boy has been allocated two tickets and this fills the house, so that it is difficult to find seats for other guests.

Peter Marsden did indeed produce plays from two years after his arrival in 1945 until he left to be headmaster of Great Yarmouth Grammar School in 1960. The fully illustrated record of his era which he assembled for archives would be worth printing. His first play, Dorothy L. Sayers' *The Zeal of Thy House,*

Importanc
1950

was an unusual choice, but he tackled five of Shakespeare's plays including *Timon of Athens*, also *Dr Faustus, HMS Pinafore* and *An Enemy of the People,* going out on a high note with *Peer Gynt.* Photographs of the cast and set of *The Importance of Being Earnest* make one wish one could have been present in 1950. It did not help that the 100 year-old Big School was declared unsafe and unusable in 1952 and other halls in the town had to be hired until the present Great School came into use four years later. The new auditorium was a more direct stimulus to drama than to music and the former improved more rapidly than the latter. Ramsey Wherrett's striking and humorous programe cover for the 1958 *Beggar's Opera* makes a fitting tailpiece to the Marsden era.

DRAMA seems to have sagged somewhat after 1960, but it revived when Richard Tucker arrived from King William's, Isle of Man, as head of English six years later just as the new Fison foyer and classrooms provided green room accommodation conveniently next to the Great School. The growth of interest and development of style in the sixties and seventies came, as it always does, from the enthusiasm of enterprising members of the common room. Dick Tucker directed annual school plays with magnificent sets constructed by Ted Herrington, appointed in 1971 in time to run the Leggett Centre. From the early seventies, the range of presentation widened to include operas, some of them for the newly founded Music for Youth in Ipswich. Each season, four or five live concerts were organised for the under-11s of the town and the Preparatory School, and such operas as *Amahl and the Night Visitors*,[3] *The Little Sweep* and Bizet's *Doctor Miracle* were staged. Some-

3 With the three kings in *Amahl* can be seen David Sawer as their page and Ben Parry in the leading part.

times a Great School full of children would in a single hour rehearse and then perform one of Malcolm Williamson's pieces, *The Stone Wall* for example, with evident enjoyment. The juniors were exhilarated by the idiosyncratic leadership of first Howard Jones (later chaplain at Alleyn's) and then Ernest Thomas in the Mermaid Society which performed a play annually.[4] In the 1975 *Owl and the Pussycat*, Mark Bailey (left) played the Quangle-Wangle with, on the right, David Broadway as the Owl and David Sawer the Pussycat. Pam Blatchly enlisted the help of many parents to begin to build up a stock of costumes which soon packed two spare bedrooms in the Headmaster's House until provision was made in school. Sixth-formers produced a play each year with a minimum of common room advice and assistance. Common Room players capped the year with an end of summer term comedy – Alex

4 The name comes from the supposed foregatherings of Marlowe, Jonson and Shakespeare at 'an Ordinary entitled The Mermaid, Southwark-side'.

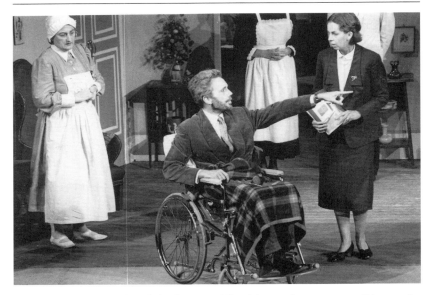

Burnett, in the wheelchair, was *The Man who came to Dinner* in 1986. In the eighties and nineties, a large number of directors (usually working in pairs) were happy to direct at any level in the school, thus opening up the stratified assumption of 'one School play plus others' into some ten or more productions a year, all of which were 'school plays', that is plays in school, or, indeed, in local churches. The broad supportive infrastructure which under Burnett[5] facilitated an even fuller programme included expertise in many fields: silk-screen posters under Mike Scoging (head of art), the wholly professional technical supervision of John Woolnough (head of physics), a tirelessly inventive wardrobe mistress in Charlotte Stewart (a distinguished painter), the stalwart efforts of David Warnes (head of history, director and adapter of anniversary presentations such as *Ivor Gurney – Out of My Sorrow*), musical support of a

5 Burnett arrived in 1978, working creatively with Tucker in both English and drama, and taking over both responsibilities on the latter's retirement in 1989.

rich variety, jazz group, brass ensemble, continuo, organ, per-
cussion or whatever the occasion demanded, as well as full-
blown musical-theatre scores. From 1989, the Little School, as
second auditorium, with raked seating usable there or in the
Great School, enhanced the house style by doubling the
options for directors. Drama at the school is still rich, varied
and non-curricular. The programmes of two typical years
(which do not include workshops, revues, class drama and
competition away from school – most notably the Ludi Scaenici tradition of junior Latin plays) illustrates this:

1981-82	*1989–90*
Requiescat for Wilfred Owen	Cain & Abel
Peter Florence, pupil in Chapel	A Sleep of Prisoners
	Fry St Margaret's Church
Unman, Wittering and Zigo	Hopeless Glory
Cooper Middle School	*Kevin Park*, pupil Sixth Form
Tarantara, Tarantara	Café Theatre
Taylor, after Gilbert and	French Set
Sullivan Senior	
The Fire Raisers	Antigone
Frisch Sixth Form	*Sophocles* Classics Set
The Children's Crusade	Captain Stirrick
Thompson 4A [Year 10]	*Taylor* Junior
The Government Inspector	As You Like It
Gogol Junior	*Shakespeare* Lower Sixth
The Soldier's Tale	The Caucasian Chalk Circle
Stravinsky Music for Youth	*Brecht* 4A [Year 10]
Broke of the Shannon	Hassan
Warnes in Library	*Flecker* Junior & Senior

1981-82 (continued)

L'Anglais tel qu'on le Parle
French Set

Toad of Toad Hall
Milne, after Grahame Prep

Gunslinger
Crane Middle School

Spring and Port Wine
Naughton Common Room

1989-90 (continued)

The Lion, the Witch and
the Wardrobe
Robbins, after Lewis Prep

The Ticket of Leave Man
Taylor Common Room

A Midsummer Night's Dream
Shakespeare Edinburgh Festival

MUSIC: Because John Ince had been mainly a chapel musician, a great enthusiast for the organ which his colleague Reginald Kell so enjoyed playing, it took his successors Keith Griffiths and Geoffrey Lavery some time to improve instrumental standards and to build a choral society capable of tackling *Gerontius* (1977) or *Elijah* (1983). The first of many chapel choir tours, to St Asaph, took place at Easter 1972, but the new headmaster's encouragement for music soon had Ian Hammond gloomily telling sporting OIs that there was now 'a piano in every room in the school'. The Chamber Music Group,

354

1991

meeting several times a term in the head's drawing room, gave rise to these remarks but, more profitably, to recitals given in Suffolk and Norfolk churches at the end of every term. The 1991 members were photographed outside chapel. Concerts in churches continue. Between 1984 and 1988 exchanges with a school in Mönchengladbach were a particular stimulus to wind and brass players.

In 1987 the school's first musician-in-residence, the oboist Mark Law, began a continuing tradition; he was followed by versatile and gifted exponents of various instruments. It was a three-man team of Stephen Orton, Richard Bainbridge and William Dore, which with Ruth Wilkinson, musician-in residence, first hired Snape Maltings for a day's rehearsal and a sell-out concert (proceeds to Save the Children) in 1990. The first half featured the Chapel Choir, Chamber Group and Orchestra, the second, Wind Band, First Form Choir, Trak 7 and Big Band. The Trad combination Trak 7 beat 2000 entries to win the *Daily Telegraph* Jazz in Education Competition held at the RNCM in Manchester. Milton's Premier Jazz band came

1993

before Trak 7, who were succeeded by Perennial Jazz (photographed in front of the Custom House) and Upbeat. Five more Snape concerts were held between the first and 2003, and others on the same scale have been held in the Corn Exchange.

In 1988 and succeeding years there were Chapel Choir tours to cathedrals in the west country, the north, and northern France. The choir is seen here processing in Beverley Minster in 1991. Under the current strong leadership of Andrew Leach, himself a fine pianist and his successive assistants Andrew Wilson and Neil Matthews, music today thrives on the enjoyment of talented boys and girls, and the breadth of musical styles and ensembles continues to grow. In autumn 2002 the chapel choir sang services in St Asaph and Peterborough Cathedrals and Southwell Minster.

Many OLD IPSWICHIANS, most of whom were both actors and musicians at school, have gone on to work in the Arts: The late Kit Pedler produced *Doomwatch* and Colin Nears ('51), who retired from the BBC after a long and distinguished career as a producer of Arts documentaries, remains actively involved in the world of ballet. Andre Ptaszynski ('71) is a West End producer. Lyn Goleby ('76) produced the Suffolk-based film *The Bridge* in 1991 and others for television. Peter Florence ('82) founded and directs the Hay-on-Wye Literary Festival and the London Orange Wood festival. Neal Swetten-ham ('76) teaches Performing Arts at De Montfort University and Tom Richardson ('79) is a production manager at the National Theatre. Dominic Taylor ('85) has appeared in *East-enders* and *London's Burning* and Julia Marsen ('88) has also acted in *Eastenders* and was Anne Boleyn in *The Wives of Henry VIII*. Tim West ('84, as Tim Freeman), Helena Lyons ('91) and Edward Lyons ('96) work on stage, in TV and film. Jo Carrick ('86) produces documentary films largely on social issues. James King ('93) is Radio One's Film Critic.

Robert Gower ('70), formerly Precentor of Radley, is now Director of Music at Glenalmond. Timothy Roe ('76) after studying musicology works with the new technology. Andrew Fryer ('79), after taking the tonmeister course at Surrey, composes and produces for his own record label and production company. He was involved with *The Full Monty*. Mark Hudson ('79), a successful and original graphic designer, surely cannot be our only working artist. Andrew Bird ('76) runs music at Bromsgrove School, his wife Tamsin (*née* Andrews, '79) a colleague. Ben Parry ('83), once a Swingles singer, from a conduct-

357

ing career in Edinburgh has been appointed to direct the music at St Paul's School. Francis Goodhand ('92), a composer and musical director, works in theatre, often with George Double ('91) as percussionist. The versatile instrumentalist Simon Wilcox ('91) has played bass for M J Cole on *Top Of The Pops* and *Later With Jools Holland*. Ned Bennett and Jon Beales (both '85) work in musical fields, and Steve Trowell ('91) is a key member of the six-strong a cappella vocal group The Magnets. Jamie Trowell ('96), now a drummer and percussionist, is seen here rehearsing with George Double in 1991. Simon Paterson ('91) and Rob Cattermole ('92) are both sound engineers. Timothy Kiddell ('98) is the most recent choral scholar, a tenor at King's. The tenor Richard Edgar-Wilson ('81) sings all over Europe in opera, oratorio and lieder and his brother Nicholas ('84), in music administration, still plays the horn. David Sawer ('79), conspicuously the most celebrated Ipswichian in the contemporary arts, has had works commissioned for The Proms and the Aldeburgh Festival; his opera *From Morning to Midnight* was premiered by English National Opera at the Coliseum, and will next be seen in Berlin.

358

XXIV
School Art and Artists

Ever since the young Thomas Gainsborough lived next door to the school in the 1750s the school has developed strong artistic traditions. The three art prizes awarded annually bear the names of the three most celebrated Ipswichian artists and the school collects works by them and others. In recent years some works by non-Ipswichian artists of the first rank have also been acquired. Stained glass made by masters and murals and screen-printed posters by pupils furnish most of the school buildings.

 WHICH OTHER SCHOOL can cite portraits of a headmaster and a senior governor by Thomas Gainsborough? Both pictures now belong to the borough and hang in Christchurch Mansion, but it was Wallace Morfey who ran to ground that of Robert Hingeston, master, acquired it and corrected its attribution.[1] Hingeston's great friend the Revd Richard Canning also sat to Gainsborough; he and others

---

1 Morfey told the whole story in 'Elusive Head OI' in *Old Ipswichian Magazine* 9, 1961. At the opening of the Morfey rooms, where the school's archives and collections have safe housing, Wallace was photographed sitting in Rigaud's chair.

drew up new regulations for the school published in 1747. In the early 1750s, long before he became famous, Thomas Gainsborough brought his new wife from his native Sudbury to Ipswich, renting houses first in Brook Street and then Foundation Street. At the latter, his garden ran alongside that of the Master's House, which was the boarders' playground. While the Gainsboroughs and Hingestons were neighbours they became close friends, and Thomas will surely have been glad to be employed to teach drawing in the school. From then on the school seems always to have had at least a part-time drawing master and they have never lacked promising pupils.

Charles Keene (1823–91) and his brother *Henry Eddowes Keene* (1824–1909) both joined the school as foundation scholars and dayboys in 1833. Their father Samuel, a London lawyer, sent them to live with their maternal uncle John Eddowes Sparrow, town clerk, at the Ancient house in the Buttermarket. Graffiti from the margins of Charles' copy of Homer's Iliad include a sketch of Ebden, his headmaster (see page 151), but the mounted officer illustrated reminds us that there were barracks in Anglesea Road, most of the officers living in Berners Street. When, later, Charles became one of the most popular Punch cartoonists he often illustrated school jokes.

One of the oldest was 'Do you collect stamps?' leading to the new boy receiving one on the toe, is set in a playground surely inspired by the one behind the Lower Brook Street school.[2] The Charles Keene Prize label reproduces a self-portrait.

Henry was also a gifted artist but always in his brother's shadow; perhaps wisely he played for safety and managed a bank. He made this sketch of the Blue Coach bringing the

brothers back to school from London. *George Ingelow*, brother of Jean Ingelow the poet, was their school fellow; he followed the Victorian topographical school.

Edward John Poynter (1836-1919) boarded at the school 1851–52 because his father Ambrose, the well-known architect, was an long-standing friend of Rigaud. Edward made the only known drawings, very much in the architectural style, of the temporary Great School behind the Brook Street School House, used only

2 Laurie Rimmer, headmaster at Framlingham College from 1971, generously presented the original to the school. See the *Punch* version on page 152.

from 1843 until the move to Henley Road in 1852. He was knighted on succeeding Millais as President of the Royal Academy in 1896, created a baronet in 1902, and made GCVO on retirement as PRA in 1918. The Edward Poynter Prize label shows ones of his pencil studies for the fresco in St Stephen's church, Dulwich.

George Thomas Rope (1846–1929), at school 1858–62, was a painter of animals and the rural landscape.

Cecil Howard Lay (1885–1956), at school 1898–1904. This artist, architect, poet and genial countryman was entirely content to live at Aldringham where his house Raidsend combines Dutch and Art Nouveau features. He was an habitué of the Parrot and Punchbowl Inn on the Leiston Road. 'Here I stay as years go by / And Suffolk knows the reason why.' Balloons seem always to feature in his watercolours of beach scenes and village celebrations. The school's liveliest Lay painting is of a boxing match on Aldringham Common.

Edward Ardizzone (1900–1979), at school 1909–12. In *The Young Ardizzone, an autobiographical fragment* (Studio Vista 1970), Edward tells how he was one of the only boys who were terrified of Miss Hunt, seen here punishing him, how chaplain de Candole was his kindly tutor and how the larger boys maltreated him in Christchurch Park. He illustrated all these scenes with pen-and-ink drawings in his delightfully clear and evocative style. For the Prize label, to the design of which the artist gave his written assent, see page 237.

Martin Squirrell (1926–50), at school 1938–44. Martin, only son of the fine topographical artist Leonard Squirrell, had three pictures hung at the Royal Academy at the age of seventeen. Leonard's prediction that his son's talent would eventually eclipse his own, was, tragically, never realised, for Martin died of cancer, aged only 24. Several of Martin's drawings illustrating the wartime school, the masters and his fellow pupils appear in Chapter XVIII.

Four Green Man roundels for the upper stage of Birkin Haward's new Library were designed by John Piper, CH, and realised by Patrick Reyntiens and David Wasley in 1981. They can be read in several different ways: as the four seasons, the Greek elements (earth, air, fire and water) or, as the faces become older, the ages of man. From spring to winter they are lit in order as the sun moves around the building each day. The Library and new Studio was opened by Sir Hugh Casson, KCVO, then PRA, on 19 May 1982. A

Spring

Autumn

loan exhibition of works of art by Old Ipswichians was assembled, the catalogue written by John Constable, then in the sixth form, seen here with two Lay drawings.

Stained glass by Walter Wilson when chaplain can be seen in the west window of the Sports Hall, at the Ivry Street entrance to the Great and Little Schools and in one of the Music rooms. There is good Victorian glass in the Chapel and more recent work by several artists including a tree of life and two artificially-lit roundels by Rosemary Rutherford. Hers also is the oil triptych in the antechapel, originally intended to have a permanent home in Charterhouse chapel but now in ours. The figures of Wolsey and Cromwell engraved on the antechapel doors are the work of Sheila Elmhirst whose twin sons were in the school. The latest chapel colour scheme is by the director of art, Michael Scoging, who also made the east window for the Sports Hall.

Work by Lida Lopez Cardozo and the late David Kindersley of Cambridge include three Welsh slate plaques: the first

364

between the Great and Little Schools, one on the Blatchly Laboratories and another at the Pre-Preparatory School entrance. Below the Vulliamy Clock of 1852 in the Little School the inscription NIL CARIUS TEMPORE [Nothing dearer than time], was lettered by Lida Kindersley and painted by Michael Scoging.

In corridors and on staircases in several buildings there are painted murals and two glass roundels made pupils over the last twenty-five years. Many striking screen-printed posters for plays and concerts have been produced by pupils over the same period; some are framed but the largest display is to be enjoyed in Room 6 in upper Sherwood (see over).

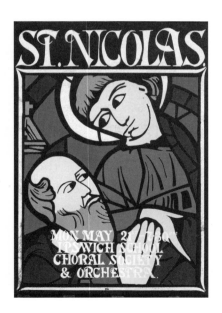 

XXV

Lists of Headmasters, etc

MASTERS, and, from Howorth onwards, HEADMASTERS

All Colleges are at Cambridge unless stated O

From ca 1325 *Chaplains of the Guild of Corpus Christi

ante 1412 Richard Penyngton

1412 Nicholas Scholemayster

1416 William Bury

1477 John Besett MA

1479 *John Squyer perhaps Magdalen O

1520 *William Stephenson

1528 *+William Golding MA King's

1538 *+Richard Argentine MA MD New College U
ante 1537

1558 *John Scott MA 1537 b.Quay 1567

1567 *+John Dawes MA Christ's and St John's

1582 *John Smith MA later BD Magdalen O

1586 *John Berkeley MA BCL New College O

1604 James Leman MA Magdalene U from 1594

1608 *George Downing MA Queens' d.1610

1611 *John Cottisford MA St John's U under Read

1612 *Alexander Read MA later DD Pembroke

1613 *John Cottisford MA St John's

1616 *Nicholas Easton MA Pembroke

1630 *William Clarke MA Trinity

1645 *Christopher Glascock MA St Catharine's

1650 *+Cave Beck MA St John's

1657 Robert Woodside MA Caius U 1630–41

1659 *Henry Wickham MA Trinity

1663	*Jeremy Collier MA Trinity
1664	*Robert Stephenson MA Magdalene
1695	* Robert Coningsby MA St John's O
1712	* Edward Leeds MA Peterhouse
1737	* Thomas Bolton MA St John's
1743	*Robert Hingeston MA Pembroke U from 1721
1767	*John King MA Peterhouse

[no Ushers after 1771]

1798	*Rowland Ingram MA Sidney Sussex
1800	*William Howorth
1832	*James Collett Ebden MA Caius
1843	*John Fenwick MA Corpus Christi
1850	*+Stephen Jordan Rigaud MA DD Exeter O
1858	*+Hubert Ashton Holden MA LL D Trinity
1883	*Frederick Herbert Browne MA Wadham O
1894	*Philip Edwin Raynor MA New College O
1906	Arthur Kenelm Watson MA Balliol O
1919	*Edward Charles Sherwood MA Magdalen O
1933	*Truman Tanqueray MA Magdalene
1950	Patrick Hassell Frederick Mermagen MA Pembroke
1972	John Marcus Blatchly MA Ph D Hon Litt D Christ's
1993	Ian Geoffrey Galbraith MA St John's

* In holy orders + See the *Oxford Dictionary of National Biography* 2004

USHERS or Deputy Masters

i = *believed to be OI*

1445	William Godyng (Master of the song school)
ante 1537	*+ Richard Argentine MA MD New College
1537	Richard Pykering ?King's
1562	Charles Ratcliffe Caius
1573	Robert Inglish Magdalene i
1577	Joseph Dawes MA Magdalene i
1580	John Sterne
1582	Robert Browne
1594	James Leman MA Magdalene i
1604	Thomas Laster
1611	Robert Sympson
1612	John Cottisford MA St John's
1613	John Coney MA
1616	John Cottisford MA St John's
1618	Robert Cade
1620	Eliezer Holt MA Caius
1630	Robert Woodside MA Caius
1641	Thomas Steffe MA Caius i
1645	Nathaniel Seaman MA St John's
1648	John Cade BA Emmanuel
1651	Henry Eades MA Queens' later DD
1651	William Dixon MA Caius
1659	Andrew Weston BA Sidney Sussex
1660	John Hildeyard Trinity later LL D
1661	Nathaniel Hudson MA Emmanuel
1663	Thomas Page MA Magdalene
1668	Samuel Butler MA Christ's
1673	George Raymond MA St Catharine's i

1679	Edward Rust BA Corpus Christi
1680	Samuel Reynolds BA Pembroke
1680	John Camplin MA St Catharine's i
1686	Henry Welsted MA Jesus
1686	Samuel Reynolds BA Pembroke i
1689	+Thomas Johnson MA King's
1691	Philip Richardson MA Christ's
1698	William Wilson MA St Catharine's
1703	James Reeve BA Christ's
1705	John Gaudy i
1713	Charles Porter BA Caius
1713	Richard Golty Pembroke
1721	Robert Hingeston MA Pembroke i
1743	Robert English MA Emmanuel i
1746	George Cheriton BA St John's
1747	Lewis Jones MA Jesus i
1753	Robert English MA Emmanuel i
1754	Charles Griffith perhaps Hertford O
1758	Samuel Hardy Emmanuel i
1763–71	Thomas Bolton BA St John's i, son of Thomas Bolton master

Chairmen of Governors since 1882

George Mason	[briefly]
Sterling Westhorp	1882
Dr John Henry Bartlet	1890
James Edward Ransome	1902
Bunnell Henry Burton [knighted 1934]	1905
Sir Percy Winn Everett	1943
Sydney Charles Grimwade	1946
*The Rt Revd Richard Brook	1952
Geoffrey Page Mason	1954
George William Pipe	1971
Geoffrey Thomas Barnard	1979
David John Coe	1989
Karl Daniels	2002

* not an Ipswichian

Second Masters since 1843

R. McNeill	1843
John G. Hawkins	1845
William Frederick Greenfield	1850
Henry A. Barclay	1858
R.N. Sanderson	before 1879
C.H. Garland	1883
A.W. Chennells	1890
R. Edmonds-Jones	1903
A.J. Agard-Butler	1905

O.P. Arton	1906
Richard Slator	1908
Harry Hughman Grimwade	1938
Ronald Hubert Frank Gleave	1964
George Stanley Notcutt	1969
Andrew Michael Gregory	1975
Darren Ayling	2001

Bursars

William R. Shirley	1950
Owen Jenkins	1967
Kenneth Pearson	1982
Peter Boughton	1987

Preparatory School Heads

Miss Hannah Hunt		1883
T.G. Powell		1912
E.C. Moir		1934
Ronald Hubert Frank Gleave	(one term only)	1939
J.G. Taplin		1940
Ronald Hubert Frank Gleave		1946
Douglas Yelland		1969
Nicholas Allen		1987
David Williams		1994
Jenny Jones		1999

Chaplains since 1907

John Alexander Corry Vully de Candole	1907–18
[E C Sherwood, HM, his own chaplain until]	
Hubert Arthur Stanley Pink	1931
John George Thomas Castle	1933
Ronald Thomas Jones	1950
William K.A. Hussey	1960
Derek M. Ryder	1972
Walter Wilson	1977
Paul Hamlet	1994
David Warnes	2002

Teaching staff with 25 years' service

Miss Gibb (Prep)	1917–49
Stanley Wilson (music)	1920–45
Norman J Stonex (Classics)	1929–63
Thomas H Glover (chemistry)	1929–69
James E Young (Classics)	1930–65
Thomas Brian Job (French)	1930–65
Noel K Sullivan (modern languages)	1948–76
Peter J Hill (history)	1952–80
Reginald G Kell (music)	1953–78
John LS Booth (Prep)	1954–86
John C Nicholson (PE and mathematics)	1955–92
Ian D Prior (English)	1956–91
Pat Yelland (née Horn) (Prep)	1958–88
John S Le Mare (art)	1958–86
Richard C Burnell (Classics)	1963–97

Derek J Chapman (chemistry and mathematics)	1968–99
John T Goodhand (English)	1970–03
Roger H Ingham (chemistry)	1970–
H Roger Holt (modern languages)	1970–
Barry J Hoskins (Classics)	1970–
Ernest G Thomas (English)	1971–97
Gordon AJ Paton (geography)	1971–99
Mike J Bannan (mathematics)	1974–
David C Fletcher (biology)	1975–
Robert L Clayton (PE and science)	1975–
Peter M Godsell (biology)	1977–
Alex J Burnett (English and drama)	1978–

Long-serving non-teaching staff

Walter 'Bunny' Howe	1905–53
Sergeant Austin	1884–1924
Albert Finch	1926–70
Cyril Perkins	1946–77
Ian Hammond	1952–94

XXVI

Presidents of the Old Ipswichian Club

1895/96	A R Malden FSA
1896/97	Rt Revd J T Hayes
1897/98	C E Hammond JP
1898/99	Revd Canon A J Worlledge
1899/1900	Edward Rose
1900/01	Sir Charles Sherrington OM
1901/02	Henry Miller
1902/03	Lord Woodbridge
1903/04	Lt-Gen Sir E A H Alderson KCB
1904/05	Sir H Rider Haggard KBE
1905/06	Brig-Gen Sir H C L Holden KCB, FRS
1906/07	Sir Bunnell H Burton
1907/08	G F Josselyn
1908/09	G S Sherrington
1909/10	Sir William P Burton KBE
1910/11	J R Geard
1911/12	Dr George Cowell FRCS
1912/13	Alan Turner
1913/19	Capt B H Chevallier RN
1920	E J Brown
1921	Revd Joseph Miles
1922	The Rt Hon Lord Roche PC
1923	S A Notcutt
1924	Lt Col F W Turner TD
1925	Major W Rowley Elliston TD
1926	Dr J R Staddon
1927	Sir Basil E Mayhew KBE

1928	J Manning Prentice
1929	Bernard Pretty
1930	Revd A A L Gedge
1931	Leonard Rees
1932	E Denham Spurrell
1933	J B Cullingham
1934	Russell Paul
1935	Sir Percy Everett FSS
1936	H Munro Cautley FSA
1937	Sir Francis E Shipway KCVO
1938	Kenneth Raynor
1939/42	Col J Josselyn CMG, DSO, OBE
1942/43	Bernard Pretty
1945/46	Col Frank L Tempest OBE, MC
1947	Col F W D Bendall CMG
1948	J B Cullingham
1949	Major G C Benham MC, TD
1950	Charles Partridge FSA
1951	Cunard T Dawson
1952	The Ven Christopher O George
1953	Major Keith W Brown TD
1954	Vice-Admiral Frank T Mason KCB
1955	Brig Ian F Hossack DSO
1956	Wallace M Morfey MBE, JP
1957	Brig Thomas L T Miller CBE
1958	Col Geoffrey P Mason CBE, TD, DL, JP
1959	John B Bantoft RASC (MT)
1960	John S Cobbald
1961	Irvine E Gray MBE, FSA
1962	The Venerable H A Stanley Pink
1963	George W Pipe JP

1964	Jack Catchpole ARIBA
1965	Dr John W Litchfield FRCP
1966	E J 'Sandy' Banks
1967	Stephen Abbot Notcutt BA
1968	E Jack W Fiske J P
1969	John B Williams OBE, TD,
1970	Hugh E N Cullingford ISO
1971	Harold R Smith
1972	Geoffrey T Barnard MA
1973	Prof John M Alexander FEng, DSc
1974	Dennis D Phillips
1975	Dr A E McLauchlan
1976	George S Notcutt BA
1977	F Guy Catchpole
1978	Prof Sir Charles Frank FRS, OBE
1979	Anthony H Greengrass
1980	John K T Webb
1981	Peter E Rolph
1982	Nicholas J Fiske
1983	Granville J Haskell
1984	John D Hennings CMG
1985	Karl Daniels
1986	Peter E Underwood JP
1987	Brig Robin C Plummer RE
1988	Michael A Philpot
1989	David J Coe JP
1990	Michael E J Williams
1991	H Jeremy G Barr
1992	Richard E Barker
1993	Lt Col Robert J Wyatt
1994	David J Moore

1995	Michael R Fenn
1996	Neil S Cawthorn
1997	William A D Whitfield
1998	Timothy G Thorn
1999	Alan T Wyatt
2000	John F Clements
2001	John S Skeates
2002	John S Le Mare
2003	Simon Woolfries

The Governing Body in June 1993.

378

XXVII
The School's Benefactors

Early Benefactors

Accounts of Felaw's bequest in 1483, of Wolsey's doomed attempts to enlarge the school permanently, Thomas Cromwell's successful plea to Henry VIII to refound it in the 1530s and give it a Royal Charter, and the confirmation of that Charter by Elizabeth I in 1566 will be found in the early chapters of this history.

In 1558, Laurence Mopted, master of Corpus Christi College, Cambridge founded a scholarship at Trinity Hall for Ipswich or Bury School boys. In 1574 Roger Barney, merchant, bequeathed merchandise, to be sold and applied to university exhibitions. In 1599, William Smarte, portman and MP for the Borough, endowed a fellowship and scholarships at Pembroke College, Cambridge. In 1601 his widow Alice and her second husband Ralph Scrivener added to Smarte's provisions.

Scholarships and Leaving Exhibitions: present-day practice

Inflation has defeated the generous intentions of all the early benefactors. Endowments which were intended to take a pupil through the school or to assist materially with university expenses are now inadequate. Some benefactors are remembered in *honorary [named] scholarships* awarded to pupils who won enabling awards at entry. Other names live on in *leaving exhibitions* which assist the ablest boys and girls going up to university each year to purchase books.

The Honorary Scholarships

The *Albert Scholarship,* originally a leaving scholarship, was endowed by public subscription in Ipswich in 1862 to commemorate the lately deceased Prince Consort and his laying the foundation stone of the present school on 4 July 1851.

The *Armstrong Scholarship* was endowed by Dr Cecilia Florence Williamson in 1964 in memory of her fiancé, Capt. James Noble Armstrong, RAMC, OI, who was killed tending the wounded near Ypres, 22 August 1915.

The *Bartlet Scholarships,* endowed by Dr John Henry Bartlet, OI, chairman of governors, were to assist boys already at the school.

The *Burton Scholarship* was endowed in 1947 by Mrs Emily May Hempson in memory of her father, Sir William Burton, OI, Skipper of America's Cup Challenger 'Shamrock IV'.

The *Pemberton Scholarship* was allocated to the school out of properties left for educational and charitable purposes in the will of John Pemberton, Portman of the Borough, in 1718.

The *Rainer Scholarships* were endowed for the sons of parents living in the county under the will of Percy Alfred Rainer, OI, who died in 1952.

Leaving Exhibitions

For the origins of the *Albert Exhibition,* the *Pemberton Exhibition* and the *Smarte Exhibition,* see above. The *Martin Exhibition* recalls that Richard Martin, Portman of Ipswich, left

Swan's Nest farm at Westerfield upon trust in his will of 1622 to endow exhibitions to Cambridge.

As the last four exhibitions are for Oxford and Cambridge entrants, two or three *St Edmunds Exhibitions* are awarded annually to able sixth formers going to other universities. They were endowed in 1985 by the Trustees of the funds of the former St Edmunds School, Kesgrave, to mark its association with Ipswich School between 1935 to 1975.

Prizes
The *Rigaud Prize*: In 1858, headmaster Stephen Jordan Rigaud left to become bishop of Antigua. When he died of yellow fever a year later, a trust fund was set up to assist his widow and family. In 1878 part of the fund was reinvested for a leaving prize for a pupil proceeding to university.

Many other prizes bearing donors' names are presented annually at Speech Day, for example those of Frederick Barnes, architect, Professor Edward Byles Cowell and Dr J H Bartlet, both OIs.

At the annual *Service of Commemoration of Benefactors* in St Mary-le-Tower the Headmaster reads out most of those named above, and also the Revd James Ford, perpetual curate of St Lawrence, Ipswich who in 1850 endowed (closed) awards at Trinity College, Oxford for pupils of this and three other schools, and Admiral Sir George Broke-Middleton who in 1884 gave the swimming bath in memory of his forebear Broke of the Shannon, OI.

More recent benefactions

Hubert Dewandelar, OI, endowed the Revd E W Porter Scholarship in 1984; Hugh Catchpole, CBE, SI, OI, endowed several scholarships to bear his name; Dorothy, Lady Foot, endowed the Rowley Elliston Scholarship in memory of her father (who was an OI), and Dr Jack Litchfield, OI, who endowed the scholarship that bears his name. The family of the late Stephen Salmon, OI, endowed a bursary in his memory. The most recent bequests to the school were from Geoffrey Barnard OI, Leslie Gibbons, Ian Hammond, Olive Hunt and J Suttle OI. Among benefactors who enabled recent developments are the Arthur Leggett Foundation, the Ganzoni Charitable Trust, the Macmillan family and the Scarfe Charitable Trust, also the Sports Council, the Foundation for Sport and the Arts and the Wolfson Foundation.

Finally, since the school became fully independent in 1945, the Old Ipswichians and the Friends of Ipswich School have supported every appeal and building project. In 1938 the OIs gave the School Field Pavilion and in 2000 raised half the cost of refurbishing it.

Index

Notes: Masters and headmasters are only indexed where they occur outside their chapters. Family members are indexed together. As the final chapters, particularly XXII, contain so many names, they have been only partially indexed.

D

E

F

J

New College ix, 27, 47, 218, 226
Oriel 193, 253
Trinity 381
Wadham 92, 202

Magdalen College School 28, 43
Siege of 91
University of 16, 27, 166, 167, 171, 190, 196, 207, 214, 241,

248, 254, 256, 260, 261, 265, 296
Oxford Dictionary of National Biography xi, 368

P

Paddie or Puddie, Mr 76
Page, Admiral Benjamin William 144
Page, Thomas 101, 103, 369
Paolozzi, Sir Eduardo 297
Partridge, Charles iv, 129, 131, 376
Pasquin, cartoonist 169
Passmore, Richard 289
Pawsey, Mrs 168
Payne, Allen 278
Peasants' Revolt 2
Peel, E. B. 265
Pemberton Scholarship 380
Penyngton, Richard {I} 367
Percyvale, Richard 4, 18, 21
Perkins, Cyril 255, 275, 316, 317, 319, 374
Perse School 225, 263

Peterborough, Bishop of 74, 270
Pettit, Mr 156
Pevsner, Nikolaus x
Phillips, Nicholas 105, 190
Phipson, Richard Makilwaine 155, 165
Pickford, Revd John 216
Pickwick Papers 143, 191
Piddlehinton, Dorset 46
Pink, H. A. Stanley 247, 249, 299, 346, 373, 376
Pipe, George W. 274, 285, 299, 371, 376
Piper, John 295, 304, 363
Poole and Pattle 303, 308
Poore, William Delta ('Dinah') 180, 183, 187
Popes
  Boniface VIIII 23
  Clement VII 31
Porter, Charles 117, 370

Potter, Gillie 273
Potter, W. E. ('Teddie') iv, vii, viii, xi, 58, 193, 259
Powell, T. G. ('Polly') 252, 335, 372
Poynter, Ambrose, Sir Edward John 155, 170, 247, 295, 361–362
Primerians 13
Prior, Ian, Marion xiii, 275, 278, 289, 292, 293, 303, 316, 317, 373
Priories suppressed by Wolsey for his College 23, 32
Privy Council 71, 72
Psalterians 338
Pudge, Simon 335
Pupplett or Purplett, Robert 108, 109
Purland, Dr Theodosius 142
Pykering, Richard 48, 369

R

Rackham, John 105
Radley College viii, 265, 266, 357
Raffe, Kay (née Foster) 273
Raimes, A. L. 5
Rainer Scholarships 380
Rainold, Alexander 79
Rames near Lillebonne 5
Ransome, R. C. 202
Raymond, George 104, 369
Raynor, Jessie (née Cursham), Kenneth, Philip Edwin {XV} 199,

229, 231, 243, 248, 316, 319, 322, 324, 344, 368, 376
Read, Alexander {VI} 367
Read, J. K. (Ken) 294, 298
Read, Samuel 144
Reading School 202, 215
Reading, Mr, writing master 119, 120
Redgrave 80
Reid, David 288
Repton School 186, 220, 332
Reymes family 5, 17

Reyntiens, Patrick 295, 363
Rheims 58
Rich, Robert, 3rd Earl of Warwick 83, 85
Richardson, William Henry iv, 193, 195, 198, 199, 219, 224
Richmond, Douglas 189, 191
Richmond, Henry 201, 322
Richmond, Yorkshire 128
Ridgard, John 2

Y

Cricket on School Field, Summer Term 1991.
Watercolour and gouache by William F.B. Cave, O.I.

WILLIAM F.B. CAVE 1991.